NIGEL HOFFMANN PhD has for eighteen years been a high school teacher, in Australian and Swiss Rudolf Steiner schools. He is the author of *Goethe's Science of Living Form: The Artistic Stages* (Adonis Press) and *The University at the Threshold: Orientation through Goethean Science* (Rudolf Steiner Press). He is the coordinator of Atelier for the Social Quest: ateliersocialquest.com

I0794726

THE SOCIAL ARCHETYPE

Realizing Society's Threefold Unity

A New Goetheanism

Nigel Hoffmann

CLAIRVIEW

Clairview Books Ltd.,
Russet, Sandy Lane,
West Hoathly,
W. Sussex RH19 4QQ

www.clairviewbooks.com

Published by Clairview Books 2024

A CIP catalogue record for this book is available from the British Library

ISBN 978 1 912992 55 3

Cover by Morgan Creative
Typeset by Symbiosys Technologies, Visakhapatnam, India
Printed and bound by 4Edge Ltd, Essex

Contents

Acknowledgements

Thanks go to Seth Jordan, Dr Luke Fischer and Tony Voss for reading through the manuscript and offering many valuable suggestions. Numerous conversations over the years with my wife Luisa have had a great influence on the text. The publication of this book was made possible through the generous support of the Ligsma Kirpe Trust Fund.

Introduction

A century has passed since Rudolf Steiner presented to the world his insights into social organization and social renewal. His idea of a threefold social order was radical in his time and remains so today—radical and insufficiently understood. We live in a time when concerns about social freedoms and rights are on the lips of very many people, in 'democratic' states across the face of the globe. As the storm clouds of crisis gather, Steiner's social vision will reveal a clear way forward if it is grasped imaginatively, in a living, creative way—for that is how it was conceived.

The artistic imaginative capacity, so important in the education of children, so valued in the life of culture and spirit going back through all civilizations to paintings on the walls of caves, might seem to have no relevance whatsoever when it comes to the hard-headed conceptualizations of economics, politics, and the sciences. Yet it is precisely this imaginative capacity that connects us deeply with the world. Could it be that our clever abstractions must also be considered a form of impoverishment?

The view persists today that artistic intelligence—or what we will be calling *cognitive imagination*—has nothing to do with the development and teaching of social science. However, a deep and powerful stream of European thought has always known otherwise. Hegel, Herder, Kant, Schiller are just a few of the philosophers who have maintained that aesthetic-creative considerations are all-important if we are to find our way to a social organization which is balanced and just. From Kant comes the view that political judgement must be aesthetic in nature. Schiller was concerned with the kind of aesthetic education necessary to integrate the psyche and prepare every individual for a healthy social existence.[1] Essentially, the idea we discover in this philosophical stream is that a genuine social science must draw upon much more than the logical intellect if we are to understand society in its deeper dimensions and wholeness.

Rudolf Steiner was heir to this tradition and made a unique contribution to it in his articulation of the threefold social picture. However, this contribution was not just another theory amongst the many theories which populate the history of social philosophy. Steiner's view that society is a living threefold unity is an artistic insight. To grasp the different dimensions of the three-membered social organism and how they relate to each other, to *enter into* this social being imaginatively, is to inwardly experience it. Philosophies of political democratic process, new socialist or capitalist outlooks, theories of liberty and human rights, even the reappraisal of Romantic social aesthetic philosophy—none of these amounts to the central imperative for our time according to Steiner. What is most crucial is the development of the kind of thinking which can engage with the creative forces at work in the social world, living forces which are *only* perceptible through an imaginative thinking. The artistic sensibility wakes up as an organ of cognition when thinking is able to dwell within these creative forces intimately; then ideas themselves become active, creative powers. Thus Steiner laid the foundations for a new social science which is the natural companion of a social art.

It is in large part the artistic quality of his thinking that still renders Steiner's social ideas inaccessible to the academic purview. Actually, although he rose to prominence as a scholar when in his twenties, he never had the slightest inclination to adapt himself to scholarly expectations in terms of intellectual content and methodology. For this he was far too much of an original thinker—but it has meant that his social outlook has to this point not been seriously considered beyond limited circles. His social thinking simply cannot be gauged in the usual scholarly ways. He produced no comprehensive volume of systematically worked out social thought which could be placed assertively on the library shelf next to Marx's *Capital* or Hegel's *Philosophy of Right*. Rather, he offered his social indications mostly through articles and lectures to a variety of audiences, each of whom he addressed with a different emphasis. This itself speaks of Steiner's artistic orientation; his social ideas are not conceived as a logical 'system' but are brought forth from different angles and perspectives, just as an artist shapes a work of art.

The fact that Steiner stands well outside the academic sphere in his consideration of physical and spiritual realities seems to be the reason that, even if one just quotes him, one can be branded a follower rather than someone who simply has made reference to his ideas.[2] In such a unscholarly state of affairs scholarship becomes impossible. If ideas are truthful and important then any author has the right and duty to quote them, or perhaps devote a whole book to them. Just because one focuses one's effort on the task of understanding and explicating the ideas of an eminent thinker doesn't mean one is bound to that thinker by some kind of emotional dependence. If that were the case then all those scholars who have spent their intellectual energies on Aristotle, Marx, Plotinus, or any other philosopher of significant standing, should all be branded followers and have opprobrium heaped upon them.

Steiner's ideas on the threefold social order most certainly warrant dedicated texts. These ideas are profound and original; they are rooted in the depths of the Western tradition of social thought yet are compelling in their quality of futurity. In the 1890s, through his involvement with circles connected with the celebrated Polish socialist philosopher Rosa Luxemburg, Steiner found himself at the epicentre of revolutionary thought in Germany. In 1902 he shared the lecture platform with Luxemburg at a gathering of the proletariat in Spandau.[3] For four years beginning in 1899 he gave lectures and cycles of lectures to workers at the Workers' College in Berlin, an institution founded by Wilhelm Liebknecht, the socialist reformer and friend of Karl Marx. Marxism, however, did not form the basis of Steiner's developed social thinking. From 1917, in the social chaos after World War 1, Steiner gave hundreds of lectures on social issues, some to large audiences of the general public, some to private circles. He wrote a number of essays on 'the social question' for journals which had been started in relation to his social thinking; he also wrote one small book—*Toward Social Renewal* (1919)—which was really only a summary of his thinking. In addition to his writing and lecturing he made appeals directly to politicians, some of whom embraced his social picture as vital for the development of a peace plan for Europe after the war.[4] Reviews and discussions of his threefold social vision were published in newspapers across Europe and America and one reviewer described his *Toward Social Renewal* as 'perhaps the most widely read of all books on politics appearing since the war'.[5] As a result of this very intense work on Steiner's part we have today a significant legacy of potent social conceptions.

In 2020 the coronavirus mayhem engulfed the world and its consequences are continuing and building. It is obvious that this is much more than a medical situation; it is a social catastrophe of immense proportions. In times of crisis people perceive in an almost instinctive way that an opportunity for change presents itself. From many directions we hear talk of possible futures but the dominant themes represent a struggle between the left and the right, just as in Steiner's time but in a new guise. What we have seen develop is a profound conflict in attitudes to public health measures. There are those in favour of public health authoritarianism—that is, placing the health of the public above the interests of the individual—and this tends to be the socialist orientation. It is opposed by those who defend civil liberties and basic rights ('my body, my choice'); this is the more libertarian orientation. Of course, there are many shades between, as there always have been on the left-right spectrum. Steiner perceived the fruitlessness and danger of the struggle between the polarities of left and right, socialism and liberalism. That is why he took upon himself the difficult task of showing that society has in truth a *threefold* constitution, the third principle being a mediating, reconciling factor. In the present climate of acute and ongoing social disruption, the task and responsibility of realizing society's threefold unity has never been greater.

Steiner's outpouring of social ideas in response to the chaos in the aftermath of the First World War was a first step in the direction of conscious social threefolding. Many efforts were made, during his time and after, to implement these social ideas, in particular through businesses, schools, and curative centres. These vanguard enterprises did not always last—some faltered, in others the founding impulse became diluted and the enterprises were forced into the mainstream. Such cases could be used to argue that Steiner's social ideas are utopian and not viable—but this wouldn't be a valid critique. Any number of examples could be taken from the history of social innovation, science and technology, to demonstrate that certain impulses may be important and groundbreaking yet nevertheless may take very many decades of trial and error, perhaps even outright rejection at the beginning, before they are finally properly understood and embraced. As is always the case with such efforts and initiatives, much is learned in the process.

It is true that some elements of Steiner's social thinking *appear* utopian; they do so until we realize that these aspects become practicable only when *other* aspects have first been realized. There are stages in any creative process and, if we picture a highly creative work of social transformation, some elements are going to seem impossible, even fanciful, before foundations have been laid and certain necessary forms are in place. For example, an associative economy as Steiner conceived it requires that we first bring a new consciousness to the forces involved in economic life and what we call 'the market'. This is still only partially the case today. Remuneration based on needs rather than a wage structure is going to require the development of a new and highly developed understanding of the nature and function of capital. Steiner asserted that, in the future, there must come about a will to work completely outside the wage nexus, and this is obviously going to seem utopian unless seen in the context of his broader assertion that such a will can only come about through a transformed cultural and spiritual life. This last point is taken up in this book in Chapters 10 and 11, on school and university education.

Each and every aspect of Steiner's social vision will require learning about new ways of organizing society and working together; the growth and circulation of capital, new forms of governance, freedom in education and so on—all will need to be submitted to the discerning eye of imaginative intelligence. There can be no predetermined programme of unfoldment, nor is an integrated threefold social organism going to arise in any miraculously rapid way. First and foremost is the imperative of gaining insight into the principles inherent in the three aspects of social life through an artistic form of thinking which enters into the archetypal forces at work within them—for without proper understanding of this social picture very little with real strength and durability could ever come of it.

The development of such a capacity of imaginative social insight requires a particularly dedicated striving because the young people of today are in no sense prepared for it through our conventional intellectually-orientated education. So here we have before us a fundamental task which is addressed in this book: to explore ways toward developing an adequate artistic-imaginative understanding of the threefold social organism, at all levels of education.

Part I
The Threefold Social Order

'Modern humanity has only a first inkling of the real nature of the social question. It will assume its real form when the structure of the social organism is such that the three life forces underlying all human existence can rise in their true form from a vague instinct into conscious thought.'

Rudolf Steiner[6]

'Citizens, no matter what happens today, in defeat no less than victory, we shall be making a revolution . . . it is the revolution of Truth. In terms of policy, there is only one principle, the sovereignty of man over himself, and this sovereignty of me over me is called Liberty. . . The common law is nothing but the protection of all men based on the rights of each, and the equivalent sacrifice that all men make is called Equality. The protection of all men by every man is Fraternity, and the point at which all these sovereignties intersect is called Society.'

Victor Hugo[7]

'. . . the most important impulses of humanity have been tending unconsciously in the direction of [the] threefold membering for centuries, only they have never gained sufficient force to carry it through . . . the work must now be taken in hand for which preparation has been made for centuries; the work of bringing order into the social organism.'

Rudolf Steiner[8]

Chapter 1

RUDOLF STEINER'S SOCIAL IMPULSE

Society On The Edge

It can scarcely be doubted that the coronavirus has unleashed a social crisis of a magnitude comparable to the world wars of the previous century. Connected more or less closely with this crisis are other immense challenges facing humanity today. New nanotechnology and genetic engineering techniques are irreversibly transforming nature and human life. Digital identity and surveillance technologies are creating intractable dilemmas in relation to human freedoms and rights; this goes together with the transhumanist agenda of marrying artificial intelligence with the human brain in the name of progress. Immense disparities of wealth are leading to rapidly growing social instability. Political structures of leadership the world over are fraught; autocratic regimes with reduced press and Internet freedom are prevalent and growing. In comparison to the power of today's political-economic alliance the hegemonies of any previous time in human history seem extremely limited.

The situation we experience today is really only a heightening of the conditions and tendencies which Rudolf Steiner saw in his contemporary world. For Steiner, the conclusion of the First World War with the Treaty of Versailles, far from resolving the social situation of Europe, cast its future into a perilous uncertainly. Into the difficult social situation he saw around him Steiner presented a vision of social renewal which he wanted to have more than just theoretical value; he wished the ideas to have an awakening power, an actual force of transformation. In this he was inspired by the German philosopher Johann Fichte whose biography he knew intimately through his doctoral studies. This is how Steiner described Fichte's work as a university teacher:

> [Fichte's] purpose was to awaken spiritual activity and spiritual being. From the souls of his hearers, as they hung upon his words, he sought to call forth a self-renewing spiritual activity. He did not merely communicate ideas.[9]

As Steiner saw it, only through an enlightened art of teaching and by means of a new art of education could a power of dynamic, self-renewing thought germinate and take root in modern humanity. During the years 1917 to 1924 when his focus was very much on 'the social question', he set about creating the kind of educational institutions in which such enlivened thinking could be cultivated in young people. He perceived conventional education to be deeply and fixedly intellectual in nature, shaped by a very old ideal of learning—the doctoral ideal—which had its origin in the medieval universities and which, according to Steiner, is unable to serve contemporary and future social needs.[10]

The schooling movement initiated by Steiner is far better known than his thoughts on world economy, work and capital, human rights and democracy, but it is insufficiently appreciated that the schools are immediate fruits of his social vision. In historical fact, this movement sprang—like an offshoot of a river—from his broad and original vision of social renewal. Everything carried out in these schools—not just in terms of pedagogical method but in their entire artistic mood and gesture—is a picture of how renewal could take place in broader social spheres. The schools are the embodiment of this social impulse. The aim of this method of schooling is to educate the child toward freedom—and freedom is the ideal behind what he called the cultural-spiritual sphere of the threefold social organism. Steiner sought an education through which every child could go forth from school in freedom so that their individual capacities could be made fruitful in social life.

One of the charges Steiner faced even in his own time in relation to his social thinking was its supposed utopianism. This was levelled at his radical views on work and human rights, on money and true price, on educational and religious renewal—indeed, his social picture was thought to be utopian as a whole and in its each and every aspect. A century later we should be very cautious about making such a claim. Let us consider what, in the early 1920s, was Steiner's 'merely utopian' view on the education of the child: 'The spiritual-psychic individuality of the child is something most sacred . . . the teacher must remove whatever might hinder the development of [the individuality of the child], and shield it with the utmost reverence.'[11] This proclamation of an education for human freedom was made at a time when school education worldwide was carried out in the traditional doctoral manner, through rote learning of a certain intellectual content primarily in order to prepare young people for a role in society (a methodology which usually included corporal punishment, something still prevalent in schools even in the 1970s). The world is evidently beginning to catch up with the respectful, reverential character of Steiner's approach because education today is by and large more child-centred and more focused on the needs of the human individual. The truth is that Steiner's pedagogy is not utopian at all but is groundbreaking, based as it is on a perception of the soul-spiritual nature and individual requirements of the developing human being. And it is equally true that his broader picture of social renewal is not 'merely utopian'; everything pertaining to it flows from a perception of the needs of the modern age and all indications for renewal are made in such a way that will allow new ways of thinking and conducting social life to become realities in our time and into the future.

In certain circles of social life Steiner's educational ideas made rapid progress and the schooling movement quickly spread to many countries. Today it is one of the fastest growing educational movements in the world. The same thing cannot be said of the broader panoramas of social renewal which Steiner entered into, such as world economy, social governance, work relations and taxation—but then, it is obvious why it is not so easy to bring about change on this level. There is always an immediate need for children to be educated and parents and teachers to take up the task of creating schools on a grassroots level. With economics, for example, with questions Steiner raised concerning capital, true price and the meaning of work, we are really dealing with the broadest possible social relations and quickly come up against deeply entrenched and powerfully resistant economic and political structures. Groundbreaking though such social ideas may be, relevant as they are to our contemporary social malaise, no one person or group in isolation will ever be able to effect significant social transformation through them. This question must then arise: How do such far-reaching ideas achieve efficacy in the world today, disinclined as we are to take up violent revolutionary causes? People nevertheless *are* seeking social renewal at a time when faith in the value of the conventional political process has become utterly eroded.

Steiner's far-reaching ideas will never become efficacious unless they are properly—that is, artistically—understood. However, such understanding does not come easily in the intellectual climate of our schools and universities, and the very notion of a threefold social organism can cause resistance because it is taken to be merely an alternative 'social system'. Steiner himself was aware that his only written work on the subject of the threefold social order had been 'fundamentally misunderstood on all sides'.[12] We need not assume that the difficulty of Steiner's social thinking lies in its intellectual obscurity; for abstruseness we already have the example of the social philosophies of Kant and Hegel. The real difficulty lies in another direction altogether, in the fact that he sought to understand human society as a soul-spiritual being, as something *alive* in a certain sense. As with Goethe's way of science from which he drew, he did not wish to impose mechanistic procedures on the living body of society. *The living, dynamic body of human society requires a living, creative thinking in order to be understood*—this is one of his key insights.

The way forward for the healthy development of society springs from a living, imaginative form of knowledge. This is a thinking which is concrete, practical, non-abstract and non-theoretical; it is a truly *living* social thinking because these ideas are not merely mental constructs but are 'saturated with the forces of reality' and 'possess the strength to take hold of the will and to live on in action', as Steiner expresses it.[13] This is a great challenge to the cultural and spiritual life of our time: the development of our thinking such that *ideas themselves become suffused with will forces*. We can gain a sense of what he means if we consider the ideals of justice and freedom which still to a degree carry within them a sense of imperative and an impulse to action. We can imagine *all* social scientific ideas having this living, dynamic quality because society itself is something living and dynamic and can only be properly understood through a thinking imbued with feeling and will.

We may come to value such a living form of social thinking more highly when we realize the cultural depths from which it has emerged. If we consider what are sometimes disparagingly called the 'Romantic thinkers'—Kant, Fichte, Schiller, Schelling, Schopenhauer, Goethe, to name only some of the more prominent—we find in all of them a rebellion against the abstract rationality of the eighteenth-century Enlightenment. In each we discover an attempt to think with more than the intellectual mind, to bring into cognition the power of imagination and creative intuition. To think is to reflect *on* life; to imagine is to enter *into* life, to cognitively participate in and actually *experience* the forces through which formation and transformation take place. Imagination, we might say, carries the impulse of creation within it. When the imagination is consciously intensified into a power of cognition, we have what Goethe called 'exact imagination', a capacity of thought which can be applied to both the natural and social worlds. The whole question of a 'will-saturated thinking' is taken up in Chapters 4 and 5 in relation to a Goethean-inspired social science and social art.

The social crisis of our time can be seen as a threshold and opportunity—a threshold to a vital, imaginative way of entering into the social question, a way which doesn't involve new political agendas or rehashed versions of socialist or capitalist theories. Only through crossing the threshold to a new kind of living thinking will the threefold nature of the social order be grasped and made fruitful for the human future.

Beyond Socialism and Capitalism

Every age has its crises and its flowerings; what is important is how each crisis is understood and how it is worked with or resolved. The influential work published in 1918 by philosopher of history Oswald Spengler—*Decline of the West*—predicted the slide of Western civilization into utter chaos. In our time there is a tendency to expect solutions from our political leaders, something which reflects our dependence on the paternal state. Yet everywhere the evidence is that our leaders are not up to this task, that the whole traditional concept of 'leader' is virtually meaningless in the modern world of highly educated 'followers'. Given this situation, the focus of this book is perhaps not surprising: it is not about political dissent, insurrection or revolution. It is about invoking and enhancing the free creative activity of individuals who make up the cultural-spiritual realm of the social organism.

When, a hundred years ago, Steiner presented the world with his picture of the threefold social order—at the very time Spengler was amassing considerable evidence for Western civilization's irreversible decline—he laid great emphasis on freedom in the cultural-spiritual realm.[14] This was a moment in European social history when events were moving decidedly away from cultural and spiritual freedom. The Great War had ended and the European social world was in a ferment, leading not long after to National Socialism in Germany and the Second World War. On another front, a struggle was taking place which resulted in the Russian Revolution and the totalitarian state of Stalin. This Russian Revolution sprang from a social programme based on the analytical philosophical system of Karl Marx and Lenin, which focused on class conflict leading to the proletariat gaining ownership of the means of economic production. In terms of this communist-socialist thinking, cultural and spiritual life is merely a reflector of class ideology and had no place in the revolution unless it supported and promoted the economic agenda.

For the suffering and alienated workers of the period around the time of the First World War, bourgeois cultural and spiritual life offered little succour. The proletariat of the early twentieth century looked to socialist ideas because they were roused by the ideal of fraternity and the promise of equality in the purely material framework of economic and political production; cultural-spiritual ideas did not press on them as a pathway to their liberation. However, at the same time, the ways of capitalism were powerful influences on them and they were moved by the possibility of freedom through financial betterment. This struggle between capitalism and communism continued through the twentieth century and capitalism is generally now said to be victorious over communism; it has risen up as a mighty and dominating force in the contemporary world. The 'free world' is the world of capitalist states, meaning states whose economic system is based on private ownership of the means of production and their operation for profit. Freedom has come to be associated with capitalism in the sense of free enterprise; it means freedom for anyone to climb the ladder to success, free from restriction, with unlimited opportunity for development and private accumulation of capital. This capitalist freedom is purely economic and in its modus operandi has nothing essential to do with cultural life. What is practical, pragmatic—where the wheels of society actually turn—that is understood by the capitalist way of thinking to be the economic-political realm.

By the end of the twentieth century it seemed capitalism had won the day; the Soviet Union had fallen and the socialist revolutionary zeal which was so evident at the beginning of that century had all but dissipated. It seemed a forlorn hope to believe that, as humanity moved into the twenty-first century, a brand new socialist political system was going to appear which would deliver humanity from capitalism's immense inequalities, from its lack of a truly inspiring economic fraternity, from its subtle and not-so-subtle social enslavements.

A striking fact is that the two social systems which have dominated the modern world as the bitterest opponents—capitalism and socialism—have something fundamental in common: *they both conceive of society and its transformative potential primarily in economic and political terms*. The reason for this is obvious: having capital and controlling the means of production gives power, whether that power is in the hands of the many or the few. In truth, the economic and political make for very congenial company and the cultural-spiritual tends to be seen as the poor relation, unwanted and uninvited at the main feast table even if valued for entertainment and other diversions. But this fundamentally distorts the social outlook, weighting it toward economic and political power.

For its part, cultural life today itself tends to resist the idea that it has any direct, practical responsibility for social transformation and renewal. The twentieth-century avant-garde's varied efforts to define and redefine itself moved it towards introspection, self-expression and experimentalism; the idea of art for art's sake was like a call to freedom and untrammelled self-involvement. To the extent that culture reflects our social life it does so as from a refined conceptual height; it perceives, it analyses and evaluates, it comments, it argues and judges. Yet it is the economic-political workers who are 'getting their hands dirty' in the actual process of social transformation. Steiner diagnosed cultural life as 'a sort of animated abstraction that runs alongside real economic and political events without having concrete effect upon them'.[15] This can come across as something strange because culture and spiritual life is normally not even *expected* to play a practical role today. Yet, just here, in this conception of culture, lies the crux of our social problem according to Steiner.

All of this can be put in more immediate, personal terms in relation to the realities facing people today. It is impossible not to see the strife and discord around us, but when it comes to actually *doing* something in relation to our greatest social dilemmas it is usually thought we have to take leave of the cultural-spiritual life and enter the political-economic arena—but, of course, that is something largely reserved for the powerful elite. Apart from the ignominious entreaties which can be made to them by means of letters of protest, lobby groups and demonstrations (which these days are always sanctioned and highly policed anyway) many people feel they must rest content with our entitlement to vote every three years or so. In truth, there is a mighty play of forces active in our time, an immense struggle impelled by the certainty that a great deal is at stake, that civil liberties are under profound threat. The struggle is taking place in the conscience of civil society—in conversations, in webinars, in educational institutions and in many other more or less 'hidden' ways. The cultural-spiritual sphere only *appears* to be impotent.

Chapter 2

THE THREEFOLD SOCIAL ORDER

Order

Inherent in the notion 'human society' is the idea of order. Disorder can reach the point of dissolution where we can no longer speak meaningfully of society; it can bring strife, violence, repression, and ultimately descent into the chaos which the ancient Greeks sensed as an ever-present danger to their city-states. The sources and potentials for social disorder have always been a central theme of political thought and in this connection we could refer to the *Politics* of Aristotle and his discussion of political enmity and disease, or what he called *stasis*.[16] Civic disorder or revolution can be a transitional stage in social evolution before a new order asserts itself. Thus, in relation to the idea of a 'threefold social order', at least the notion of 'social order' is relatively straightforward. But how and why such order is *threefold* is something strikingly unfamiliar.

Throughout the history of social philosophy order has normally meant *political* order, the order which is instigated and maintained by a ruling individual or elite group. Thus the history of human social life is charted by the interminable struggles of the different political ordering forces—pharaohs, caesars, monarchs and their vast armies, the modern state with its judiciary and police executive, the determiners and maintainers of 'law and order'. Said erstwhile American president Woodrow Wilson in his *The State*: 'The authority of governors, directly or indirectly, rests in all cases ultimately on *force*. Government, in its last analysis, is organized force.'[17] Wilson makes the point that this force is not always asserted but that order depends on its readiness-at-hand. And the notion of the 'new world order' which rose like a spectre in the first decades of the twenty-first century—this is a political order, a totalitarian form of world governance which will undoubtedly require policing on a global scale, a vast magnification of the kinds of political ordering methods which currently prevail.

In times of crisis the veils fall aside and we are able to see a situation in its stark reality. This is what has occurred in the coronavirus crisis; democratically elected governments the world over have revealed, in an extraordinarily short space of time, a normally more hidden, inherent authoritarian tendency in the ways they have asserted ordering measures. The methods of the Roman oligarch linger on in our democratic social processes—we are still very Roman in our laws and approaches to human rights, as Marx and Engels noted.[18] In this recent crisis our elected leaders have shut down the economy, prohibited the greater part of cultural-spiritual life, and dramatically curtailed human rights—all at the stroke of a pen. The concern here is not whether such modes of order enforcement are *necessary* in terms of public health; what is important is that it reveals to us the very tenuous and actually juvenile nature of our democratic forms and processes. The 'free world' prides itself on its democracies, but the fact is that only through profound and undaunted efforts toward social renewal in our time will the democratic spirit be able to advance and mature.

Because order has mostly been conceived and enforced politically, the political state is considered to be the only possible source of order in society. It is for this reason that the state is felt to be the enemy of freedom by libertarians—and in fact, this has largely been justified when we consider humanity's long history of enslavement and tyranny. Anarchism rose up in the nineteenth century as a movement of radical opposition to the threat to human freedom posed by the hierarchical ordering power of the state, the control of the many by the few. Anarchism is a celebration and assertion of human individuality, the free human creative spirit which does not wish to be 'ordered' in any way whatsoever. Anarchism has remained a powerful voice in political philosophy but its significance has often been clouded because it is associated with the very opposite idea, with chaos or lack of order—that is, with anti-social forces.

In fact, anarchist philosophy is only saying that there are sources of social order, of balanced social existence, other than from a centralized unitary government and its law-enforcement agencies. Anarchism puts the focus onto the integrity of the individual as the source of social wellbeing. Nevertheless, because anarchy is an 'anti' position, it perpetuates the dilemma which has always existed in political philosophy—namely, the unresolved conflict between individual and society, freedom and authority. As the philosopher Martin Heidegger sagely comments: 'Everything "anti" [is] held fast in the essence of that over against which it moves.'[19] Thus it follows: anarchism is held fast in the essential thrust of centralized political power against which it struggles. It should be noted that in recent history anarchistic, anti-authoritarian struggles such as the Occupy movement, whatever they may have achieved, have also served to reinforce the idea that if 'people power' is let loose then the power of the state will reassert itself in the most forceful way.

We need and expect order in our social lives and normally entrust this order-making role to the unitary political state when we elect a government. In doing so we take for granted that we are giving to that government the power to enforce an order which extends into all areas of society, including economic strategy and regulation of education. The order-making, controlling powers of the modern democratic state are vast and encompassing. The 'democratic moment' of the general election of government is held to be of key importance in that it distinguishes democracies from dictatorships. What is false is the idea that this vote is fundamentally a gesture of freedom, even if this is the general belief. The essence of the 'democratic moment', its fundamental gesture, is not freedom but *equality*; it is the fact that it grants every human individual the equal right to have their say—'one person, one vote'. Of course there is a degree of freedom of choice in a democratic election but this is a very limited choice and it is not the hallmark of freedom in modern society. It is absurd and dangerous to conflate freedom with equality, and if that happens then both are diminished.

In truth, freedom has its primary expression and reveals its predominating ordering gesture in a realm of society quite distinct from the political. Freedom is the ideal of the cultural-spiritual sphere and it is here that we can assess a society in terms of its fundamental liberties. Steiner writes: 'Man is free in so far as he is able to obey himself in every moment of his life.'[20] This is something entirely different from political order; freedom is *self* order, *self* creation. It means that the only sovereign power over a person is her or himself. The reality and potential of freedom is something immensely more than what takes place in the political realm. It is the condition which a free culture and free education strives for: to bring forth human beings who are free because they are masters of themselves, not because they are mastered or managed by others. Freedom only becomes a 'social problem' when we insist that it is fundamentally a political determination. The political determines the equal *right* of human individuals to be free but only individuals who, through a proper education and through self-development, can become free in themselves. The political state cannot create freedom, and freedom does not belong in its essence to the political-rights sphere. When freedom is properly valued in human life, the recognition will arise that freedom is the essence and ideal of a realm of society entirely distinct from the political-rights sphere.

Further, there is a social ordering force which works in the way people cooperate with each other to produce goods and provide services, and to utilize those goods and services. The vast majority of people spend their waking hours working cooperatively in this way. This ordered form of human activity is what we call 'mutuality' or 'solidarity'; it is a social order not determined politically but simply through the way people live and provide for each other. This cooperative activity defines the economic sphere of society. The political-rights sphere does not and cannot control how individuals work together economically; what it can do is only to formulate and maintain the *rights* which allow people to live their lives fraternally. These include the right to freedom of movement and freedom of association.

Thus, if we examine how different order-creating forces shape the form of human society, we see that what emerges is a threefoldness in relation to the cultural, political, and economic spheres of society and their respective ideals of freedom, equality, and fraternity. It is as if a spell has been broken which has held human consciousness in its thrall down the ages, from Plato and Aristotle, to Locke and Rousseau, and into our own time. The spell has made it impossible to see social order as anything other than the interminable struggle between freedom and authority, between the individual and cooperative life, between monarchy and anarchy. In truth, society is a three-membered unity, not a 'one' in the ancient, traditional sense which is still so engrained in our thinking. There is a right and proper place for the ideal of freedom to be fully realized—this is the cultural-spiritual sphere. And there is a right and proper place for the ideal of fraternity to be realized and most fully expressed—this is the economic sphere. Between these two there is an area we call the political-rights or legal sphere whose task is not to control the other two spheres but to determine and maintain human rights in the spirit of human equality. The three spheres of society express and embody the three ideals at work in every individual: liberty, equality, and fraternity.

The three spheres are not separate, as if side-by-side in a physical sense. Each of us belongs to all three spheres and every human individual expresses this threefold wholeness, more or less consciously. In every person works the ideals of freedom, equality, and fraternity, and each of us lives in the three spheres. Some may belong to the economic sphere only as consumers but many are entirely devoted to working in that sphere. We all belong to the sphere of rights because every person is equal before the law. And whenever we are undergoing any individual developmental process—which can be stimulated in myriad ways but is most clearly epitomized in the work of the educator—we are participating in a cultural process.

The eminent German sociologist and philosopher Jürgen Habermas has noted the three principal spheres in differentiated societies as a matter of observational fact—he refers to them as sub-systems of the total social system, and also as the three life-worlds of society.[21] These three interrelated spheres he calls the economic system, the political-administrative system and the socio-cultural system, each with a separate 'control centre' in organizational terms. Habermas's chief concern is the coordination between these three systems in advanced capitalist societies and the question of the legitimacy of the political sphere when the economic has become so dominant. What he doesn't do—and doesn't set out to do—is to explore the implications of the notion of society as a threefold wholeness—for example, the fact that each sphere requires its own, independent governance rather than the overarching political authority. And, most significantly, he doesn't develop the kind of imaginative thinking which makes it possible to actually perceive the dynamic, health-giving relationships between the three spheres as expressions of a living wholeness. The three clearly differentiated spheres which Habermas accurately observes in contemporary society are not yet the threefold social order which Rudolf Steiner articulated as the possibility of social renewal in our time.

Viewed imaginatively and artistically, society appears as a threefold unity with no sphere more important or higher than the other two. Each of the three spheres has integrity and significance unto itself yet all are organically related. As we ease ourselves into this social understanding, the absurdity of thinking that the 'political-rights' domain is the higher and most important can dawn almost like an epiphany. Yet it is actually only as obvious as saying that the brain and nervous system are not higher and more important than the digestive or respiratory systems in the human organism. The brain does not 'order' the metabolic functions from on high but plays a role in metabolic process, just as the metabolic plays a role in brain function. The thrust of Steiner's threefold social impulse is that social order must come in the first place, not from political authority and might, nor from the onrush of revolutionary zeal which tries to counter this political authority with the assertion of individual freedom, but *from seeing the rightful place and meaning of the different spheres of society in relation to each other*. That is to say: social order must now—and in the future—derive from an act of consciousness, from living, imaginative understanding.

When we, as contemporary humanity, take the first steps in creating social order out of understanding rather than political might, we become true representatives of what Steiner calls the age of the consciousness soul. The belief that social order is political order, that it is only ever the outcome of political might, has its origins in the instinctual life of humanity which goes back into the mists of time, to what Steiner calls the age of the sentient soul—a fundamentally feeling relationship with the physical and spiritual worlds. The belief that the political sphere is higher, is supreme, is still bound up with religious sentience, the feeling relationship with a 'higher power' as in the divine right of theocrats or kings. The revolutionary feeling—the raging against one's oppressors, the urge to violent insurrection—is still governed by the sentient soul and feeling compulsion. Autocracy and insurrection are two sides of the same social reality.

The consciousness soul means waking up from instinctive life, but not just to a theoretical knowledge which has no inner will and resolve. Consciousness soul, in the way Steiner describes it, involves an understanding which is not just a conceptual elaboration but a living thinking which pertains to the whole human being, to thinking, feeling and willing, active as a whole. In other words, in this new social understanding, 'thinking' and 'doing' are united, or we could say: science and art are conjoined. This is what will be explored in further chapters: a new social science which pertains to cognition yet is inherent in a new social art, which pertains to the 'doing' aspect of the human being. It means the power to both understand the threefold social order and to realize it in deed.

Polarity in Nature and Society

We have been looking at the key polarizing tendencies in society, specifically the opposition between free individuals and what we can call the social collective, which is society as a whole, and the ordering forces which give it stability and coherence. It takes very little to perceive that social polarity is a cause of great social tension and strife. We speak of 'polarization', usually giving it a pejorative connotation, meaning oppositional, conflicting force—in ideas, in worldviews, in social strategies and policies. Politically, this opposition and tension on a broad social level can easily reach the point where it cannot be tolerated and is generally resolved through a punitive act of authority. For government which rests on force—that is, for all absolutist forms of social order—it has to be like this, for, logically and practically, one pole cannot tolerate its opposite. A society simply cannot be both free and cooperative/fraternal in all of its aspects.

It is assumed that oppositional, polarizing forces must be overcome through establishing social unity—through political compromise—but that inevitably means either subtly or forcefully silencing dissent.

We need to understand polarity, we need to be able to properly think it, not to just refer to it in an abstract or theoretical way, but get to know it artistically, imaginatively. Here we can first turn to nature for guidance, for in nature the phenomenon of polarity is everywhere present. We don't do this merely to find analogies or similes between nature and the social realm in a superficial sense. We do it to undergo an apprenticeship in imaginative cognition, for the reality of polarity comes to singular manifestation in certain natural forms and here we can learn to understand its significance. This is the kind of study carried out by thinkers such as Kant, Schelling, Fichte and Goethe, whose endeavours are finally beginning to be appreciated by scholarship in the English-speaking world.

The magnet was what Goethe called an 'archetypal phenomenon', meaning that in it the polar forces, which work throughout nature and govern world phenomena in a more or less hidden way, show forth as a physically experienceable manifestation. He also spoke of such phenomena as 'pregnant points', declaring that 'nature has no secret which she does not somewhere place openly before the eye of the attentive observer'.[22] Polarity is inherent also in the world of living form—in plants, animals and in human physiology. For example, the principal polarity in the plant world is that between root (orientated to the Earth), and the floral chalice (orientated to the Sun). In Chapter 4 ways of studying polarity in these living forms are presented, working with the methods of artistic science developed by Goethe. This is about not merely recognizing polarity in nature but entering into it, inwardly working with it and getting to know it intimately.

Goethean studies of polarity in nature lead over to the contemplation of the archetypal polar forces at work in human society—human society considered as something living and transforming. For indeed, a definite polar characteristic has worked more and more to the surface in the long history of human social development: this is the polarity of 'individuality' (inspired by the ideal of freedom) and 'communality' (inspired by the ideal of fraternity or mutuality). Polarities come into existence concomitantly; light obtains its being by virtue of darkness—and vice versa. The 'individuality pole' becomes highly differentiated only to the extent that the 'communality pole' shapes and differentiates itself—not necessarily at exactly the same time but in relationship. Before we had individual freedom we also had no conscious fraternity; work within the absolute authority of a theocratic or aristocratic social order was not fraternal in the sense of self-willed cooperative activity. Medieval serfdom was not fraternal but, rather, utter subservience and a form of bondage. Fraternal work depends on the evolved human consciousness which has its concomitant in cultural-spiritual freedom; freedom and fraternity are distinct yet interdependent and not possible without each other. Original forms of communality, such as tribal and related forms of association, were the result of more or less instinctive forms of social feeling based on family ties. This, likewise, was not a conscious form of brotherhood or sisterhood.

The polarity of 'individuality' and 'communality' can also be understood as the polarity of 'anti-social forces' and 'social forces' which Steiner calls an 'archetypal phenomenon of social science in Goethe's sense'.[23] The 'individuality pole' in which human beings strive for the free realization of self—this has an essentially anti-social gesture. We may think most characteristically of the poet; when a poem is created the poet is impelled by the need to realize the creative idea of the work. The poem in the first place is not created 'for others' but for and out of itself. Likewise, the wish to discover who we are as a person, how we can find our way through life, the search for freedom in the sense that Steiner described it as learning how to obey oneself in every moment of our lives—these are entirely healthy activities yet essentially anti-social in nature. As Steiner notes, anything anti-social is normally thought to be immoral and wrong, yet it is a vital part of human nature—anti-social forces are 'the pillars on which personal independence rests' and something, he suggests, which will become even more powerful in the future.[24]

By contrast, the inner gesture of the 'communality pole' is essentially social. The whole meaning and quality of the fraternal life is working to serve the needs of others—through the manufacture and distribution of goods and through the provision of services. Now it might be objected that in modern economic life the most characteristic gesture is not fraternal at all but self-serving—in other words, expressing an overtly anti-social character. Here those most lionized are the 'self-made men' who have profited for themselves through the system of free enterprise. However, as we shall see in Chapter 6, such self-orientated gain is precisely a sign that the 'communality pole' has not yet been realized, that the essentially social, mutually-benefitting forces of the economic realm have not yet come fully into play. In terms of a healthy balance of anti-social and social forces, this emphasis on freedom in the modern economy can be read as a symptom of disease.[25]

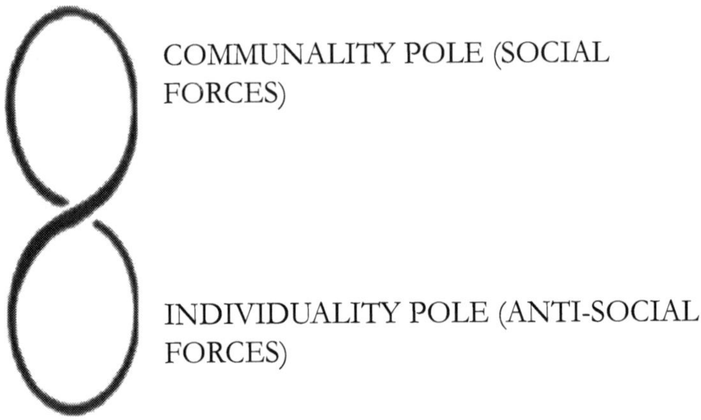

Figure 1

Today it is the anti-social aspect which predominates with results evident in every area of the social fabric. Herein lies the particular challenge of our times as enunciated by Steiner: social behaviour leading to healthy communality is no longer instinctive but must be consciously brought about by us. The impulse to actively take an interest in others leading to outward activities which promote harmonious relationships—this can only come about through a conscious acting against the tendency to allow anti-social forces to predominate in oneself. Freedom, when truly realized in oneself, can lead to profound perceptions of the needs of others—to what Steiner calls moral imagination and ethical individualism.[26] There is an important role for education here; it is also a question of creating social forms through which a balanced condition of social and anti-social forces can flourish. Such indeed is the aim of the impulse toward a threefold ordering of society.

The opposition and strife of the individual-collective polarity will never be 'worked out' logically; it is ineluctable, a reflection of polar forces at work everywhere in nature. It will ever be a source of social strife as long as the nature of polarity is inadequately understood. The polar forces must be entered into imaginatively, artistically grasped and inwardly experienced. Then it will be seen that all true polarity is not merely duality—it is a *threefold*.

The Threefold Archetype

Polarities are not just opposites—or, better said, polarities are opposites of a certain kind. Opposites—like hot and cold—intermingle and neutralize each other. Polarities are generative; as Goethe observed, the intensified poles 'will produce a third thing, something new, higher, unexpected'.[27] When we think of a magnet with its north and south poles it may appear as a twofoldness but the poles of a magnet have a field of forces relating them, expressed in the gestures of attraction and repulsion. Polarity is thus a threefold relationship, comprising the two poles and the relating element called by Goethe and his colleagues the *copula,* or uniting principle (from the Latin, meaning 'that which binds'). Immanuel Kant had already come to the idea of the *copula* as the reciprocal relation between two polarities; for Schelling the copula became fundamental to his thinking on the dynamic equilibrium of nature.[28]

In Schelling's philosophy of nature, this threefold unity becomes significant in relation to his theory of identity and his ontological world-picture. Schelling explored philosophically the idea of the copula as the mediating principle in the polarities of freedom and necessity, self and nature, subject and object, being and becoming.[29] It was Goethe, who,

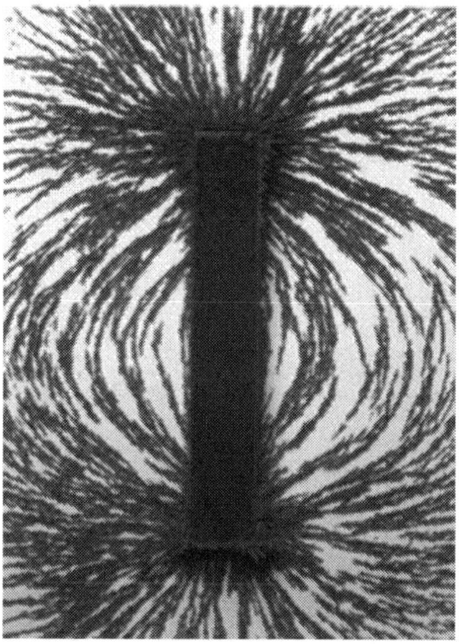

Figure 2: Iron filings allowing the field relating the poles of a magnet to become visible.

through actual phenomenological study, showed that the threefold principle emerges in nature, in particular through his colour studies in which he demonstrated that colour arises through the interplay of the polarities of light and darkness. These insights were taken up by Schelling and particularly by Hegel in his *Philosophy of Nature*. Rudolf Steiner recognized the idea of polarity as a threefold unity in relation to the plant and animal kingdoms and the human being.[30]

From such studies of natural form and relationship we can turn again to the phenomenon of human society, considered as a living being. It now becomes possible to perceive in society the threefold archetypal principle as a structuring, formative force. To do this we can firstly work with the fundamental threefold relatedness in terms of personal pronouns which take us into the realm of lived experience.

The aspect of human life which cultivates and celebrates human freedom, creativity and individuality is the 'individuality pole'—it relates to 'I'. Freedom here rests on the acknowledgement that anti-social forces in the human being are healthy and not to be suppressed or 'ordered'. On the contrary, they need to be enhanced to the highest degree. The polar aspect of society which requires a conscious cultivation of social forces through cooperative activity is the 'communality pole'—it relates to 'we', what we are and do together fraternally. Like a chord in music, only the sounding together of the tones is important, not the tones in and of themselves.

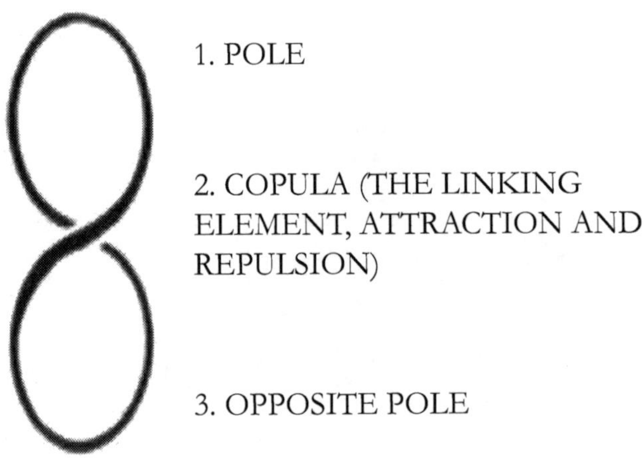

Figure 3

Individuality pole — freedom and individuality — 'I'

Copula or mediation sphere — equality — 'you'

Communality pole — fraternity and interest in the other — 'We'

Figure 4

Freedom and fraternity, 'I' and 'we', will ever appear as contradictions and antagonisms unless a third principle of human life is consciously articulated as the mediating sphere. Such a mediating principle is certainly present and at work in society but it is not normally recognized as such. Working with 'I-we' as the fundamental social polarity it becomes evident that the copula is 'you'. We say 'you' in recognition that *you are also an 'I'*, just like myself. If I consider myself to be free, then freedom must equally be the possession of every other individual, every other 'I'. 'Real freedom presupposes others who are free' declared the philosopher Hegel, and when we refer to 'others' we mean 'we'.[31] Thus it follows that the copula 'you' pertains to both poles, to both 'I' and 'we', to individuality and communality.

Spirit and Matter

All social forms and processes take shape within—and are reflections of—the encompassing polarity of spirit and matter. Human society develops between the poles of spirit and matter and is 'rooted' in both. We can call one pole the world of nature (matter) upon which society depends for its every material need; and we can speak of the mental realm (spirit) which we draw upon in relation to everything to do with our cultural-spiritual lives. This sense of polarity is precisely what Karl Marx lacked in his thinking; he saw social history purely in terms of material processes and developing from an original material base, so that everything cultural and spiritual he considered as deriving from the material. He endeavoured to understand society one-sidedly in terms of the matter pole.

Matter is what is of substantial reality; spirit means immaterial reality. We do not need to spend much time on the argument that what is immaterial has no reality, for we know that our thoughts, concepts and feelings are real yet, in terms of their experiential content, are immaterial. There is nothing solid about the concept of freedom, the feeling of joy. We also know, from experience in our own lives and from a consideration of human civilization, that it is from individual impulses of a spiritual nature—from concepts, insights, inspirations—that nature is worked on and transformed into everything we have around us in society: technologies, architectural constructions, furniture, forms of cuisine, artworks and so on. Spirit is creative, formative, an active principle; matter is shaped by the impulses of spirit and, conversely, it is matter which allows spirit to take embodied form.

Societies of the past were much more orientated toward the spiritual pole than is the case today. For example, in ancient Indian society, labour and economic activity were bound up in their entirety with the religious life. All forms of manual labour and social relationship were carried out as forms of devotional service. This spiritual identity of the people was otherworldly and conceived as the transcendental and absolute Self or Brahman. By contrast, the common expression 'modern materialism' obviously points to an emphasis on the material aspect of the polarity to the point of denying the reality of spirit altogether. Spirit and matter are ever in dynamic interaction.

It is not fruitful to try to understand this relationship of spirit and matter merely conceptually or logically; the interaction of the two needs to be pictured with the eye of the imagination as a dynamic, creative

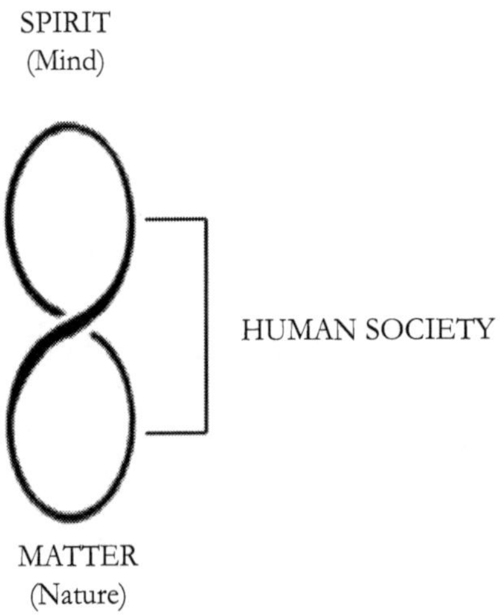

Figure 5

Figure 6

process of one pole working upon the other (or it can be carried out physically by walking the lemniscate and so bringing it palpably into the will).

We can imagine the dynamic relationship of the lemniscate—or physically experience it—starting at the marked point and moving in the direction of the arrow. We hold our right arm out and move through the form, returning in the end to the same point. In the first sphere our arm will be pointing inwards toward the centre and then, at the moment of the crossing, it will be pointing out, towards the periphery. When the arm is pointing in, it is the centric orientation, as if to the centre of the Earth, to the centre of gravity; this we can call the material pole. The other way, the arm will be pointing to the cosmic periphery which we can call the spiritual pole.

Now, in a similar way, we can experience the relationship between the poles of the social organism. We have already discussed that the 'individuality' pole—the pole of 'I'—bears the closest relationship to spirit, to ideas and inspirations individually conceived. In terms of society as a whole, we call this the *cultural-spiritual sphere*. If we again move around the lemniscate from the cultural-spiritual sphere, the peripheral orientation (spiritual inspiration) turns into a centric orientation which is matter or Earth; this is the 'communality pole'—the pole of 'we'. In terms of society as a whole, we call this the *economic sphere*. Individual freedom is not what is important here; we cooperatively work the Earth and shape its raw materials into products for the use of others.

This is one way of experiencing the polarity of individuality and communality; there is another way which can also be discovered as we move through the lemniscate. With regard to creative inspiration the individual is certainly orientated peripherally into the world of the spirit. However, in order to do that a person needs to be closed off, to a greater or lesser extent, from outer social influences and intrusions of the world, to develop their talents in solitude. Conversely, we see that for people to cooperatively work the Earth a turning outward towards others is necessary, a connection to the greater social whole must be fostered.

The point of this exercise is not just to think about the relationship of the cultural-spiritual and economic spheres abstractly but to actually *enter into* this relationship. This is 'a doing which is a knowing'. We move from the cultural-spiritual sphere to the economic sphere and in so doing 'carry' the spiritual impulses so that they now bear upon the centric pole,

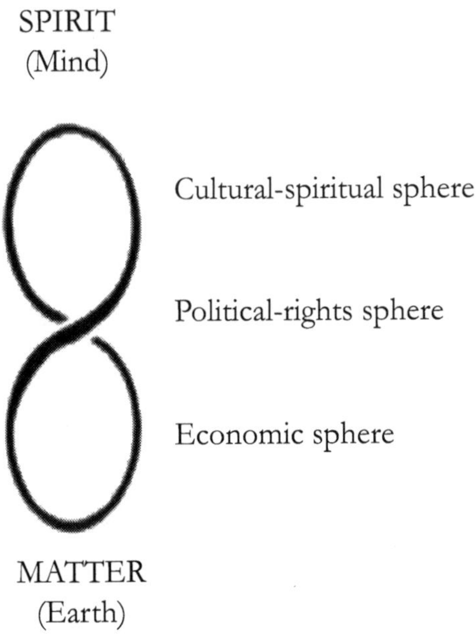

Figure 7

the Earth. They become the inspiration for collective work, for acquiring and maintaining the means of production, for setting up businesses, for everything which comes within what we mean by entrepreneurship. And as we 'carry' the products of the economy back into the cultural-spiritual sphere we experience the arising of *capital* which is creative potential; it is capital which supports and makes possible cultural-spiritual life. Thus the cycle continues in creative fashion.

We need to repeat the backwards and forwards movement between the poles numerous times to bring it deeply into the will. Working through the lemniscate in this way we can experience inwardly the interaction of the cultural-spiritual and the economic poles as a living process, as an actual inner event with a certain gesture and meaning. We may ask at the moment of the crossing-over: What is it in our society which regulates the pure freedom of creative inspiration with the activity of cooperatively working the Earth and otherwise providing for each other? The answer is: our *laws* which embody our rights. A law does not limit inspiration; it simply regulates what is good for me in relation to what is good for everyone. A *right* is what I can do in relation to another—this relationship is implied in every right. Every right comes into being at the crossing-over of the lemniscate, between the opposing gestures of Spirit and Matter, individuality and communality. Because laws are legislated in the political realm we may call this crossing-over point the *political-rights sphere.*

Thus the threefold social order is shaped through the creative interaction of Spirit and Matter and is the manifestation of the archetypal threefold as it expresses and reveals itself in human society. In civilization this threefold membering has not always been evident as it is today with modern society expressing three largely emancipated spheres. In archaic societies we do not find a distinct cultural-spiritual, economic or political-rights spheres. Nevertheless, what was present in these early societies was the seed of the threefold social order—for the archetypal threefold was active then as it is now. In the next chapter the emergence of the contemporary articulated threefold social organism is further explored.

Chapter 3

THE DIFFERENTIATION OF THE THREE SOCIAL SPHERES

Thinking Social History

Jürgen Habermas sees the threefold differentiation of modern society as a matter of simple observational fact—there are three principal interrelated centres or functional hearts of activity: the economic, the political, and the cultural. This is true and is an important observation as far as it goes; it points to a definite contemporary social phenomenon. But in terms of Rudolf Steiner's conception of the threefold social order it provides only a starting point. Through this phenomenon of social threefoldness we can think into the creative, differentiating forces which *give rise* to the threefold organization, forces which have been active throughout human history and which continue to be active.

Without question the emergence of the differentiated threefold social organism was (and still is to a certain extent) instinctive or at least semi-conscious; the forms of trade and first use of money, the appearance of different forms of religion, art, and social governance—all these began in time immemorial and were not the result of some kind of deliberate, conscious strategy. Through this largely instinctual evolution, social life has been shaped into the three distinct spheres which Habermas observes today. If we follow this evolution from the past into the present and then gaze towards the future with the eye of the imagination, it becomes evident that what has arisen instinctively must in the future become something deliberate. The threefold organization of society will only attain a higher level of realization as an entirely conscious creation.

This capacity to enter into and participate in the activity of formative forces in civilization over aeons is what we can call 'cognitive imagination'. The imaginative approach to the study of history, which draws upon both the scientific and artistic sensibilities, was described by Wilhelm von Humboldt following the methods of Goethe. Humboldt writes in his seminal essay *The Task of the Historian* (1821):

> If the historian . . . can only reveal the truth of an event by presentation, by filling in and connecting the disjointed fragments of direct

> observation, he can do so, like the poet, only through his imagination. The crucial difference, which removes all potential dangers, lies in the fact that the historian subordinates his imagination to experience and the investigation of reality. In this subordination, the imagination does not act as pure fantasy and is, therefore, more properly called the intuitive faculty or connective ability. . . [32]

> Through a study of the creative forces of world history, the historian conceives for himself a general picture of the form of the connection of all events ... They are not being projected into history but are the essence of history itself.[33]

These are the words of a man who was highly experienced in Goethe's way of science, having worked with Goethe over several years on the dissection of anatomical specimens. What Humboldt would have learned through such study was to move between contiguous parts with 'exact imagination' and so to reach towards the underlying forces, acting lawfully, that come to expression in those parts; it was this way of thinking that he took and exercised in other realms, including in linguistic and historical studies. Humboldt notes that hidden behind or within historical events are 'creative forces' which are invisible to normal perception. He writes: 'One can only grasp that which is right, subtle and hidden, because the mind is properly attuned to grasping it.'[34] This *attunement of mind* is the key point here; what he calls the 'connective ability' is the capacity of the imagination to participate in the facts of history and thereby learn to read their language, to perceive how these events 'speak' of the creative, formative forces that shaped them.

Rudolf Steiner, taking forward the phenomenological approaches of Goethe and Humboldt, conceives key events of history as 'symptoms' of the creative, differentiating 'driving forces' as he calls them, at work below the surface but revealing themselves in certain phenomena in human history. Thus Steiner indicates the way towards a historical symptomatology:

> These significant points are distinguished by the fact that what is otherwise hidden comes here to the surface . . . Here, in a particular phenomenon, [it is possible to become aware of] something which otherwise is at work everywhere, but which does not show itself in such a significant manifestation.[35]

These 'significant points' can be phenomena of different kinds. They can be dramatic social events such as the French Revolution but also significant works of art which reflect and magnify the underlying forces which shape human history in a broad sense. In the free, creative act, the artist's mind is particularly 'attuned' to these driving forces of life beneath the surface of social reality which creative act brings to cogent expression. Through looking at works of art we can gain creative act clear imaginative picture of how these underlying driving forces have progressively structured and differentiated human society, from the most remotely ancient times up to the present.

With the above considerations in mind we can now turn to look at the evolution of civilization as perceived through particular works of art understood as 'significant points'. Here we are focusing on the progression through the birth of Europe into the modern world. This is not Euro-centrism in the negative sense; it has a definite intention which is to uncover the way the creative forces bring forth a threefold social differentiation in this particular historical progression. It is a limited study even if vast in terms of its time span. But there is a further reason for this focus: the three spheres—the cultural-spiritual, the political-rights and the economic—underwent an intense differentiation in the Western world which has to do with its particular destiny as a world civilization. How this threefold differentiation is developing in other world cultures in our contemporary globalized situation is a broader question.

The Threefold Social Organism: An Evolutionary Picture

The Germinal Unity

We can bring to mind a picture of humanity in its most archaic seed-condition in which the embryo of the threefold social organization was sleeping, as it were. Common knowledge based on decades of anthropological and archaeological research tells us that archaic society was profoundly different from society as we know it today and relatively undifferentiated in a material, operational sense. It was this society which nevertheless slowly gave rise to modern civilization.

No matter which of the world's ancient peoples one considers it will always be found that these archaic societies were religious in their governing, ordering process; all of social life was conducted according to spiritual principles. In tribal society such as that of the indigenous people of Australia, there was no human ruler; it was the spiritual principle itself which ruled their lives in every respect, including economic activity. Specifically in terms of Aboriginal culture, this spiritual rulership is what we call 'the Dreaming', the creative workings of the ancestral deities.

These peoples couched their insights and cosmic-creative understanding in mythical, pictorial terms—myths which were the governing stories of their entire social existence.

From these stories—which had different artistic expressions including dance and song—one element becomes clear: these ancient peoples lived primarily in relation to the spiritual element. Spirit was the reality, and spirit filled everything—mountains, plants, animals; everything had a soul or spirit inhabitant because these 'material' entities were created by spiritual beings and still contained their spiritual essence. This unity of archaic peoples with the spirit is what the British philosopher and poet Owen Barfield called 'original participation' meaning that they lived in direct communion with spiritual beings.[36]

Although it is right to speak of a 'germinal unity', early peoples believed that their connection with the spiritual could be broken and their union had to be maintained as it was 'in the Beginning'—*ab origine*—when spiritual beings created the world.[37] Thus, within the 'seed-unity' of archaic society we can identify, not divisions, but three fundamental foci of experience. Firstly the realm of the gods, the 'Dreaming', was the dominant reality and this was a realm of creative freedom because each god was a unique individual Creator, animalistic in nature and not compelled by anything other than its own creative mission (for example, the Rainbow Serpent in Aboriginal culture). Freedom and creative individuality was an attribute of the gods alone.

The 'earthly' collective life of archaic society, by contrast, was not free at all; it was entirely determined by ancestral law. Tribal society was the second life focus. Social or kinship groupings were familial and had an almost crystalline symmetry and rigidity in form and function. There was no freedom of choice about who a person partnered with—this was already 'laid down'. Also determined by tradition was the yearly cycle of ritual life and—for hunter-gatherers—the movement through the landscape which also related to economic activity. All activities of trading and bartering were set by the cosmic cycles and traditional patterns—there was no 'free economic enterprise'.

Thus we can identify the archetypal polarity of individuality and collectivity in the life of ancient peoples—the first spiritual, the second earthly. And thirdly, there was the focus which bound together the spiritual and the earthly, the free and the determined: this was the mythos and ritual life, the religious lore. It was the responsibility of the tribal elders and shamans to preserve this mythos and maintain the ritual life. The shamans could undertake 'celestial journeys' in order to communicate with the

SPIRITUAL POLE : Realm of the gods — individuality and creative freedom

COPULA : Religious lore and ceremonial life

MATERIAL POLE : Collective material life, hunting, gathering and trading

Figure 8

gods on behalf of the community; their task was to heal unrest and resolve community issues by delivering gifts to the spirits. Myths were no mere stories, they were governing principles of the entire human collective. This was the copula, the principle binding the spiritual and the earthly which in archaic Indian culture was depicted through imagery of actual copulation, of male-female sexual union.[38]

Figure 9: Shiva, the Nataraja dancer.

While archaic society such as that of the Australian aborigine remained largely unchanged over millennia, in other parts of the world differentiating, driving forces brought the archetypal threefold 'seed' to a more realized state. This was the case in ancient Indian civilization. The traditional sculptural form of the Nataraja dancer shows the 'cosmic dance' of Shiva, the god of creation and destruction, standing on and crushing the dwarf Apasmara which symbolizes the individual human self as *maya*, illusion or ignorance. The cosmic lawfulness asserts itself as absolute in the freedom of the dance, filling the entire cosmic sphere. However, significantly, this cosmic power with the name of Shiva takes a *human* form in ancient India as distinct from the animalistic gods of Australian Aboriginal religion; the quality of freedom has in a sense approached and 'touched' the human being as the potential of the liberation of the human mind which is what the ancient Indians called *samardhi* or 'god realization'. The freedom of the gods, this attribute of the divine, becomes a human possibility. At that moment, we could say, begins the emancipation of the human being. The seed of the threefold social organism has germinated.

The Birth of Theocracy

We pass now to the time in which theocracies arose in the East and Near East; this is government by officials or priests who are regarded as divinely guided. Ancient Indian society was composed of kingdoms ruled by different theocratic monarchies and great theocratic states appeared in ancient Persia and Mesopotamia. Ancient Egyptian theocratic society took form in the same time period—around the middle of the millennium before the Christian era. Ancient Egyptian culture bears strongly upon Greek and Roman civilization and the birth of Europe.

It was noted above that the quality of freedom approached and 'touched' the human being in the ancient Indian world; this advanced to a higher degree in ancient Egyptian civilization and is strikingly depicted in a statue of the Pharaoh Chefren. In this work the pharaoh's head is embraced by the wings of the god Horus, symbolized as a falcon (see Fig. 10). The head is the centre of consciousness which is here being seeded with the 'divine word' or power of creative freedom which otherwise is possessed only by the gods. A comparison can be made with the Shiva image; in the latter the god assumes a human form but is still a cosmic figure. The pharaoh however is very much an actual living human being, seated on his throne on Earth. Nevertheless, in his consciousness the pharaoh is 'on the level' with the god which is why the theocrat is called a 'god-man'.

In the sole individuality of the pharaoh a god-like power resides and this power passes to the population, binding and guiding it. It is rendered into the written word by the scribe and into images by the artist-priests. Here we recognize the profound difference between the tribal elder or shaman and the theocrat. The role is mediatory in all cases but the direction of activity is opposed. The elder or shaman remembers and propitiates the gods, visits the abode of the gods; the activity of the theocrat is directed downward, to the people.

Humanity was 'touched' with divine freedom but it is not possible to speak of the pharaoh and the society beneath him as free in the way we mean it today. We see that the Pharaoh Chefren in this sculpture is transfixed and held by the power of the god, and historiography tells us that the ancient Egyptian social structure fanning out beneath the pharaohs was rigidly hierarchical. This is not an image of a free society; the human beings who made up ancient Egyptian theocratic society were not an aggregation of individuals in the modern social sense. It was more like a collective consciousness and child-like absorption in the power of the pharaoh, a 'folk-soul'. Nevertheless, in the individuality of the pharaoh (and through him the social whole) a potential has been born; it has 'descended' from the cosmic heights of the creatively free deities, onto the Earth.

This seed-potential of freedom was accompanied by other social formative processes which made the form of ancient Egyptian society something immensely more complex and differentiated than archaic cultures such as that of the Australian Aboriginal. Ancient Egyptian society was divided into classes of priests, scribes and workers, with the pharaoh presiding over them all. In terms of legal processes, pharaohs held supreme authority in settling disputes but they often delegated these powers to other officials such as governors, viziers, and magistrates, who could conduct investigations, hold trials, and issue punishments. Here we see the beginnings of a distinct legal sphere although individual human rights was a notion which had not yet emerged in the evolution of consciousness.

Economic life was also far more complex. In the obligatory 'dreaming journeys' of Aboriginal people between the territory's sacred sites, economic activity mainly took the relatively simple form of hunting, gathering and trading; little permanent settlement and agricultural activity was possible although so-called fire-stick farming was integrated into

Figure 10: Statue of Pharaoh Chefren embraced by the god Horus.

Figure 11: The hierarchical structure of ancient Egyptian theocratic society.

nomadic life.[39] However, in the formation of city-states of the Near East there was intense agricultural cultivation through sophisticated irrigation and farming techniques which made food production more efficient. This enabled society's needs to be produced by a limited class of workers and at the same time made possible the establishment of a priestly class. In ancient Egyptian theocratic society economic life involved extensive trading routes which included the use of boats traversing the Mediterranean Sea. The economy was primarily agrarian which was an expression of how this people, as a folk-soul, related to the Earth in a material sense. The only true individual, the 'god-man', presided over the agrarian life of the people. Only with the individuation of the human being in general could a more developed calculating thinking come about, the kind of thinking which led to commerce.

Thus we see that, in the world of the ancient theocrats, the formative forces of the archetypal threefold were active and here we can discern the beginnings of a threefold social differentiation—inchoate yet quite distinct. This social structure, we could say, was approaching the more differentiated threefold form which we call Graeco-Roman civilization.

The Birth of Democracy, Aristocracy and the Emancipation of the Political-Legal Sphere

It was indicated above that all three spheres of the threefold social organism are continually differentiating. In the emerging threefold archetype the three principles determine each other as a threefold wholeness. This is what comes to light when we look into and *through* significant points in the development of Western civilization seen as a whole, with the necessary 'atunement of mind'—that is, with an exact imagination. In the development of civilization the three spheres arise mutually but in different

SPIRITUAL POLE : The pharaoh or 'god-man' — receiving and possessing the divine creative Word which creates and maintains the whole society; the artist-priests and scribes

LEGAL POLE : Governors, viziers, and magistrates

ECONOMIC POLE : Agrarian workers, artisans, and traders

Figure 12

cultural epochs one or other sphere undergoes a particularly intense differentiating process in relation to the cultural milieu of that epoch.

In the Graeco-Roman civilization the threefold differentiating process which was evident in the ancient Egyptian world was further heightened. The particular cultural conditions and form of consciousness of the Graeco-Roman world—in particular the evolution of a logical, ordering form of intelligence—meant that the political-legal sphere during that time took shape in a most pronounced way, with the two other spheres reflecting this emancipation. To move with a living, imaginative form of thinking from one civilization or cultural epoch to another, experiencing how the dynamic archetypal relationship of the three spheres transformed, is to enter into a living metamorphic process.

We can find our way into the particularities of the Graeco-Roman world by considering several key works of art. Two works from the early Greek period exemplify what developed towards a pinnacle in the Classical Greek age. The first *kouros* (young man) figure is very similar to the ancient Egyptian in its rigidity; the figure is held within the folk-soul by the force of authority which we have identified as the theocratic principle in that civilization (see Fig. 13). In the second *kouros* figure, a life permeates every feature and the figure seems almost to breathe (see Fig. 14). A new expression of freedom is entering into human self-consciousness; it is

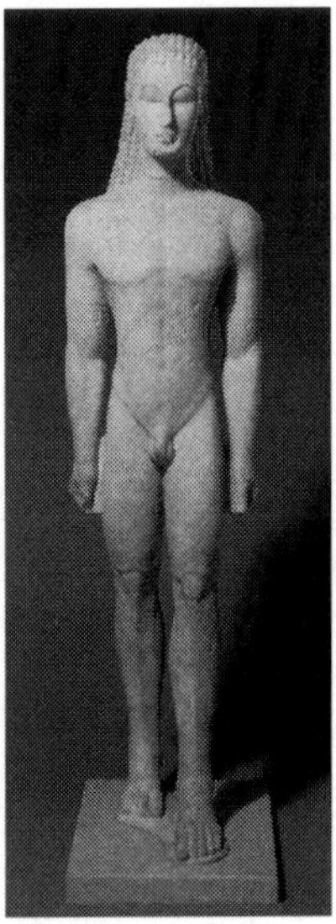

Figure 13: Marble sculpture of a kouros (youth)

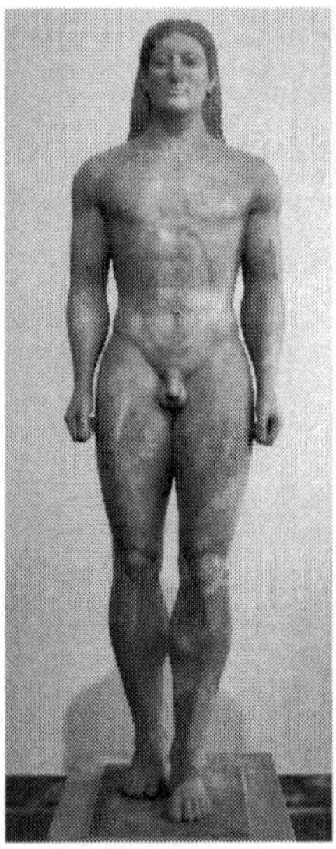

Figure 14: Kroisos kouros

the freedom to stand on the Earth with the sense of oneself as an individual, not 'bound' by the god, even if there is still something strongly ideal and godlike about this figure.

This new sense of self is also reflected in the beginning of the democratic impulse in the Greek city-states during the Classical period. When human beings experience themselves as individuals, when the differentiating forces bring it about that human beings experience existence through the power of their own inner centre of life forces, then there is a dawning in the social order of what we term *rights*. This, in its germinal form in the Greek world, was the right (at least in certain classes of society which didn't include women or slaves) to participate in the governing process.

In relation to the Roman era we can look upon a work such as the frieze on the *Ara Pacis* altar in Rome and feel quite close to the kind of people in the procession (see Fig. 15).[40] In a sense this is a 'modern' work; these people are very much more like individuals as we know them today. This sense of individuality awoke at this time and was the reason why the values of love and salvation in Christianity could appeal to all people equally—including women and slaves. The individuality and freedom possessed only by the ancient Egyptian pharaoh was passing into society as a whole.

Yet Roman society was still essentially aristocratic—that is, controlled by elite groups or by tyrants, with more democratic elements only evident in the late Republic. The sense that the Caesar was still a 'divine' figure

Figure 15: Ara Pacis frieze

meant that the Roman world was still relatively close to the 'god-governance' of ancient Egypt. The locus of power was still in the spiritual sphere in Roman times even while the political-legal sphere was differentiating, taking the form of the constitution of the Roman Republic with its senate, assemblies and magistrates and its system of elected consuls, its courts and jurists. More progressive and more retarding elements shape every cultural epoch; in the case of the Graeco-Roman world, the progressive element was certainly the legal aspect which set the tone for European social development for centuries to come.

The legal evolution of the Roman world culminated in the Justinian Code, part of the Corpus Juris Civilis (AD 529), a compilation of Roman imperial law, which became the basis of civil law up to the present. Although there was an intense differentiation of the legal aspect of society in Roman times, it was really only after the eighteenth century, through the work of the French philosopher Montesquieu who advocated the separation of legislative, judicial, and executive powers, that European civilization arrived at a decisively differentiated legal-rights sphere. This 'separation of powers' or *trias politica* which became the basis of most modern democracies, means that the judicial process is now outside the control of the ruler or ruling group, and thus can be said to have truly emancipated itself.

All these changes and developments were the outward expression of inward driving forces in the evolving social organism. Human consciousness was transforming and in the Graeco-Roman era we see the emergence of the kind of logical thinking which bestows on thought an inner confidence and certainty. The logical mind continued to evolve in the centuries after the birth of Europe and in the medieval period the universities came into existence as heightened expressions of this kind of thought structure. All aspects of the differentiating political-legal sphere were shaped through such thinking; evident particularly in the Roman era was the kind of logical mentality we could term 'juristic'. It was such juristic-logical thinking which, in the Roman period, also began a profound transformation of the economic life. Within the more ancient theocracies the economy was fundamentally agrarian; from the Graeco-Roman period forward the commercial aspect of the economy began to grow and consolidate. This is because all commercial arrangements depend on a sense of rights, on what kind of contracts and commercial arrangements are just, on how money can be used in an equitable way.

With the birth of a new sense of individual self in the Graeco-Roman period and the coming about of a logical-juristic kind of thinking, the three spheres were differentiating together. However, the *emancipation* of the particular spheres happened at different times.

SPIRITUAL POLE : Both aristocratic and democratic methods

LEGAL-RIGHTS ASPECT : Culminating in the Justinian Code, the basis of European civil law

ECONOMIC POLE : The development of commerce based on contracts

Figure 16

The Emancipation of the Economic Sphere

In spite of the fact that seeds of democracy germinated in the ancient Graeco-Roman world, the aristocratic principle of governance was maintained throughout the Middle Ages in Europe, expressed in the feudal system and manorialism. And the Christian Church, from its humble egalitarian beginnings in the Roman catacombs, rose to be a profoundly aristocratic power of governance in Europe and, in the case of the papacy, almost theocratic in nature. 'Divine right' was the key feature of monarchies right through to the eighteenth century. We could say that the whole of the medieval period continued to be Roman in this respect.

Unconscious driving forces within European civilization continued to bring it about that the three spheres gradually differentiated although, even into our own time, they remain tangled with each other. The system of serfdom in medieval times, an aspect of feudalism, meant that the peasants were owned and controlled by the lord of the manor and that economic life was completely bound to the political and religious life (as was the rest of the cultural life). Yet in the medieval period a very particular awakening of economic fraternity and autonomy took place in the towns in the forms of the guild system. The many who wished to escape the servitude of serfdom moved to the cities and guilds of workers were formed under the principle of mutual aid—that is, true fraternity.[41] The economic work and transactions which took place within and through the guilds were self-determined—that is, not subject to a 'higher' controlling power. For example, the idea and practice of right price came about through what the members of guilds themselves determined to be good through the principle of mutual help, not through supply and demand requirements of 'the market' in the more modern sense. The guild system persisted until around the beginning of the nineteenth century and the advent of the Industrial Revolution; it came to be thought of as a hindrance to free trade and business development—that is, to the advance of capitalism.

Let us consider two images by nineteenth-century artists. The image of the Dutch peasant by Van Gogh could equally be of a medieval serf to the extent that the lives of these workers are bound to the rhythms of nature. In the case of the peasant the produce may be just for himself and his family or perhaps for a market economy. Into the gloomy fecundity of the fallow soil the sower casts the sun-imbued seeds of the life which will rise again with the new crop; this is the overwhelming reality of the peasant (see Fig. 17).

Let us now bring to imagination the picture of the very same kind of human beings in the same period, those who are plucked out of the binding rhythms of nature, uprooted and relocated by the mechanism of the train, as depicted in the image by Daumier (see Fig. 18). The peasantry now has turned into the *proletariat*, bound not to the rhythms of nature but instead to the owner of the means of economic production, the capitalist.

In the mixture of the workers in the third-class carriage we have an image of what in fact became the differentiated workforce of the Industrial Revolution, with its intense division of labour. Such a workforce brought about an explosion of productivity in the seventeenth and

Figure 17: Vincent van Gogh, Sower at Sunset, *1888.*

Figure 18: Honoré Daumier, The Third-Class Carriage, *1864.*

eighteenth centuries; this meant that the economy developed in a way which went far beyond the system of guilds and could become something separate from the control of religious-political life. As a result of the great accumulation of capital, in England in particular, through the combination of industry and colonialism, what we call a 'free market economy' developed—that is, a form of trading that takes place with freedom from centralized monarchical or governmental control. A free market economy works through private ownership of the means of production and voluntary exchange of goods.

Thus the emancipation of the economic sphere in the evolution of European civilization has depended on two main things: firstly on the development of a logical, ordering kind of mentality which first appeared in a pronounced way in Roman society and developed further in the creation of mechanized industrial production; and secondly through the extraction of human beings from the natural order. This was part of the process of human individualization and was, in a sense, a liberating process—liberating from theocratic and aristocratic forms of governance and from the strictures of rural peasant life. Yet, as depicted by Romantic artists such as William Blake, it also had a destructive aspect, for what arose across the European landscape were the 'dark Satanic Mills' of the Industrial Revolution with its destruction of the relationship between humanity and the natural world.

The Emancipation of the Cultural-Spiritual Sphere

If we follow this cultural metamorphosis with the 'inner eye', the eye of the imagination, then it is possible to perceive how the driving forces at work within the developments we have been considering have to do with the human being becoming an *individual*. We spoke of the theocrat as the proto-individual; this individualization of the human being was then expressed in the emancipation of the legal sphere in the Graeco-Roman world and centuries later in the emancipated economic sphere in European civilization. The threefold social order which was embryonic in the most archaic form of humanity comes to expression progressively as human individuality 'wakes up' and realizes itself through self-consciousness. The emancipation of the three spheres, the gradual separation of the social threads, has to do fundamentally with this driving force of human individualization. Today we may consider ourselves greatly advanced in relation to our primitive ancestors and to the medieval serfs, but the fact is that individualization is an ongoing process. The archetypal force driving this differentiation continues to be active, more or less instinctively but unquestionably rising to a new consciousness in our time. It was the heightened consciousness of self in the modern world which allowed the cultural-spiritual aspect of social life to separate itself from the all-embracing aristocratic power, monarchical and religious, which contained and controlled cultural and spiritual life in Europe for almost two millennia.

Victor Hugo defined liberty as 'the sovereignty of man over himself', this being one of the ideals of the French Revolution.[42] We see this heightened individualism expressed in the image by Caspar David Friedrich from the Romantic period whose thinkers lived in the spirit of the French Revolution (see Fig. 19). The figure depicted is alone in the sublime landscape, separated from society and situated at a height on a mountain top. He is seemingly in the process of finding a new relationship with nature from the perspective of the individual. No longer is he bound to nature's rhythms like Van Gogh's peasant. No cultural or economic bonds restrict him, no tradition or political order limits him; he considers himself free to express himself and determine his life in whichever way he chooses. From the Romantic period into the twentieth century we see a great striving towards self-expression as well as continuous efforts, through all forms of cultural life and especially avant-garde art, to achieve freedom from tradition and any other intrusive or suppressive influence.

The gradual emancipation of the cultural-spiritual sphere in the modern period came about through concerted freedom-seeking deeds with a high degree of conscious intention. The philosophy of Friedrich Nietzsche had an extraordinarily great influence on the culture of the twentieth century—on artists, writers, and political thinkers. Steiner illuminates Nietzsche's key point as follows: 'The strong, truly free human being will not *receive* truth, he will *create* it; he will not let something "be permitted" him; he will not obey.'[43] The free individual wishes to be responsible only to him or herself, to be subservient or obedient to no 'higher power'. Through such self-responsibility it becomes possible to play a responsible role in society, a role which is self-chosen and which springs from a person's own sense of mission. Freedom does not necessarily equate with egotism.

When individual freedom doesn't awaken the sense of social responsibility it leads to the particular quality of alienation which is a characteristic of the modern period, the kind of imprisonment in the self which Nietzsche suffered from and which existential philosophers like Jean-Paul Sartre identified. In the sculptural works of Giacometti the figures are upright and individual yet in every other respect stunted, physically and spiritually (see Fig. 20). Yet they are 'free'—or, as Sartre put it, 'condemned to be free'.[44] The same gesture can be found in the immense glass and concrete uprightness of skyscrapers; economic freedom is

Figure 19: Caspar David Friedrich, Wanderer above the Sea of Fog, *c.1817.*

Figure 20: Alberto Giacometti, detail from The Forest, *1950.*

powerfully asserted yet they appear spiritually stunted and self-enclosed. No relations of love are possible in Giacometti's figures and love is not what finds its primary expression in our contemporary skyscraper cityscapes. We can assume that we are only at the very beginning of what it means to be culturally and spiritually free; we are certainly still only on the way to achieving the wholeness of the human condition which Steiner called the threefold social order.

A Conscious Evolution

The idea expressed above is that, while the evolution of civilization and the differentiation of the three spheres has been something instinctive or at least semi-conscious, it now needs to be a highly conscious process. Nothing occurs suddenly; the entire differentiation process over millennia has been a kind of slow dawning, a waking up to self. Nietzsche and others before and at the beginning of the twentieth century brought a particularly accentuated consciousness to what it means to be an individual and what it means for individuals—rather than 'higher powers'—to chart the course of their own destiny. These thinkers laid the foundations of a new social art, an art which can only come about through a truly liberated cultural-spiritual sphere.

Modern society expresses three distinct spheres, the economic, the political-legal and the cultural-spiritual, shaped and defined through a very long span of cultural evolution. But this is not the threefold social order, the consciously realized threefold social organism. It takes very little to perceive that, far from being a healthy organism, in many ways society today is still highly disordered, riven, politically and economically diseased, wracked with inequality, corruption, and narrowness of thinking, and encumbered with immense economic debt among many other debilitating factors. The threefold social order is not our condition—but nevertheless we can learn to see what it might be, just as in a state of illness we can learn to understand health and thereby provide ourselves with a positive and health-bestowing orientation.

Society is in a constant state of movement and development—not just in its large political events but in the most inconspicuous human relationships. Since time immemorial human beings have lived in social situations but only in very recent times has there been what we might call a 'social sense' in people generally. We are now considering humanity in general, not just the Western stream of civilization where—as we have seen—the three social spheres gradually underwent a definite differentiation and emancipation. Through telecommunications, the spread of the printed media and through education, people in all parts of the Earth are waking up to the 'social question'. They are becoming aware, not just of the political and economic realities of their own society, but of political and social issues in the global context. With the social sense awakening in people's minds—far more so than even a century ago in Steiner's time when he observed it waking up among the proletariat through the influence of Marxist ideas—comes the natural question: What can we do to bring about a world which is just and which is healthy?

The differentiation of the three spheres occurred in the Western stream of civilization—or, more accurately, *is* that history. That has been its destiny in world events and has nothing to do with Eurocentrism (in the pejorative sense) or racial superiority. Democracy, legal thinking and its codification, the separation of political powers, the free market economy, scientific advancement in all areas of life and in particular the development of sophisticated machines, the self-expressive approach to art—all this was shaped in a particular way in the West and has now been taken up by societies the world over, both capitalist countries and countries which maintain socialist structures to some degree. In human society everywhere today it is possible to discern—with Habermas—that there are three principal centres of activity: the economic, the political-legal and the cultural. For people across the whole face of the planet it is possible now for anyone to see that their society has a threefold nature; what is equally apparent is that nowhere yet has society been *consciously organized* as such.

Part II
A New Social Science and Social Art

'No matter what social programmes are thought out, no matter what ideal social conditions we may desire to bring about, if the point of departure is not an understanding of the human being as such, if the objective is not in accordance with the more intimate knowledge of man, everything will remain fruitless.'

Rudolf Steiner[45]

'Modern sociology seeks to be great by taking no account of anything that could lead to social will, social impulse, merely noting historically and statistically the so-called sociological facts, to prove, or so it appears, that the human being is a kind of social animal living within a community. It has furnished strong evidence of this, unconsciously it is true, furnished it by not advancing anything but the most insipid sociological views which are the common property of everyone — mere trivialities. Nowhere is there the will to discover social laws and how they must affect the social will of man. Hence in this sphere the force of all life of spirit is crippled . . . Social will is non-existent just because, where it is meant to be cultivated, namely in centres for higher education, sociology has replaced social science — an ineffective sociology in place of a social science which pulsates in the will and stimulates the human being. These matters have their roots deep in the cultural life; it is there that they have to be sought if they are ever to be found.'

Rudolf Steiner[46]

'We are called on to form the world.'

Novalis[47]

Chapter 4

SOCIAL SCIENCE RE-IMAGINED

The Human and Social Organisms

There is a philosophical tradition of viewing society in organic terms going back at least to Plato.[48] For this reason there is nothing radical about Steiner's use of the phrase 'the threefold social organism' to mean the way a healthy society works as a living whole. Nevertheless it continues to be a somewhat provocative expression, as challenging today as it was in Steiner's time. It is still likely to be taken as something poetic, a mere metaphor. However, a metaphorical reference was not his aim; he wanted to give concise expression to a perceptible reality. Steiner's discussions concerning the 'threefold social organism' were intended to open the way toward a social science which is a genuine life science. To this it must be added that such a science is still only on the horizon of modern consciousness, notwithstanding the great development and diversification of the social sciences within academic spheres.

It stands to reason that it will be difficult, even impossible, to find our way toward social renewal on a scientific basis if it remains unclear exactly what kind of phenomenon we are dealing with. If society is claimed to be an organism then it will surely be objected that it is impossible to categorize and study it like a plant or animal which are organic productions of nature. Nevertheless, it is true that society is made up of living human beings and while it does not have a discrete body like an animal it does exhibit the character of a 'super-organism' like a hive of bees or colony of ants. Here we can imagine that, whereas the cells of an organism or an organ such as the liver, are held in a coherent wholeness as a single entity, the 'cells' or individual entities of the super-organism—the bees and the ants—are spread out in space yet nevertheless form an integrated whole in the way they work together. The immediate and obvious difficulty with this is that, beyond a certain point, it is impossible to equate a human self-conscious individuality with a bee or ant which does not possess the power of volition.

Then it might be claimed that we are on safer ground if we say that society is *like* an organism, so that we can analyse it by means of analogy.

This is the approach which was being taken in Steiner's time by Woodrow Wilson, the American president and academic social scientist. Wilson advanced the idea that the social organism (like Steiner, he called it that) could be compared to the human body, with its organs and cells serving the whole organism. In developing this analogy, Wilson paralleled the governmental and political entities to limbs, sense organs, blood and spirit.[49] These political organs and their constituent human 'cells' serve and are given meaning by the greater whole (the whole human organism) within which they are granted their existence. This greater whole, by analogy, is the state according to Wilson. If we proceed in the way of a living social understanding there is no possibility of ending in the same place as Woodrow Wilson and his conception of the social organism as merely analogous to the individual human organism. It might be argued that Steiner, because he referred to 'the social organism', wanted, like Wilson, to explain society through logical correspondences with the human organism. He did not—and, indeed, went to some pains to disavow Wilson's approach.[50]

Wilson's ideas bore a connection to the organicist social outlook which rose to prominence through the views of the philosopher Georg Hegel. It was Hegel who said 'the true is the whole' meaning that the form and development of the social whole or state has primary significance for human life.[51] Hegel has many interpreters but a key reading (propagated in particular through Marxist thought) is that the human individual has significance only in the sense of the part he or she plays in the communality. Individuality, to this way of thinking, must be considered subordinate to and less real (and in this sense less important) than the whole. If we consider the social whole to be the reality then there can be no truly individual rights and freedoms—for what is right and good is only what is right and good for society as a whole. The role of every part must be determined by the lawfulness of the whole.

The lawfulness of the whole is the meaningful way society unfolds over time. Society can only be called a 'whole' if we understand it as something with inner integrity or coherence rather than as something formed of random human actions. Hegel had presented this inner integrity in terms of the evolution of 'the idea' through logical phases of opposition and resolution. Hegel's philosophy was transformed into the socialist philosophy of Marx with its historical materialism, meaning the evolutionary advance of civilization as a whole as a result of struggle between different social classes rooted in the underlying economic base. In this way Marx conceived the inevitability of communism arising from socialism, through the 'transcendence of the proletariat'.[52]

This claim of inevitability in social philosophy is what Karl Popper decried as the 'poverty of historicism'. Popper defined historicism as:

> an approach to the social sciences which assumes that historical prediction is their principal aim, and which assumes that this aim is attainable by discovering the 'rhythms' or the 'patterns', the 'laws' or the 'trends' that underlie the evolution of history.[53]

Popper admitted no sense in which the organic wholeness of society could be understood scientifically and rationally. He saw in those who claimed they could intuit these laws (and his focus was principally on Marxism and its totalitarian manifestations) an immense danger to the freedom of the human spirit because all social change is implemented through wholesale planning and no change at the individual or small-group levels is considered important.

An entirely contrary approach was taken by the great nineteenth-century German libertarian philosopher of human individuality, Max Stirner, who said society has no reality but rather that 'the individuals are its reality'. He considered that the individual is subordinate to nothing, that the individual is not determined by a 'greater whole' but is free and responsible only to him or herself.[54] Stirner's ideas became the basis for modern anarchism. An echo of this way of thinking was heard well over a century later with the well-known neo-liberal proclamation of Margaret Thatcher who said 'there is no such thing as society, there is a living tapestry of men and women . . . '[55] She does concede that there are natural, organic groupings but that they go no further than the family unit. The individualist approach is also reflected in the 'methodological individualism' of sociologist Max Weber, who claimed that all social phenomena on the macro level must be explained by showing how they result from individual actions and the 'intentional states' of individuals.[56] From this point of view political institutions, businesses, and cultural entities are not organs of a great organic whole; they are not natural productions at all but are human artefacts, created by individuals like works of art. Society, thus considered, is a free human creation.

What then is society in truth? Is it an organism with a complex of functional parts, developing lawfully and organically in predetermined phases, or is it an aggregate of many free human individuals, free creators who determine their own lives, who are not bound to any organic law at all? Each yields insights which have a certain truth but each, taken by itself, appears one-sided or partial and we never catch sight of society in its living wholeness. This seeming contradiction can be put in a nutshell: are we as a human society determined or are we free? But life is not a philosophical puzzle and to take it as such is not to grasp it at all.

Firstly, we need to keep firmly in mind that human society is a specifically human phenomenon. Animals too are social—for example, groups of lions ('prides') move together and perform certain acts like hunting. We will understand lion society by understanding lion nature; just so, we will only know what human society is if we understand human nature. We have already noted the obvious fact that a human being cannot be equated with an ant or a bee—but neither is it the same as a lion nor any 'higher' animal. Human beings have a physical body, as do all animals; like animals too, humans have an inner or sentient life of feeling. But human beings, unlike any being of the natural world, say 'I'—they have a self-consciousness or ego. Human society is a human phenomenon and is a particular form or manifestation of the human being, a being of body, inner life (sentience or soul nature) and selfhood (spirit).

In that we are physical beings we, like any natural being, are determined by the laws of physics and of biological growth; we are born, we grow and physically develop and we inevitably die. In that we are a self, an 'I', we have the possibility of becoming free and self-determining. In the living human being there is no contradiction whatsoever between determinism and freedom—it is simply what it means to be human. Consider how, during the predetermined, unalterable stages of childhood and puberty, we gradually come to realize who we are; we wake up to ourselves and to the options we have for our life. We gradually become conscious of what our own gifts and capacities are and even, as we move into adulthood, what our individual mission in life is. Then we try to guide our own lives, through our free choices and creative deeds, so that what is unique about ourselves can best be realized in our lifetime. The predetermined reality of ageing and death may become a 'problem' in terms of what we are trying to achieve, but confronting and coming to terms with ageing and impending death can also be part of the way we forge our existence creatively as subjective agents.

Determinism and freedom are in no sense a 'problem' in relation to human society, although it appears so if we proceed merely theoretically. Conventional social science talks about different perspectives, contradictory theories concerning the nature of society. It will say: 'according to Woodrow Wilson society is a whole composed of many parts (individuals)', or: 'according to Marx society develops in a determined way' or: 'according to Stirner society as a whole doesn't exist and there are just individuals creating their lives'. But presenting such theories abstractly like this is actually only preliminary to a re-imagined social science, a true life science of society. Through cognitive imagination we develop the kind of understanding required to grasp the living relationship of what appears as contradictions or 'opposing positions'. We look through these apparent contradictions and oppositions to perceive the unitary nature of the human being which, on the one hand, expresses itself in every human individual, on the other in the form of society as a whole.

Goethe's Way Of Science

Steiner insists that society can only be properly understood through the power of imaginative thinking, and he emphasizes that such thinking requires a special cultivation. In his words:

> . . . a spiritual contemplation of nature will provide means for the kind of training in thought which, among other things, makes it possible to comprehend the social organism.[57]

When Steiner speaks of 'a spiritual contemplation of nature' he has something specific in mind. He is referring to the methods of conscious participation in living form developed by the German poet and 'nature observer' Johann Wolfgang von Goethe. In one place Steiner uses the expression 'a new Goetheanism' to mean that these methods can be heightened and extended into the social sciences.[58] Elsewhere he comments: 'My book *Towards Social Renewal* is Goetheanistic, if properly understood . . . '.[59] This provides us with a very good starting point. It highlights a pathway toward the entire re-imagination of the social sciences. It also makes it clear that what he himself put forward as social conceptions are of little value if interpreted merely theoretically.

Goethe worked by participating imaginatively in the forms and qualities of colours, plants and animals; his approach to understanding the natural world is sometimes called a 'science of qualities'. Quantities are expressed in abstract numerical form; however, an intimate, living thinking is not the possibility of a thinking which remains in the realm of the objective, quantitative and merely logical. Qualities can be understood only by a highly cultivated feeling capacity. This qualitative understanding is not abstract; the forces, gestures, dynamic tendencies of living things have to be *experienced* in an exact way. A new Goetheanism means that we are endeavouring to study social forms and processes according to the same participatory method—'extremely intimately' as Steiner puts it.[60]

Presented below are indications towards the kind of training in thought 'which . . . makes it possible to comprehend the social organism'. In the context of a university which has dedicated itself to this end, this training would be the task of an orientation programme of studies, undertaken by students from all faculties in all years of a degree course.[61] Some aspects of this orientation programme are likely to deal specifically with social scientific issues of a general nature and here the training would seek to cultivate the social scientific imagination. In the context of the social science faculty itself it could be expected that such a training would no longer be required and that the teaching staff and students would have developed the faculty of imaginative thinking to a high degree and be able to apply it to every aspect of teaching and research.

Goethe's Phenomenological Method

In the text which was the outcome of his colour research Goethe details the nature of his method:

> In reality, any attempt to express the inner nature of a thing is fruitless. What we perceive are effects, and a complete record of these effects ought to encompass this inner nature. We labour in vain to describe a person's character, but when we compile his actions, his deeds, a picture of his character will emerge. Colours are the deeds of light, what it does and what it endures. In this sense we can expect them to tell us something about light . . . [62]

We begin in the realm of exact, objective perception—just like any scientist. We carefully observe each colour or whatever object or process of the world of nature we are dealing with. This is the empirical phenomenon. But we must go much further; in practice we enter into each observed aspect or part and allow its quality or gesture to 'speak' with each other aspect or part. Feeling assumes the precise form, configuration, or quality of the part, which may be a colour, which may be the organs of a plant. This is no facile requirement. It must be carried out in a reverential manner, exactly as we would when opening ourselves to a master work of art with genuine wonderment; in a master work every single part will have significance in terms of the whole, and as students we cannot presume to be able to rapidly understand that whole. We are not seeking to bring the phenomenon down to our level but just the reverse—to raise ourselves up to its height, to allow ourselves to be on a level with it. Gradually, from a total 'conversation' of parts, a vivid inner picture of the whole can emerge.

The Goethean scientific approach always seeks the whole and endeavours to understand the parts as reflections of the whole, how the whole has 'imparted' itself in its parts. Through this holistic approach Goethe identified three key principles or orientations which could also be considered the three primary 'letters' in the language of living form. These principles are polarity (which Goethe called 'one of the driving forces of creation'), metamorphosis, and intensification (*Steigerung*). All three are connected; none can be understood without the others in the practice of Goethe's way of science. Below, firstly, are indications of how a study of natural form cultivates the faculties of cognitive feeling and cognitive will, through entering into the wholeness of living form, polarity, metamorphosis, and intensification.[63] Following that are applications of cognitive feeling and cognitive will in the realm of social phenomena. The faculties of feeling and will, normally considered as having nothing to do with the practise of science, are 'raised up' to become powers of knowing.

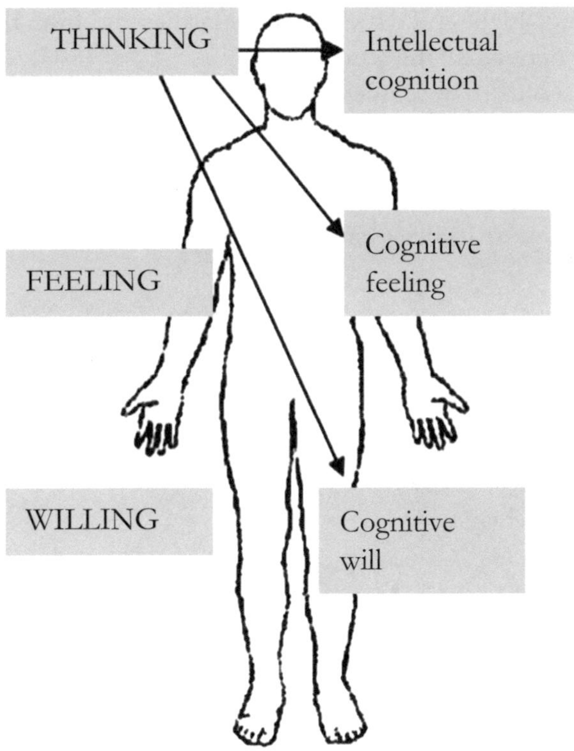

Figure 21

The Realm of Colour

Goethe's phenomenological approach is clearly evidenced in the way he explored colour phenomena. Here the observational facts of light, darkness, and colours are actually entered into and inwardly experienced. Experiments can be carried out with prisms and other apparatus but the central task involves the observation of simple colour phenomena. We are thinking *in* the colour but equally we can say that the colour phenomenon enters our thinking. We abide in 'the phenomenality of the phenomenon', in the experienced quality of the colour, and are not merely concerned with thoughts *about* the phenomenon such as its wavelength and hue.

Participating in the colour yellow we experience its essential gesture—an outward radiation in all directions. In this gesture we see that yellow is closest to light; Goethe called it the first darkening of the light. When we enter into a colour phenomenon in such a way as to bring to consciousness its language of gesture we speak of *cognitive feeling*; our power of feeling assumes the quality or precise dynamic of the gesture. Entering into blue we find the polar gesture of inward contraction or indefinite inwardness. Blue is closest to darkness and Goethe called it the lighting of the darkness. Light and darkness are polarities and from their interrelation can be derived all the other colours.

Yellow and blue may combine to produce green, the colour we see at the centre of the spectrum of light (see Fig. 22). When we enter with the 'eye' of cognitive feeling into this colour we discover that its inner activity or gesture is neither outward nor inward—like yellow and blue—but a harmonization or neutralization of the two.

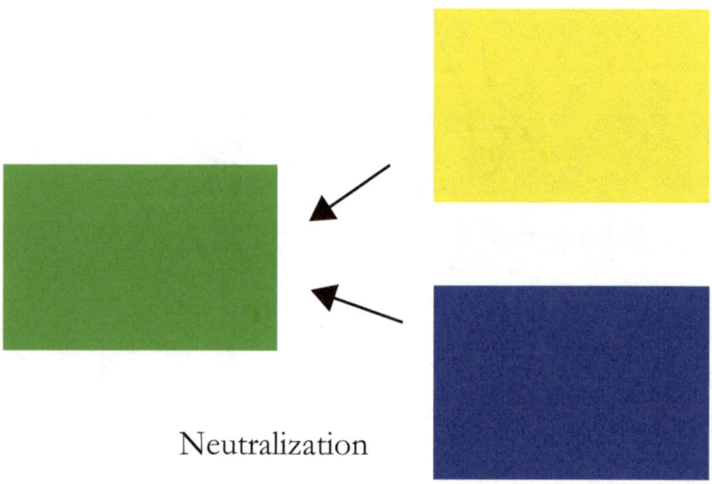

Figure 22

But yellow and blue can be related in another way which Goethe called intensification or heightening (*Steigerung*). It produces a colour which is not in the normal visible spectrum defined by a specific wavelength—this is magenta (see Fig. 23).

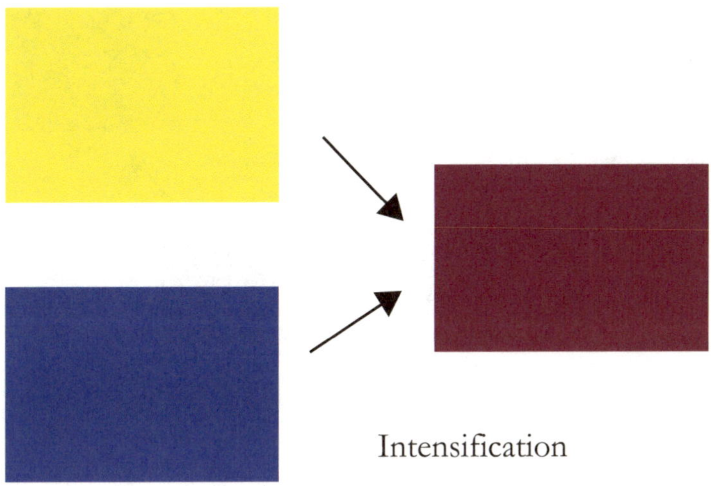

Figure 23

Yellow, as we have just seen, has a diffuse, outward radiating quality. If this outward radiation is intensified or heightened it becomes something forceful and direct; this increases progressively from yellow, to orange, to red. This constitutes a metamorphic sequence. In magenta this forcefulness 'meets' the intensification-metamorphosis of blue, to indigo, to purple. If we intensify blue the 'inward radiation', the retreating into itself, becomes concentrated and enriched. The colour magenta represents the culmination of both intensifications coming from the polarities of yellow and blue, uniting both as a colour which could be described as 'an intensity of inner richness offered powerfully outwardly'.

Thus, through cognitive feeling, we inwardly explore each colour in a way which leads to the perception of the total coherent form in which all the colours are related—the circle of colours (see Fig. 24). Each colour is allowed to have a 'conversation' with every other. Gradually the picture develops of the colour circle as an 'organism', a self-relating organic wholeness. Each colour is intelligible in terms of every other colour and in terms of the whole. Now we have moved beyond perceiving just the gestural expression of particular colours; we now experience the *arising* of colours, how colours are creating each other mutually, how each colour is

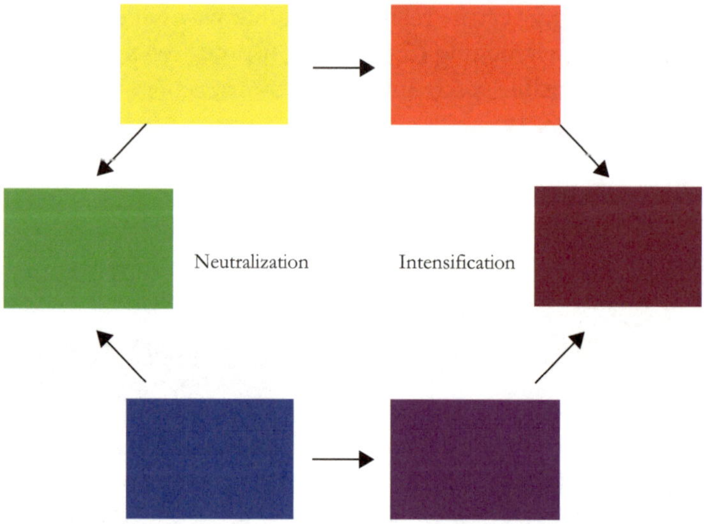

Figure 24

the metamorphosis of another. The polarity of yellow and blue neutralizes into green and intensifies into magenta. Inwardly, we *will* yellow into orange and red, blue into indigo and violet, both yellow and blue into green and into magenta. The formative dynamic of the colours in the creation of the self-relating colour organism we experience in the cognitive will.

The Plant

In terms of a training of thinking toward a re-imagined social science, the goetheanistic study of plants offers a step beyond the realm of colours. The powers of thought cultivated in colour work—exact observation, cognitive feeling, and cognitive will—are further exercised in the more complicated phenomena of plant form.

In the 'higher' phenomena of the plant kingdom Goethe discovered the archetypal qualities of polarity, metamorphosis and intensification which he also identified in the colour realm. Goethe perceived the polarity of root and flower but it was Rudolf Steiner and authors associated with his work who took Goethe's insights further and described how the plant takes form between the encompassing polarity of Earth and Sun. In the Earth where the seed rests and the root takes shape there is relative darkness and coldness. The normally bitter taste of roots expresses something of this inward contraction to a centre. By contrast, the flower with its colours and sweet nectar, opened upward and outward in some degree

Figure 25

of cup shape, expresses qualities of lightness and levity which are related to the Sun.

The leaves of the plant express the relationship of root-seed and flower and as such constitute the copula, the 'in between' of the poles, in their growth and unfoldment. The seed 'sleeping' in the earth is in a state of potential in which the future form is hidden. It is in the polar gesture of the flower in which the plant is most unfolded and expressed. This unfoldment, we could say, represents the metamorphosis and intensification of Earth into Sun. Some plants express this in clearly visible stages of transformation; the rounded seed leaves express the quality of an undifferentiated watery expansion; differentiation takes hold of the leaf form and close to the flower the leaves draw back to the stem in pointed forms, preparing, as it were, for the event of the flower. The flower represents the most intensified or heightened form of the plant; what is hidden in the seed is fully revealed in the flower.

If we look carefully at the sequence of leaf forms, from the bottom to the top of the plant, we can begin to practise exact imagination in two stages. We begin, as with colour work, with exact, empirical observations, with careful, objective perception. Now we inwardly participate in each leaf by assuming its exact shape through cognitive feeling; feeling moulds itself to the leaf form as water does when it takes on the configuration of a vessel into which it is poured. We then move to the next and in this way run through the sequence.

In order to cultivate this flexible, metamorphic thinking we move backwards and forwards along the sequence; each leaf belongs together with the contiguous leaves and to the sequence. One leaf does not physically turn into the next; what develops as we rise up the plant is the *gestural language* of the leaf, a language only visible to the eye of the imagination. At the base the rounded leaf-forms are outstretching; as we rise the leaves become more differentiated and finally pointed and contracted onto the stem. In this way we gain an understanding of the sequence as a single, formative movement. We inwardly *enact* this metamorphosis which is why we speak of a 'cognitive will'. In a more developed Goethean practice the whole leaf metamorphic sequence is worked with in this way and the flower and fruit forms are incorporated into a total study.

The Whole Animal

Grasping the coherent wholeness of the 'organism' of colours is an important training of the living, imaginative thinking necessary to comprehend the wholeness of animal form. Goethe himself did not proceed very far in this direction but others who have taken up his approach have made significant contributions.[64] An animal is a complex creature and even with the simplest animal a very large number of attributes or 'parts' could be compiled in relation to the empirical phenomenon. In practice, such a lengthy compilation is not necessary for a basic study; we list the parts or qualities most apparent, most distinctive of that animal. For our purpose here we can refer to the study of the elephant by Goethean scientist Craig Holdrege. Holdrege makes a preliminary compilation of ten characteristics which here will be formed into a circle, as with our organism of colours (see Fig. 26).

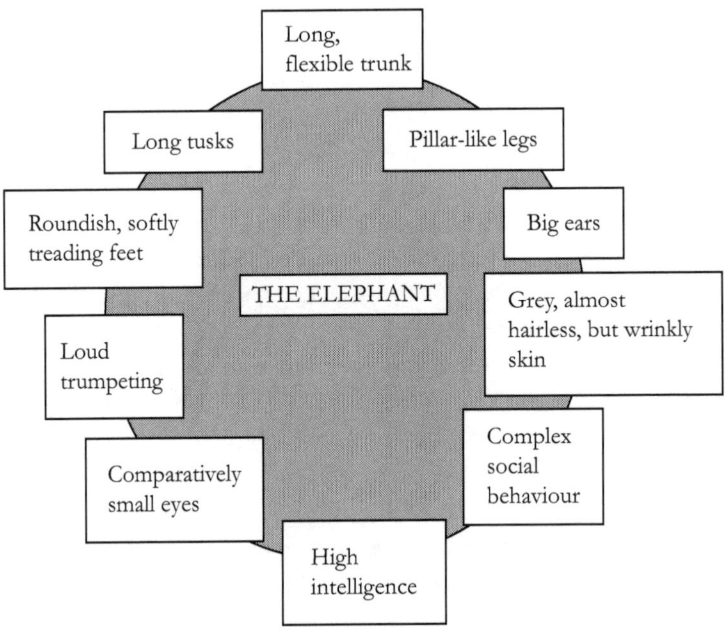

Figure 26

With the characteristics presented in a circle suggesting the whole animal, this whole-seeing being the aim of our striving, each characteristic can be allowed to 'speak' to every other. In an animal study the characteristics must firstly be understood in the ordinary analytical way, as empirical phenomena. When we Goetheanistically deepen our study by imaginatively participating in the characteristics or attributes and their relationships, each attribute reveals its gestural character in relation to the whole. For example, 'big ears' and 'comparatively small eyes' have a purely descriptive, quantitative aspect (the empirical phenomenon) which, through imaginative engagement, can come to reveal something about the character of the animal. They become, in other words, a kind of physiognomic language, the outer form revealing something of the inner. A picture of 'who' this animal is begins to build. Writes Holdrege:

> When I am studying a given phenomenon or reading what others have discovered, I make as vivid a mental picture as possible . . . By utilising imagination and staying as close to the phenomena as possible, I try to create an exact picture. The goal is to achieve saturated inner images of the elephant's characteristics. The remarkable thing is that when one builds these exact pictures over and over, moving from one characteristic to the next, patterns emerge. You begin to recognise how the characteristics form a whole—the unity begins to reveal itself.[65]

Holdrege describes how the quality of flexibility, most immediately apparent in the trunk, is actually intrinsic to its whole being. The elephant shows flexibility in its feeding behaviour, social interactions, in its learning overall, 'even flexibility rooted in the anatomy of its immense feet'.[66] Holdrege indicates that his goal is, in Goethe's words, to 'portray rather than to explain'.[67]

Human Physiology

On the educational pathway toward artistically comprehending the threefold social organism, the Goetheanistic study of human physiology is a particularly important step. This is because it cultivates the faculty of 'perceiving the balance of the threefold in the parts'.

It was Rudolf Steiner who, using the fundamental methods and approaches of Goethe, brought forth a picture of the human organism in its threefold unity. Through cognitive imagination Steiner revealed three principal centres that he called the *nerve-sense organisation*, the *metabolic-limb organisation*, and, between the two and forming the copula, the *rhythmic organization* (see Fig. 27). How these organizations are expressed in a specialised way in different groups of mammals has been explored by others.[68]

For our apprenticeship in living, imaginative thinking, studying natural form as a pathway towards a genuine social thinking, it is important to experience through cognitive imagination how these three organizations relate to each other. When we become intimate with the dynamic quality or gesture of the different organizations, through cognitive feeling which progresses to cognitive will, we are learning to perceive the mutual creative arising of the three aspects of the whole physiological organization. These organizations are by no means compartmentalized, existing side-by-side in a spatial sense. They interpenetrate in a living, dynamic way and in different proportions depending on the nature of

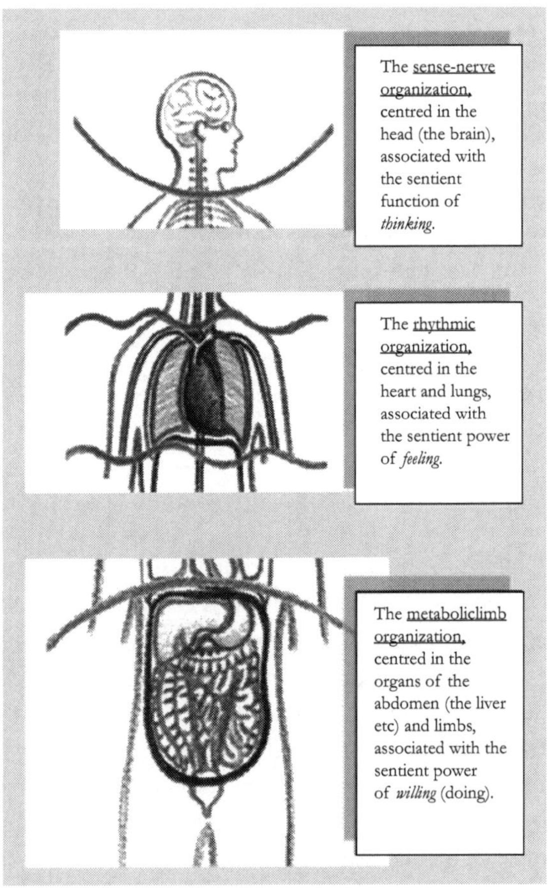

Figure 27

each particular organ. As we shall see, exactly the same thing applies with the social organization.

The *nerve-sense organization* has its seat in the head, in the brain, but is also spread throughout the organism in the form of the nervous systems and the sense organs. The brain is the centre of apprehension and cognition. Its polarity, the *metabolic-limb organization*, includes all the metabolic organs, for this is where food substance becomes energy for use by the limbs (as well as by all tissues and organs throughout the body, in order for them to carry out their functions). Metabolic process is almost completely unconscious. Between these two poles is the *rhythmic organization* with its seat in the heart and lungs. Breathing generally takes place unconsciously but it also can be consciously controlled. The processes of respiration and blood circulation are fundamentally rhythmical and, as such, extend throughout the organism. So while we find the principal focus of the third organization in the thorax, rhythmic process takes place throughout the organism.

Working Goetheanistically we enter into these phenomena, in the first place, with cognitive feeling. This is no facile task; it demands a dedicated and lengthy exact imaginative work. The exact cognitive imagination participates in the form and function of each organization as a whole and discovers the manner in which the three interpenetrate in every organ and process in the human organism. We move backwards and forwards, entering into the forms and qualities of the head and the metabolic organs, allowing the polar qualities of these phenomena to permeate our thinking. In this way an ever-more luminous picture of the dynamic wholeness arises inwardly. The nerve-sense organs are immobile and relatively unregenerative whereas, by contrast, the functions of the metabolic-limb organization involve constant muscular activity and are highly regenerative. The activity of the in-between rhythmic organs involves a constant oscillation between movement and rest, with the lung tissue non-muscular, largely symmetrical in form and immobile (non-muscular, and in that sense closer in nature to the brain) and the heart asymmetrical, muscular and mobile (and in these ways closer to the organs of the metabolic-limb system).

The heart is primarily a rhythmic organ but it is enervated and is thus an aspect of the nerve-sense organization of the body. Further, it is related to the metabolic-limb organization in that it plays a role in moving blood carrying energy substance to the limbs and other bodily organs. Likewise, the brain is primarily a nerve-sense organ and is characterized by its immobility and lack of regenerative power. Yet on the level of ideation it is highly mobile, and through the formation and dissolution, production and reproduction of thoughts, it partakes of the will activity typical of the metabolic-limb organization. Through its blood supply it is related to the rhythmic organization. The liver is the primary metabolic organ but, in a similar way, it likewise is connected to the other two organizations.

Each organ of the body can be imaginatively appraised in this manner, based on at least a basic understanding of physiological form and function. The whole is reflected in every part and that is not just a theory but needs to be inwardly *seen*. We weigh up—through cognitive feeling and cognitive will—the balance of the three systems expressed in every part. The deeper one penetrates with one's understanding, the more comprehensive, mobile, and vivid the picture becomes of the whole human organization as a three-membered unity.

Animal Physiology

The three physiological systems exist in a balanced condition in the healthy human being. Through undertaking the exercise above it becomes possible to perceive that no physiological system is 'higher', more dominant or accentuated than the other two systems. This balance comes to particularly overt expression in the human dental structure—neither incisors, canines, nor molars predominate, there is a balance of all three tooth forms (see Fig. 28).

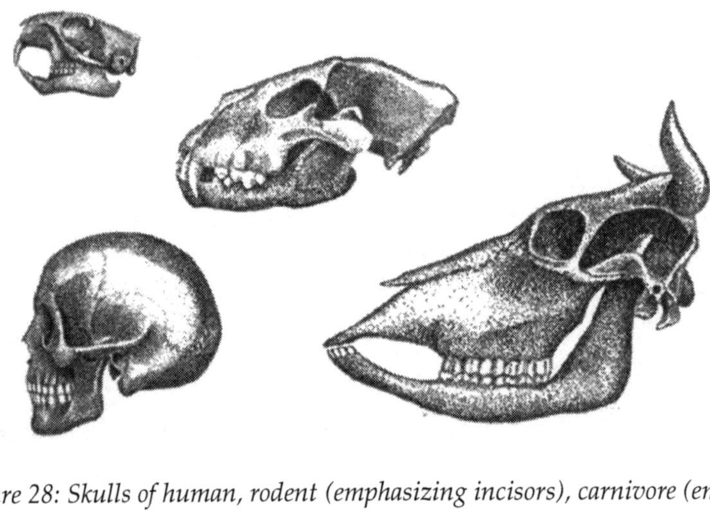

Figure 28: Skulls of human, rodent (emphasizing incisors), carnivore (emphasizing canines) and ungulate (emphasizing molars).

It is different with animals; for example, each mammal type emphasizes either the nerve-sense, rhythmic, or the metabolic-limb aspect. This one-sidedness is expressed in animal dentition; rodents (nerve-sense animals) emphasize the incisors which they use for incessant gnawing. Cows, as ungulates, (metabolic-limb animals) emphasize the molars which grind grass; lions as carnivores ('in between' or rhythmic animals) emphasize the canines which are used for tearing flesh. This physiological emphasis is reflected in the social nature of the animal. Rodents (emphasizing the nerve-sense aspect) are characteristically nervous, quick moving, diminutive animals, and tend to be solitary and reclusive. Cows (emphasizing the metabolic-limb aspect) by contrast are focused in their deep metabolic processes—they are large and slow-moving and their social existence is characteristically in a herd, a collectivity. A lion's social existence falls between these poles, rhythmically alternating between collective life of rapid movement on the hunt and a lengthy digestive process at rest, largely solitary.

A New Goetheanism: Exercises Toward A Living Social Imagination

The Social Whole in Historical Study

Any phenomenological study, in relation to the natural and human worlds alike, begins with clear observations, with gathering together 'solid facts' to the extent that they can be ascertained. Social phenomena do not have the sense-perceptible, objective definiteness of a mineral, plant or animal form. In the social realm we are dealing with creations of the human spirit, with cultural forms and processes; but all such social phenomena can be recorded in different ways, and clearly described. The journey of imaginative thinking sets forth from this firm foundation.

Wilhelm von Humboldt, using Goethe's approaches, guides us towards the perception of the social whole.[69] He states that the historian, just like the poet, can only find the truth which gives meaning to disjointed social realities through the active imagination which enters into these realities in such a way that their connections may come to light. Thereby, writes Humboldt, the historian gradually forms an exact 'general picture' of the creative forces working behind the objective social phenomena, forces which are 'the essence of history itself'.[70] We are seeking the 'essential character' of a particular historical event, episode or period of history.

Let us consider an event which stands out in its significance in the history of European civilization—the French Revolution. Set out in a circle are some key objective aspects, presented as starting points and guides to a phenomenological way of working (see Fig. 29). Each names a whole area of research. The only aspects which are not the production of the human spirit are the French climate and other geographical features. However, in terms of the event in question, it is not the geographical features in themselves which are important but *how the French people responded creatively to these features*: their lifestyle, their architecture, their customs, their language—all formed over a very long period of time.

The French Revolution is considered to have taken place between May 1789 and November 1799. Whether we are dealing with short-lived occurrences or longer historical processes, our Goetheanistic method is the same: we enter into a phenomenological engagement with the key aspects (the 'particulars'), deepening our understanding through feeling and will cognition. We allow a kind of 'conversation' to take place, one particular with another, over and over, testing the quality of each with all others. Nothing is forced about this process; by entering each fact openly and sensitively, the facts or particulars are being allowed to speak for

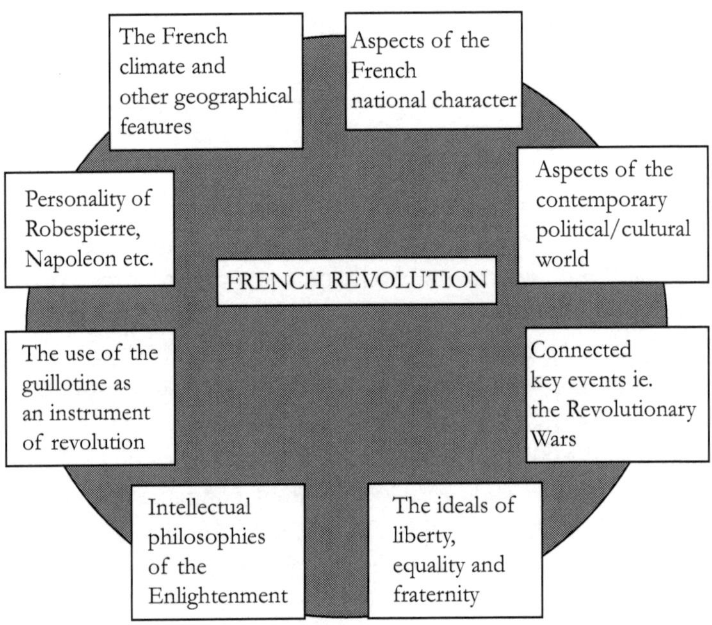

Figure 29

themselves, to reveal what they are without being constrained or constricted in any way.

Let us consider one of the 'conversations': between the ideals of liberty, equality, and fraternity, and the personalities of Napoleon and Robespierre. We may suppose that each of these areas has been researched thoroughly and that we are familiar and flexible with this material. Then it becomes possible to allow them to come into relationship, just as we did with the colours in the colour circle and with our whole-animal study. The result of this process is not what is important here, only the way of working. Each of the ideals of liberty, equality, and fraternity relates to a very different aspect of human nature which can be inwardly experienced; each ideal has a characteristic gesture. The personalities of the two prominent individuals can also be entered into in an exact, imaginative way—including Napoleon's sharp intelligence and Robespierre's asceticism. It is these gestures which 'converse' with each other; nothing telling may emerge immediately but, if worked on over and over, also in relation to the other particulars around the circle, a 'general picture' of the essential character of this revolution can emerge, vividly living and comprehensive.

The Individuality/Communality Polarity

Already in Chapter 2 a way of working with the fundamental social polarity has been indicated. Here it is stated that we get to know the polarity artistically, imaginatively; we actually enter into the reciprocal relationship of the poles. Thereby we can come to understand, not just theoretically but as actual experience, how the communality pole is essentially social in character and how the individuality pole essentially anti-social.

We can now connect the two social poles with the two social scientific outlooks—*individuality* with the approach of Stirner and Thatcher ('the individual is the reality') and *communality* with the approach of Wilson, Hegel and Marx ('the true is the whole').

Certainly the words 'individuality' and 'communality' have a definite, conceptual meaning and this provides the 'solid' basis for the further journey in thinking. In the practice of a 'new Goetheanism' we do not remain with this polarity as something abstract; we learn to enter into it and inwardly experience it. Working as we have done with the polarity of yellow and blue colours provides the training of thinking necessary; we participate in the exact inner gesture of each colour. In just the same way we enter into the inner gestures of 'individuality' and 'communality'. This is a deed of the imagination. It becomes possible to inwardly

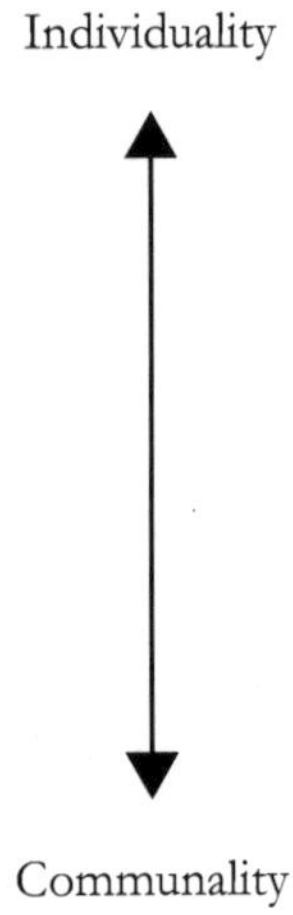

Figure 30

experience the polar dynamic of these two social realities; inwardly we can move between the two, backward and forward, deepening in the will the nature of this polarity.

The individual is the reality is proclaimed because we sense in the self-hood or 'I' of every single human being an irreducible, unassailable truth. *The true is the whole* is proclaimed when we sense that humanity only has reality when people live with and for each other; social wholeness sounds a gesture of goodness and completeness. The opposition of individuality and communality is not something abstract and logical; it needs to be felt and willed *exactly*.

The Living Threefold Social Wholeness

If the reality of individuality and communality has become an experience of the cognitive will, then we will grasp the creative forces which have shaped prominent conflicts in social life. Firstly, we can consider the antithetical theories which have dominated social life in the twentieth century and continue to exert enormous influence—this is the opposition of capitalism and communism. Capitalism, to the extent that it promotes free enterprise, the 'self-made man', and private ownership of property, is connected with individuality and the ideal of freedom. In these ways it is aligned with the traditional philosophy of liberalism. Communism relates to the pole of communality in that it promotes collectivism, communal property ownership and the ideal of the common good or fraternity.

CAPITALISM
Liberalism
Individuality

↕ Opposition

COMMUNISM/SOCIALISM
Communality

Figure 31

The polarity capitalism-communism has been experienced for over a hundred years as the central social strife. Politics and social theory have been devoted to trying to solve or harmonize this strife. It can only be neutralized or harmonized through a lessening of the extremes, just as yellow-blue is neutralized into green. Throughout the twentieth century and into the present, political life has taken the form of different degrees of compromise between the opposing positions (see Fig. 32). Political parties or groupings can be more or less left wing or right wing; there is the 'centre right' and the 'centre left' and so on. For example, in the 'left of centre' position, the communality aspect remains strong (the common good) whereas the individuality aspect (specifically, individual rights) is considerably diminished.

Going back to the individuality-communality polarity which stands behind the capitalism-communism opposition: the pole of individuality, for reasons already entered into, belongs primarily and natively to the cultural-spiritual sphere of society where the ideal of freedom is cultivated, educated, and practised above everything else. Communality belongs primarily to the economic sphere where people work with and for each other, to serve the needs of the other, inspired by the ideal of cooperation or fraternity. When this polarity is properly expressed in the social whole

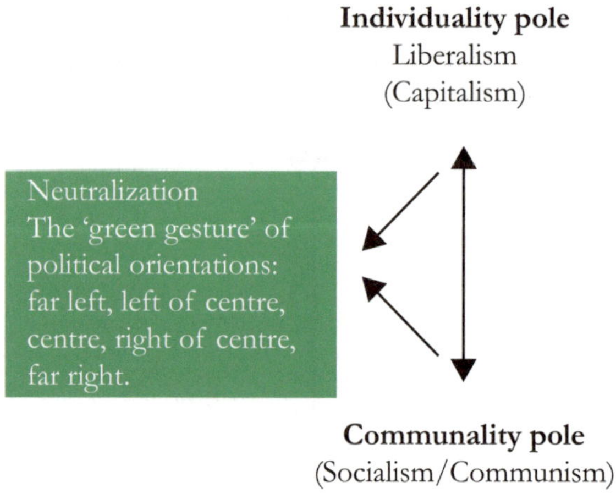

Figure 32

it becomes creative and not just a source of strife. It can be intensified into a 'third thing'.

In magenta neither yellow nor blue is diminished or compromised; magenta is not merely a blending but a 'raising up' or intensifying, a creating. In a 'magenta gesture' the poles unite at the height of their intensification so that a 'third thing' is engendered with the heightened qualities of both (see Fig. 33). The character of magenta is a 'fullness and depth which gives itself forth of itself'. If we undergo such intensification within the social realm we can experience in a creative way how an independent sphere of rights comes into existence as the copula or mediator between the economic and cultural-spiritual spheres.

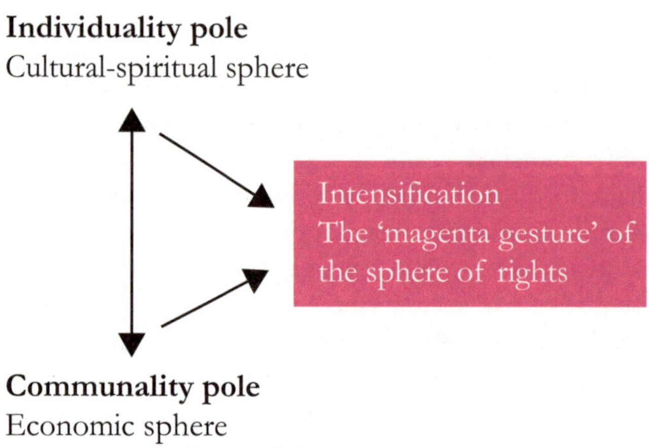

Figure 33

In the acknowledgement of a right neither individuality nor communality is diminished or compromised; on the contrary, both are enhanced. In every recognized right the dignity and independence of every single human 'I' is being celebrated. I feel myself to be a free being; I value and love my freedom personally. But society is not just 'me'—personal freedom is the experience of very many 'I's. The 'I' experience is also a 'we'. When individual freedom is recognized as a legal right (and this is something relatively recent in human cultural evolution), it is immensely enhanced by becoming a formal agreement within the social whole (that is, also by the enhancement or intensification of the 'we' or communality pole which collectively recognizes this right). Thus every right has something of a 'magenta gesture'; the rights-legal sphere we could call a magenta phenomenon. The 'common will' and the 'I' are inherently polarized; only the sphere of rights mediates and enhances both.

Thus the understanding of the threefold social whole emerges as a creative-cognitive deed, not as merely a thought-out formula or philosophical social theory which is foisted upon a limited aspect of the social reality, leading to a distortion or imbalance. In imaginative cognition we inwardly create the threefold social unity.

The Whole Manifesting in the Parts

Through creative will-thinking we have inwardly generated the imagination of society as a threefold unity. In relation to the threefold archetype—two poles and the relating principle or copula—the human social organism is a balanced formation in its healthy condition. We perceive with the eye of the imagination that neither the economic, political-rights, nor cultural-spiritual sphere predominates over the others. If one or the other social sphere becomes exaggerated or dominant we perceive it to be in a state of social illness. Most commonly today the political sphere dominates (most extremely in forms of totalitarian government) and tends to want to repress, control, or even eliminate the free cultural-spiritual life.

We have also seen that balance in healthy human physiology, in its overall formation. However, to understand any particular organ (or 'part') of the human being, we need to train the power of cognitive feeling to sense how one aspect—the sense-nerve, the rhythmic or the metabolic-limb—predominates and how the other aspects are nevertheless present. The same kind of training of thinking takes place in the goetheanistic study of animal physiology. In animals the threefold archetype manifests in a one-sided way, depending on the animal type.

Just as with human physiology, so every 'organ' of the social organism—which includes every form of organization and institution—entered into imaginatively, reveals its threefold constitution and how one or the other of the three social spheres is emphasized. The whole is manifest in every part but in a one-sided way. For example, a school is primarily a cultural-spiritual organization (within the ideal of freedom), yet nevertheless expresses, to a much lesser extent, economic (fraternity) and legal-rights (equality) aspects. In the case of the school, the school board expresses the economic aspect, and the administration the legal-rights aspect. A community bank may be thought to be an economic institution; however, it is actually primarily a legal-rights entity relating to the ideal of equality (this is something which will be discussed in Chapter 6). As such it mediates the economic and cultural-spiritual spheres; it deals with capital which has come into being through economic activity and how this capital is directed toward initiatives in the cultural-spiritual sphere.

These exercises in a 'new Goetheanism' are very important, for they show how the threefold social order comes into being. The threefold social order will never be the result of a theory or a strategy—it is a creative work. Such exercises are the means of cultivating the social art, which in the future can be practised throughout the social fabric and which involves the conscious creation of this social order. In the next chapter a case study is documented which shows how medicine in all its forms is primarily a cultural-spiritual phenomenon and only to a much lesser degree pertains to the economic and political-rights spheres.

Social Metamorphosis and Intensification

Everything set forth in Chapter 3 can be used as an exercise for the development of living social thinking. This study is intended to be something far more than an historical survey. The emergence of the threefold formation of human society, seen over millennia, is a vast process of metamorphosis and intensification. What intensifies is the threefold social archetype; it begins in a seed-like state in original societies and, through stages of emancipation, gradually emerges and differentiates into the essentially threefold structure which is modern society. The whole progression needs to be entered into, inwardly enacted, so that it is perceived as a continuum with the eye of the imagination.

The exploration of the economic sphere in Chapter 6 needs to be treated in the same way. It could be called an 'encompassing economic imagination'. The 'hidden' potential of the Earth is what intensifies; hidden in the sense of being visible only to the eye of the spirit. Through stages of metamorphosis this potential becomes something concrete in the form of financial capital. This economic distillation of the Earth is truly a creative, formative work of the human spirit and, as with formative processes in nature, it can only be grasped in the will, the cognitive will. A re-imagined economics is much more than an intellectual pursuit; it calls upon the most finely adjusted power of artistic discernment.

The 'flower' of the economic process—that is to say, the point of greatest intensification—is the formation of capital. One expression of capital is money and it is normally assumed that money has a single property or potential, no matter how it is used. But money itself reveals a different potential or value in relation to the economic, political-rights and cultural-spiritual spheres. It arises in the economic sphere through the activity of working upon nature guided by the human mind (spirit), but its revealed, intensified form pertains to both the rights-legal and the cultural-spiritual spheres. Money as capital—pure potential—assumes different forms within the social organism; one form transforms into another in a developmental process.

Described in what follows are three steps in a particular metamorphosis of money. What drives this metamorphosis is the intensification of capital (= potential). In the form of purchase money the potential which capital represents has reached a certain limited state; in the form of gift money that potential is free. This is the intensification which needs to be inwardly enacted.

Purchase money is that which is given in exchange for a good or a service within the economic sphere. The key point is that something specific is received in exchange for what is given; barter functions in the same way and has the same gesture of balance. Purchase money has value only for the person giving it; upon payment that value is transferred to the recipient. A purchase is immediate—it happens the moment the purchase money is handed over. If it is not immediate—for example, if an IOU or a promissory note is written—then it becomes more of the nature of a loan. *Because of its exchange character (the goodwill between a buyer and a seller) it relates primarily to the motivating ideal of the economic sphere which is cooperation or fraternity.* The ideal of freedom, however, is at work to a degree because the purchaser can choose which product to purchase for the same amount of money.

Loan money arises in the economy when excess capital is generated through profit; in most cases loans are issued by banks which are repositories of loan capital. Loan money has value for the person who receives it—yet its value is not lost for the giver because the loan is sooner or later repaid (most commonly with interest). Nothing is immediately received in exchange for the issuing of a loan—this is its fundamental difference from purchase money. The loan has value for the recipient because it allows that person to realize something they wish to create, do or have; loan money is unrealized potential. Therefore loan money—which arises in the economic sphere as capital—reaches beyond toward the cultural-spiritual sphere as a potential for the human spirit to realize something. Because of its nature as potential it has a gift character; but because the giver receives back its value (upon repayment) it has something of the give-and-receive-back character of purchase money. Loan money is thus mediatory between purchase and gift money. Because it has an obligation attached to it (the obligation to repay which is either an informal IOU or a legal contract) it is primarily a legal-rights phenomenon which always relates to the ideal of equality and justice. In accounting terms, a loan is equity.

Gift money is a further development of loan money because it has value *only* for the recipient as potential; no interest is accrued and nothing needs to be returned to the giver. Gift money is addressed to the creative intentions and inspirations of the human spirit and that is why its primary locus of activity is in the cultural-spiritual sphere of society (even if it straight away is turned back into purchase money by the recipient). At the moment it is received it is entirely free and to that degree it is an

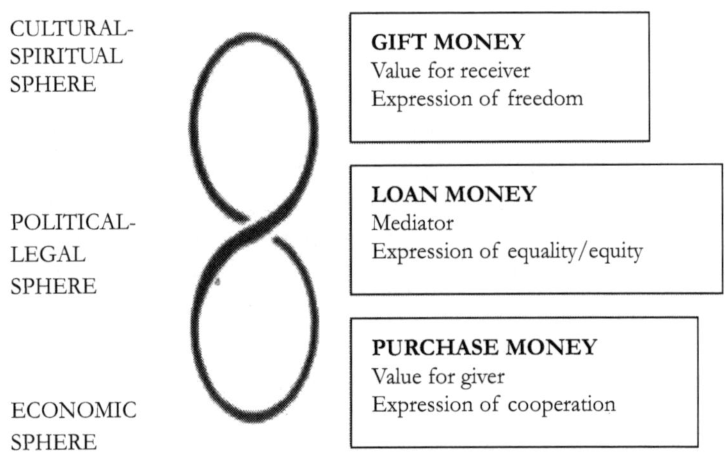

Figure 34

expression of the ideal of liberty which works as the primary motivating force of the cultural-spiritual sphere.

The theory of money in its most death-like abstraction should turn around cold, hard facts, but these facts must be resurrected into life on the path of true understanding. Money only has reality within the *living* social fabric. As with our method of developing a living picture of the economy as a whole, the three states of money and their transformation must be entered into to the point where a vivid 'feeling-picture' of the whole process takes shape. This is one of the pathways toward a re-imagined social science.

Chapter 5

SOCIAL ART

Social Science and Social Art

Even when external forms of social protest are met with guns and walls of steel, nothing can prevent the yearning for social renewal from ever rising anew, born of care. Conscience makes resolute the will to build our world in the best possible way. This is not something which can be left to the politicians and technocrats; the task of social transformation is a profound form of creative art.

The work of the artist has always carried a socially transformative—even revolutionary—impulse. Art does not just passively mirror the world; it builds it, transforms and enriches it, often by penetrating to its darkest recesses. Art is world-transformative, no matter on which level or in which form we consider it. Whether through expression, insight, revelation—social transformation is a form of creation, the bringing about of the new. Nature is forever bringing about the new, in multifarious forms and expressions; the cosmos as a whole is creating and recreating itself. Art is for human social life what creative, evolutionary forces are for the natural world.

When social scientific understanding reaches the level of cognitive will, we are already within the domain of art. Cognitive will is a 'creative knowing'; it thinks in terms of the language of creative forces active in the living social body and in this sense we can speak of science reaching toward the artistic, science calling upon an artistic sensibility. When social science has attained to will-imbued understanding it becomes the impetus for a social art, an art which, as we will see, has awoken in the present even while it still in many ways belongs to the future.

The Gestation of Social Art

The notion of social art is meaningful only in the light of the aeonic process of human individuation. The existential philosopher Paul Tillich talks about different dimensions of what it means to be a modern human individual, one of them being 'the courage to be as a part in the creative process of nature and history, as developed in Western civilization'.[71] He discusses how men like Pico della Mirandola, Leonardo, Giordano Bruno, Kant, Goethe and Schelling were inspired by the idea of participating in the creative process of the universe, by the recognition that 'the unconscious process of nature breaks into the consciousness of man'.[72] This process is borne, Tillich writes, by the human individual through whom creative potentiality can be actualized. All such creative actualization gives rise to what we call 'progress'.

The basic structure of progress is that everything actualized has potentialities for further actualization. This is the freedom of radical existentialism, the will to act because we live and seek to affirm our being through action (although a distinction must be drawn here between Tillich as a religious existentialist and atheist existentialists like Sartre).[73] The courage and the possibility of creating the world into the future, of actualizing potentiality, is to enter the kingdom of our freedom. It is an existential state filled with anxiety because it cannot depend on the traditional religious worldview which gave the human a secure place in the cosmic order. We live on an Earth thrown out of the centre by Copernicus and Galileo and made minute in the infinity of the universe. This courage 'had to take into itself the deep anxiety of nonbeing in a universe without limits and without a humanly understandable meaning'.[74] We are free to create our world—but more than that, we are *called on* to be such free creators out of the very condition of our individuality. The modern belief in progress through individual action, Tillich goes on to say:

> is something completely different from the attitude of Aristotle and the whole ancient world. In Aristotle the movement from potentiality to actuality is vertical, going from the lower to the higher forms of being. In modern progressivism the movement from potentiality to actuality is horizontal, temporal, futuristic.[75]

The way Tillich describes the horizontal nature of creative potentiality is exactly how we can contemplate the meaning and role of a social art in our time.

The gradual emancipation of the cultural-spiritual sphere of society in the last two centuries has to a great extent been propelled by the arts which were seen as the vanguard, the epitome of what it meant to be free. In the eighteenth and nineteenth-century Romantic period artists began to sense that the way to freedom comes about by dissolving the links to tradition, to religion in a formal sense, and to enter into a chaotic process—inspired by the natural world. Goethe and thinkers around him sought the *Urgrund* or 'procreative chaos' as the mystic Jacob Boehme had called it, the creative source at the heart of living nature. Novalis declared that 'the chaos must radiate from every poem'.[76]

All of this anticipated the intense forces of emancipation at work in the cultural-spiritual sphere of society in the nineteenth and twentieth centuries. Freedom was the governing impulse of the twentieth century's art movements, of Surrealism, Expressionism, Abstractionism, and many others. Amid the turbulence of war at the beginning of the century a vanguard art appeared which did not want to have the characterization of an elite 'fine art' placed upon it. We see this in Marcel Duchamp's dadaist found-objects and the whole movement of subversive, 'anti-art' spawned from it. We see how it proliferated into the kind of Land Art and Performance Art where the privileged gallery space is eschewed. With much more lofty aims yet still fundamentally subversive was the future-orientated *Mysterium* of Scriabin, an artwork conceived as a grand act of spiritual transformation and renewal involving whole populations of people in musical and architectural settings. These so-called 'total works of art' sought to dissolve the separation between artistic expression and the social organism. A grotesquely distorted form of 'total art' was the theatre of politics of National Socialism. The Nazi festivals enabled a kind of mystic communion with the Führer, the 'master artist' who presided over the millions of selves fusing ecstatically with the social whole.[77] The traditional 'frame' of art is ruptured and a 'procreative chaos' opens within the cultural-spiritual life.

Viewed as a whole with the eye of the imagination which looks through the representative works to the underlying creative currents and formative forces, the arts in the modern period underwent an extraordinary transmutation and diversification in the name of freedom; sculpture, poetry, music, drama, and movement arts all came into flux, dissolved or intermingled. Art reshaped itself, subverted and dissolved itself. The void it created is not a nothingness—it is a fullness of the potential of the liberated human spirit. From within this matrix of potentiality it is possible to discern the emergence of an entirely new form of artistic striving.

The Rebellion Against Forms: Beyond The World of Art

A revolutionary power has been at work in modern culture. It is a life process and condition of human nature. Nietzsche identified as the Dionysian the tendency towards flux and transformation, opposing the Apollonian tendency toward purity and fixed form. There are periods in the development of civilization when this Dionysian aspect of human nature breaks to the surface with particular intensity and predominates over every retreat into fixity. We have seen the tendency towards breaking out of the frame of limiting forms and conceptions about art in the culture of the modernist avant-garde, in an exuberant and often courageous fashion. This can be understood as one outward sign of a Dionysian struggle which is impelling humanity from the depths of its own nature.

The Russian symbolist poet Andrey Bely was writing at the time of the Russian Revolution when, after the mayhem of the First World War, European society ached for a new civilization. He formed a connection with Rudolf Steiner at exactly the time when Steiner was formulating his ideas for the threefold social order and shared with Steiner a sense of revolutionary potential in post-war European civilization, not in a political but in an artistic-creative sense. In his essay *Revolution and Culture* Bely invokes this creative revolutionary power as he senses it gathering at the surface of the modern world:

> Inside the life of art a rebellion against forms is rising. It is becoming recognised that creation is in the creation of new spiritual-emotional elements. Its form is not transitory. No; it is not clay, not paint, and not sound. No, it is the soul of man.[78]

It's as if the traditional art forms had become encumbrances, garments which no longer fitted, no longer suited the individuality that the modern human being had become. They had to be flung off so that the human being could stand naked in freedom, or at least soul-naked before—itself. Nietzsche had already glimpsed it: '[The human being] is no longer an artist; he has become a work of art.'[79] The revolutionary power through which human beings free themselves means finding the source in the human soul out of which all the different traditional art forms have been extruded.

Bely writes that 'the first act of our creativity' is the creation of the world of art.[80] In all civilizations the world over the ubiquity of architecture, sculpture, painting, music and poetry is striking but to be expected when we consider that the origin of the arts lies in the nature of the human being. When we lift ourselves to an encompassing imagination of the evolution of all civilizations, as Bely and Steiner endeavour to do, we perceive that the arts are in a sense shaping a consciousness of the whole human being, a being of body, soul (sentience) and spirit (selfhood). We learn about our physical incarnation, especially through architecture which most strongly relates to the body and the way it stands upright, rooted on the Earth and rising toward the heavens, providing for the needs of the body in external space and time. In sculpture that externalizing impulse is somewhat held back and we gain insight into the dynamic, living forces of our own living being. Through painting we bring consciousness to our inner sentient life, through gestures of colour and form, by learning how to 'hear' the colours and gestures of this inner life. In music these gestures are literally heard as disembodied patterns and movements of tones; in poetry attention is turned more to the gesture and flow of our thoughts, to the way we sense our own identity; language speaks directly of the self, the 'I'.[81]

The world of art, over millennia, has shaped and formed us as individuals, brought us to self-knowledge, liberated us. Now, as free individuals, we become creators in a new sense, even if the traditional arts continue and evolve in their own way. We are no longer just products of cultural determinations but creators of ourselves and our future. This is what Bely means by 'a rebellion against forms', the path beyond the 'world of art'. He refers to it as 'the second act of creation'.[82] By this Bely is suggesting that human artistic nature will begin to take creative responsibility for the world in an entirely new way. It is the existential responsibility grasped by Tillich when he speaks of 'the courage to be as a part in the creative process of nature and history'. It is also how the German conceptual and social artist Joseph Beuys conceived the task of 'social sculpture'—that is, the shaping of the total artwork of the future social order in which every person potentially plays a part. Beuys calls the human being a 'freedom being' because every person is potentially a social artist.[83]

The creation of the society of the future is not the commission of a political elite, the class of our political masters; it is the responsibility of every person. This is a radically democratic picture of social transformation and social creation. Bely speaks also of a third act of creation and this, he says, must be imagined to take place on the far horizon of the social future: 'The third act is the entry into the kingdom of freedom and the new joining of absolutely free people for the creation of a commune of life . . . '[84]

The Threefold Social Order As Social Artwork

To be free means to be unconstrained, to have the immediate potential and ability to act in a way which, to the greatest possible extent, realizes our unique capacities and powers. The social artist acts in freedom but that freedom is inspired and guided by understanding, by social scientific perception. The social activist Ulrich Roesch puts it as follows:

> As social scientists we can experience the social organism as an inner spiritual picture, but then we have to become artists when we act socially. For the artist then creates a new, unique piece of art out of the archetype.[85]

Every element of society, every process, every phenomenon, can be seen in relation to the threefold social wholeness, the archetypal threefold. That is the task of the social scientist, working with exact, living imagination. Every aspect of society becomes meaningful in relation to every other as each comes to shine with the light of the social whole. Just as every colour in the circle of colours shapes every other colour to form a self-subsistent wholeness, so it is with the social organism. This is the 'inner spiritual picture' which is nothing abstract or merely 'thought out'; it is dynamic and enlivening, as is a mighty work of art. Because any aspect of society is perceived to be an expression of the whole, that aspect gathers to itself a living force, an impulse of social will. When, as a social artist, I create a new, unique piece of art out of the archetype, I am shaping the threefold social organism; this is how the threefold social unity comes into being as a conscious creation, and this is how it is maintained.

When does social scientific research end and social art action begin? In truth they are not divided but are a continuum. The social scientist needs to be a social artist as well, otherwise all research will represent unrealized potential. The social artist needs to be a social scientist to a degree, to carry out the research and come to the level of understanding necessary to act creatively. At the mid-point of this continuum is the 'inner spiritual picture'. This is not a 'picture' in the sense of a static mental image; it is formed through cognitive feeling and cognitive will, which means it is both a feeling and a will impulse. Because of its will nature it already has the character of social art action (see Fig. 35).

The case study on medicine and the coronavirus crisis, documented in this chapter, builds from the examples presented in the previous chapter; it is intended as an example of 'new Goetheanism'. We begin with some key empirical, objective facts concerning this crisis; these are presented in a circle. These facts are now entered into, participated in with exact feeling, so that each empirical phenomenon is allowed to show itself forth as a specific gesture or quality. Masks, injections, social distancing—each of the phenomena 'speaks' in a language of gesture,

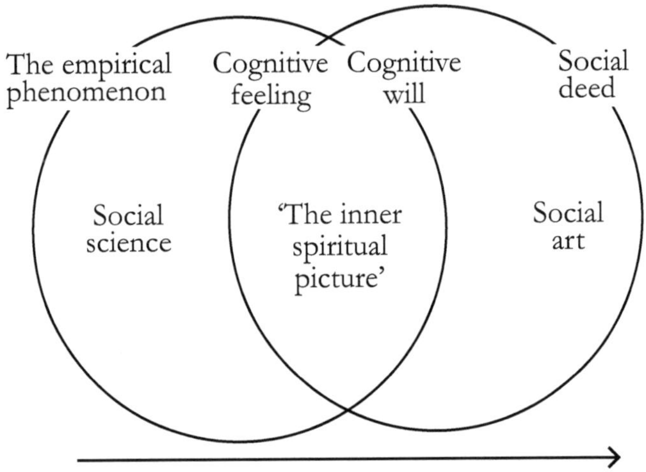

Figure 35

a qualitative language, and this is the language in which the different elements, around and across the circle, 'converse' with one another. The social scientist becomes a listener—not with the physical ear but with the ear of the spirit—in order to 'hear' the relationships of the different elements, their dissonances and harmonies, the degree of their affinity. Gradually an 'inner spiritual picture' is formed of the totality. The question then becomes: In what way is this crisis a distortion, a lack, a need, in relation to the threefold social wholeness? This gives the incentive and direction of the social artwork.

A Social Art Case Study—The Coronavirus Crisis and Its Aftermath

The focus of this study is the social crisis which engulfed the world in the second decade of the twenty-first century. It might possibly be asked: Isn't this coronavirus crisis just a medical issue—why should it be made into a social art case study? *Everything* which comes within the scope of the social, which is everything in the human world, is potentially the focus of a social artwork. A social crisis, like a war or a revolution, is a highly significant point in social history because it brings to clear manifestation forces and tendencies which are active throughout the social organism in a more or less hidden way.[86] This means that a crisis has great creative potential, because these forces can be perceived in an immediate way and worked with directly.

The following study does not pretend to encompass every element of this complex, multidimensional phenomenon. While some aspects like 'lockdown' and 'social distancing'—perhaps even 'COVID 19 vaccines'—may seem to be no longer relevant, the study makes it clear that the coronavirus situation is part of an evolving social crisis on a global scale. Moving from social science to social art, some of the actions which are developing out of the coronavirus crisis and its aftermath are indicated. What is presented here is rudimentary, preparatory, more illuminating possibilities than finalities.

A guiding idea of this research is the following social artistic insight from Rudolf Steiner: 'Mechanisation of the spirit, vegetisation of the soul, animalisation of the body' . . . this is what we must face without delusion'.[87]

Social Scientific Research Stage

The empirical phenomena—The illness and its preventative measures

In a medical situation which rapidly involved every country the broad symptoms of the illness became known to most people through the media. This is principally a respiratory illness which bears a strong resemblance to influenza; it mainly affects the elderly. The illness is called Coronavirus '19 (COVID 19) and the virus is called severe acute respiratory syndrome virus 2 (SARS-CoV-2).

This illness affects primarily—and in an acute way in some cases—a seat of rhythmic system of the human being—the lungs (it can also affect the heart but not in its initial stages). Many experience mild symptoms like runny nose and flu-like aches and pains; with others, particularly the elderly, it can become a respiratory emergency leading to death.

The situation of the illness is immensely complicated and one of the main complications is how deaths from COVID-19 are assessed and reported. Most people who die from the virus are the elderly with comorbidities, so it is never clear exactly what caused the death. For this reason the numbers of deaths in any country and worldwide are problematic; but, one way or the other, this illness had an enormous social impact during the years 2020 and 2021, much more than the seasonal influenza. Illness and mortality were so widespread and significant that it has been called a pandemic which is defined as an illness which crosses national boundaries and affects a large number of people. Actually seasonal illnesses such as influenza fit within this definition but are not termed pandemics. The measures introduced universally to diagnose, limit and treat this illness are: PCR swab testing, mask wearing, social distancing, lockdown, curfew, DNA and mRNA (nucleic acid) vaccines.

The PCR (polymerase chain reaction) works by taking a segment of DNA and 'copying' it through 30 or 40 cycles of amplification. A machine called a thermocycler denatures and synthesises the segment, producing more than a billion exact copies of the segment in a few hours. The specimen for the test can be taken, using a long swab, up the nasal cavity or from the back of the throat; spit which has been collected in a tube can also be used. The worldwide application PCR testing for the Covid 19 virus (and also the rapid antigen test) was central to the course of the Covid 19 pandemic, from 2020 forward, because a person who tested positive to this test was considered to be infected with this virus, even if they displayed no symptoms. Soon after the introduction of the PCR test it became known as the 'gold standard' for diagnosing infection with this virus. Nevertheless, the use of this PCR test was highly contentious from the beginning because of the doubt about diagnostic accuracy and usefulness of what is produced after 30 to 40 cycles of amplification. What is unequivocally true is that, under conditions of states of emergency, only the 'gold standard' view of this test gained currency and universal acceptance.

Virus particles are extremely small; they average 100nm, about 2,000 times smaller than a dust mite. The only masks which can prevent particles of 300nm and less passing through are certain kinds of N95 respirators which form a seal between its outer edges and the face; these masks restrict breathing to an extent which is why some models have exhalation valves.[88] Nevertheless—and here the example of Australia is highlighted—the use of N95 respirators is neither specified nor mandated; only a 'fitted face mark' is spoken of. Most people wear barrier face covering (like cloth masks) or surgical masks which are loose-fitting around the edges but cover the mouth and nose. The latter two are designed only to form a physical barrier to contaminants in the immediate environment such as fine droplets of fluid which may possibly hold viral particles.

The preventive measures of social distancing (in Australia it is 1.5 metres), lockdown and curfew were either recommended or mandated on the basis that they can either prevent or minimalize transmission of the virus. The effectiveness of these measures was in question from the beginning of the Covid 19 pandemic. Even in the very long lockdown which took place in Australia, people were still able to go out to buy food and go to work if they couldn't work from home. Only in China (for example, in Shanghai in mid-2022) was lockdown applied rigorously, with no one allowed to leave their home for any reason and with food brought to them by workers in medical plastics (along with mandatory PCR testing for every citizen). Even so, it remained unclear as to whether this measure halted infections (that is, people testing positive with the PCR test).

The nucleic acid vaccines are strictly only 'vaccine-like' in their effect because they are neither the usual live or live-attenuated type. World Health Organisation information makes it clear that, due to emergency authorization, effectively the whole world population has been engaged in a clinical trial of these drugs:

> The nucleic acid approach is a new way of developing vaccines. Before the COVID-19 pandemic, none had yet been through the full approvals process for use in humans, though some DNA vaccines, including for particular cancers, were undergoing human trials. Because of the pandemic, research in this area has progressed very fast and some mRNA vaccines for COVID-19 are getting emergency use authorisation, which means they can now be given to people beyond using them only in clinical trials.[89]

All the above measures have been introduced under states of emergency—either national or territorial. In laws relating to states of emergency, normally accepted individual rights are suspended and public-health measures are determined (dictated) by chief health officers who are brought into the political arena for this purpose. Normal parliamentary process may also be suspended in the state of emergency in order to expedite these public health measures. In some countries the states of emergency are ongoing, two years after the commencement of the pandemic.

At the time of writing digital identity and smart cities are still not a reality; they are on the very threshold of becoming significant social phenomena, ushered in by the COVID 19 crisis. The current means of identification—the passport, driver's licence or some form of bank card—is in the possession of the individual him or herself and to be changed it has to be physically removed from that living individual. Not so with digital identity; all data, all information regarding a person, is held in cyberspace—that is, in centrally located mainframe computers. Identity data will include personal and biometric details, vaccination record, banking details, medical history and so forth. For the planned global digital identity there would need to be a location in one country at which all data for all world citizens would be held.

Digital identity is integral to the working of a smart city. This city is a technologically modern urban area in which data is gathered through sensors, cameras, Internet usage and other mechanisms, to manage assets and resources efficiently and to control and regulate human activity according to sustainability criteria. The entire smart city will be controlled by artificial intelligence, relying on 5G technology to achieve the greatest possible power of data collection and processing. It is planned

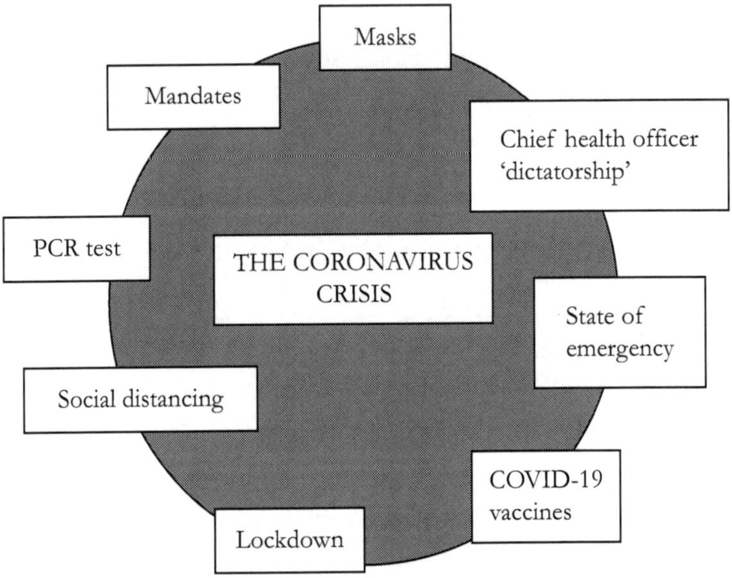

Figure 36

to transform cities all over the world into smart cities within which '15 minute zones' will be set up. These are areas to which one's car usage is monitored and restricted, to a greater or lesser extent.

Qualitative Research through Cognitive Feeling

Masks

Face masks stop contagion—it is said. The question is, what results from universal, enforced mask-wearing? Enforced mask-wearing enhances the animalization of the body—this is its gesture. One can have the experience, walking down a crowded street in which everyone is masked, of being amongst a herd. Some more pointed masks are uncannily like snouts. The rules state that the mask must cover the mouth, high up the nose, and even the chin. As a result, one's human presence is largely obliterated. Human beings fall away from the human social order and enter, to a greater or lesser degree, a social order of an alien kind.

The musico-sculptural form of the human face is the signature of the 'I'. The ego-presence, markedly expressed in the uprightness of the entire face and most 'nakedly' in the forehead, is diminished to a high degree when the lower face is masked. 'One who has a human head before his sculptor's eye has the whole man before him' comments Rudolf Steiner. In the rounded cranium the sense-nerve system is brought to fullest expression. The 'eye-nose-formation' is 'an expression of the man as a man of courage—as a man who sets his inner self, in so far as it is courageous, in opposition to the external cosmos'. The sculptural form of the mouth is 'an expression of what he is in his inner being'.[90]

When we obliterate the wholeness of the eye-nose formation with the mask, we express the diminishment or even extinguishing of the courage of the inner self. We become more like animals. And of course that diminishment of courage is exactly what is necessary when people are required to follow rules, to simply obey. Not courage for individual volition and action but compliance is what is necessary and what is expected. With the mouth entirely covered, and even the chin, what is extinguished is the individuality of the human being—the 'man of limbs and metabolism' as Steiner puts it—which asserts itself in the world. In other words, what are lost are the very attributes of individuality which are the signs, we could say, that a person lives in freedom within the cultural-spiritual sphere of the threefold social wholeness.

When everyone around is masked the impression is that sickness is all-pervading and scarcely being kept at bay. Sickness animalizes us to some degree; we lose ego strength and become more like the illness than our own real self. We become unbalanced, one-sided as an animal is one-sided—a nerve-sense creature, or a rhythmic creature, or a metabolic-limb creature—depending on the form of the illness.[91]

PCR testing

A saliva sample for a PCR test can be spat into a tube, in private and discreetly in most circumstances, by the person who is doing the PCR test. However, this is not the style of PCR test which became favoured worldwide. Normally the person receiving the test, seated below the standing tester who is commonly in blue or white medical plastics with a mask or even shield on, tilts back their head and receives a long swab deep into their nasal cavity or mouth.

The gesture is one of submission. Just as the mask obliterates the eye-nose formation and the mouth, the principal outward expressions of the courage and strength of the inner human self, so the PCR swab breaches and penetrates just the same external formations. The head is bent back and up; the face—the profoundest expression of one's individuality—is offered toward the tester. The whole enactment is of the human being submitting themselves to the imposing, faceless figure of the medical establishment; it is submission even if the person acts out of trust, with the most positive wish to support 'the common good'. This image of submission-by-testing has been projected through the media countless times as an act of advocacy.

If everyone is assumed to be possibly ill—whether they have symptoms or not—then it seems justified that they can all be tested and treated en masse, as cows in a herd are tested and vaccinated for illnesses like mastitis. Mandatory PCR testing and vaccination for COVID 19 comes into that category and it is noteworthy that mandatory anal PCR swabbing was rolled out in China at the beginning of 2021—a highly rigorous 'herd measure'.[92]

'Vaccine' administration

While the PCR swab penetrates the body to a degree, the injection of anti-COVID 19 'vaccine' both enters the body and unites with it. It does this much more profoundly than a traditional vaccine which remains in the blood; mRNA 'vaccine' enters the cells where it is biochemically interactive with cellular components.

From the beginning of the COVID 19 'pandemic' in 2020, or near to the beginning, mRNA 'vaccine' could have been delivered orally in the form of a capsule.[93] The application of the oral administration would only have been as experimental as the mRNA 'vaccines' themselves. However, the favoured method globally immediately became the injection, and that remains so towards three years after the beginning of the 'pandemic'.

These 'vaccines' in oral form could be taken in the privacy of a person's home for those who wish to be protected and who are willing to take the risk with this very new medical technology; they do not have to be administered at a clinic or vaccination hub. Importantly, a pill can be taken in a dignified way by the individuals themselves and not, as with the PCR test, submissively. This gets to the most important feature of the formal injection: whether the injection is carried out by a doctor, nurse or pharmacist, it can be registered that individuals have definitely been inoculated and this information can be gathered and processed electronically by the government and its agencies. This wouldn't be possible if people ingested the drug in their own space and time. With a herd of cows the same thing happens through a branding, tagging and a tallying of numbers. What is critical is that the whole herd is inoculated.

Social distancing and lockdowns

Essentially, in relation to the anti-transmission strategy of social distancing, lockdown and curfew: people were required to stay out of the personal space of others.

The phenomenon of social distancing and lockdown is a symptom of something far more than a straightforward, if controversial, public health measure. It has a qualitative nature of a very specific kind. When we are within the personal space of others many things happen on a soul-physical level which cannot take place when we are not. We can shake hands; we can tenderly or brusquely touch another person on the shoulder. We can hug and kiss someone. Our eyes—'the windows of the soul'—can meet in a way which takes us far beyond merely verbal communication. An intimate soul space is required by little children when they are learning by imitation, as they naturally do. After all, they have not long left the nurturing embrace of the maternal arms and breast. During the pandemic, in classrooms and playgrounds all over the world, children were carefully socially distanced.

When we are locked up at home the whole reality and significance of real human community dissolves and we vegetate within our own reality and the reality which comes to us through digital technologies. We engage in only a virtual community on the Internet. When a person is positioned in a certain place by mandate, freedom of interpersonal expression and freedom of movement is dramatically curtailed; we become somewhat like plants which can be cultivated in isolation from other members of their species, from their natural community.

The medical consultation and treatment

The act of a medical consultation has a very specific social gesture. The medical practitioner and the patient form, as it were, a unity. A payment is made but this is not an economic transaction. The doctor is not selling something to the patient but is seeking to help draw something forth from the constitution and inner powers of the patient, physical and spiritual; namely, their health. In this way the work of the doctor can be directly related to the work of the teacher who is drawing forth capacities and understanding from the students, in order to 'set them free'. The work of both the teacher and the medical practitioner belong to the cultural-spiritual sphere of society, to the ideal of freedom, even if we do not usually think of medical practice as 'cultural' or 'spiritual'.

The way we relate to the COVID 19, or any illness, is individual and ideally free. Human beings are not just bodies; they process an individual spirit, a conscious self. Symptoms of an illness on the bodily level are largely the same for everyone but—just as with the process of ageing and death—how we relate to these symptoms is an individual matter and indeed may open a way toward profound self-knowledge.

Whether we seek medical assistance, and the *kind* of medical assistance we seek, is an individual matter. The entire aspect of illness and its treatment 'sounds' the gesture of freedom and individual consciousness.

At the bodily level we have the same symptoms but that has nothing to do with *equality* as an ideal of the human spirit and of the human social organism. The expression 'herd immunity' belongs to a scientific reading of the disease which considers human beings in just the same way as disease in animals is understood—that is, all humans have the same symptoms and respond in the same way to the same treatment. It could be called the veterinary approach to the pandemic. In terms of the illness and its treatment the only aspect which is in harmony with the ideal of equality is the equal right of every person to receive medical treatment and the right to receive medicaments and treatments which have been properly tested for efficacy and safety.

Likewise, there is no relationship of the illness and its treatment with the ideal of fraternity, even if the idea of 'the common good' is frequently given as the reason for forced general restrictions and treatments of the population. Being ill is an entirely individual affair and healing, as we have already noted, is likewise individual. They belong in gesture to the 'individuality pole' of the threefold social organism—to the ideal of freedom. True modern fraternity which distinguishes us from people in much earlier stages of social evolution, this fraternity comes about through how an individual human *wishes* to be with others, not through an imposed collectivity or mass process. Forced medical procedures have nothing to do with the ideal of fraternity and relate to the 'common good' only in the way someone who is maintaining the general medical health of a herd of cattle carries out similar procedures for the whole herd.

States of emergency

According to laws pertaining to 'states of emergency' in force all over the world, medical officers are trusted to protect and care for the 'human herd'. Plucked, as it were, out of their rightful place within the cultural-spiritual sphere, doctors or professors of medicine have been granted dictatorial powers within the political sphere, dictatorial in the sense of acting outside any parliamentary or democratic process. This extraordinary possibility comes down to us from Roman times in which states of emergency were permissible—but, significantly, for no longer than six months.[94] In Roman law the Senate could grant powers to an individual to deal, during this half year, with situations like warfare, natural disaster or pestilence. *Dictator* was the term for this person. The following comment is noteworthy:

> Though fairly uncommon in democracies, dictatorial regimes often declare a state of emergency that is prolonged indefinitely for the life of the regime, or for extended periods of time so that derogations can be used to override human rights of their citizens usually protected by the International Covenant on Civil and Political Rights.[95]

The idea that a doctor or professor of medicine could be brought in from the cultural-spiritual realm to serve as *dictator*—that is something which could happen in much more recent times in which chief scientists or 'medical experts' have a very high social standing, something equivalent to warrior heroes or demigods in the Roman era.

Societies the world over—and this certainly includes the self-proclaimed 'strongly democratic' states—became dictatorial regimes during states of emergency related to the pandemic. Many continue to be so to a greater or lesser extent—the pre-pandemic conditions have not returned. Many human rights were derogated under states of emergency presided over by chief health officer 'dictators'; all talk of rights and freedom was regarded as selfish under pandemic conditions. In Australia, for example, there are laws at both the state and federal levels which allow health ministers to do 'whatever is necessary' in terms of public health (the common good) to prevent or minimize a pandemic—and 'whatever is necessary' does not mean consideration for what is wanted or needed by individual citizens. A further development of this 'whatever is necessary' exigency began to take place in the middle of 2020 when numerous countries sought to enact laws to make illegal the posting on social media and other platforms of 'disinformation' concerning vaccines and related matters.

One example of well-established rights which were derogated during the time of COVID 19 comes from the Australian state of Victoria which has its own bill of rights—the Victorian Charter of Human Rights and Responsibilities Act (2006); this is a law of this state. Part 2 (10c) of this Charter states:

> A person must not be subjected to medical or scientific experimentation or treatment without that person's full, free and informed consent.[96]

Nevertheless, under an officially declared state of emergency during and after 2020, the Chief Health Officer of Victoria was able to override this law and mandate COVID 19 vaccines for all authorized workers in the state, on pain of losing their employment. The operative word in this statement of medical rights is 'free'; according to this law no form of coercion is possible. Sometimes one hears compulsory seat belt wearing being equated with vaccine mandates, the idea being that both mandates serve the common good. However they are not the same at all; seat belt wearing is not a medical treatment. The gesture of intended protection is entirely different; seat belts, like airbags, and like numerous of other features of modern cars including disc brakes and the rigid, strong enclosure of the car frame, are designed to shield or protect the body in different ways. Vaccines enter and are incorporated into the body.[97]

States of social emergency will happen in the future, as they always have in the past. The issue is whether the time has finally come to go beyond Roman law to bring about an altogether new form of social creation. In the realized threefold social order no form of governmental-medical dictatorship is possible because there is no centralized governance. In any emergency, whether it be a natural disaster, warfare or a pandemic disease, all three spheres are equally represented: the economic, rights-legal and cultural-spiritual (which includes all aspects of medical treatment). Emergency decisions are never made by just one person, but neither by a triumvirate of dictators.

Digital identity and smart cities

With digital identity, submission is disguised as efficiency, convenience, and sustainability. When we carry our identity on our person we physically *possess* this identity. With digital identity this is reversed—we belong to *it* in the sense of being enslaved by it. This identity is not a living human being, a being of body, soul and spirit. The identity is merely a correspondence—a correspondence between a biometric or alphanumeric login and a set of data held in cyberspace. It is a tagging operation, regarding a human being as just a body and electromagnetic code. AI controlled identities means humans submitting almost entirely to a non-living, electromagnetic form of intelligence. If a digital identity is mandatory to obtain goods, services, government benefits and to travel, then it represents a profound mechanization of the spirit and animalization of the body.

With smart cities exactly the same thing applies and the scope of animalization is very broad. Here not just the *ability* to travel, but how much travel and the kind of destinations can all be digitally monitored and adjusted; not just *ability* to purchase, but what is purchased and how much is purchased can be tallied. These won't be cities and human identities in the sense of recognizing and providing for beings of body, soul and spirit—the 'liveable cities' which in the 1980s was a much-publicized goal of urban design. The new cities will be large-scale corral-type arrangements and extremely sophisticated branding and tagging mechanisms for the complex activities of human animals. The only way to live in such a city will be to submit to it.

Shaping an 'Inner Spiritual Picture' Through Cognitive Will

Two counter-pictures emerge in the time of COVID 19 and its aftermath in relation to the threefold social archetype.

The first represents a profound challenge to the ideal of freedom which inspires the cultural-spiritual sphere. We form the picture of millions upon millions of people, worldwide, in postures and attitudes of submission, in animalized and vegetized bodily and mental states, even if these people themselves believe they are doing the right thing for the 'common good'. Through this picture we can sense the obliteration of individuality and, to a great degree, the free human spirit. Declared states of emergency and the springing up of public health dictatorships bring about conditions in which the passage to submission is very rapidly formed. Digital identity and smart cities emphasize the 'common good' as being the same as the 'ecological good'. This is a picture of intentionality, calculated actions and strategies to bring human individuals into states of submission in order that the 'common good' be expedited. Freedom has no place in this situation; the only thing required is to yield to what is considered best for the whole.

The counter-picture draws upon the threefold social archetype to illuminate a pathway of creation. We can form a picture of a worldwide movement with human freedom as its ideal, taking shape on every level and in every sphere of society. This is far from the first time in the history of social revolution and social crisis that freedom has been asserted and demanded; at each of these significant points society is re-imagined in a new way.

The freedom movement we are picturing here is working toward a social condition in which human freedom can never be merely a governmental or judicial determination, never again be brushed aside under a regressive state of emergency. Scarcely yet formulated, this movement is working toward a new form of society; there is no manifesto, no formal written statements of intention and agreement exist. The society to which this movement aspires could be called 'a society of individual wills', individuals who are free to develop themselves and who cooperate creatively and productively with others, out of their freedom.

The Initiation and Potential of a Social Art Action

The social art action has already begun with the impulse of the 'inner spiritual picture'. This inner picture is a knowing which is a doing; artistic feeling and the creative will have shaped it. All further social action is the attempt to bring this spiritual picture to further states of realization.

Large numbers of individuals and groups of people are active in many different ways in response to the coronavirus crisis and its ramifications which include the powerful movement toward digital identity and surveillance systems, greatly increased censorship of social media, and the planned herding of people into smart mega-cities. Social artists worldwide are setting up new kinds of food cooperatives, people's assemblies, online forums, home-schooling networks, new forms of media and news channels, and the like. Beyond these grassroots actions there is also the potential for social artistic creation to be effected through formal education, legal, and economic processes. All of these 'freedom fighters' have, in their own way and to a greater or lesser extent, formed an 'inner spiritual picture' in response to the coronavirus crisis, a picture which has impelled them into action.

The fight for freedom in the face of tyranny and authoritarianism always has the appearance of an assertion of freedom *from*. It seems, in the first place, to be bound to the thing it is seeking to counter because it is shaped as a reaction *to* that thing. But then this assertion of freedom transforms, matures, and reveals itself as a positive act. The creation of this book represents an effort—in connection with those working creatively in a similar direction—to perceive this crisis and related social phenomena in the light of the threefold social archetype. Social art working groups could, worldwide, begin to develop every possible aspect of the threefold social outlook in relation to specific local political, cultural, and economic conditions. The aim is to help transform the understanding of freedom, from a reactionary slogan to the guiding and inspiring ideal of an entire domain of social life—the cultural-spiritual sphere.

Part III
The Three Spheres and Their Governance

'We can never found a real science of economics without developing pictorial ideas; we must be able to conceive all details of our economic science in imaginative pictures. And these pictures must contain a dynamic quality.'

Rudolf Steiner[98]

' . . . if we want to make sure that the rights that we have encoded into our laws are reliable . . . this will never be the work of politicians—this can only be the work of the people . . . If we want to have a better world, we must build it ourselves.'

Edward Snowden[99]

'. . . we are educating people out of their creative capacities. Picasso once said this—he said that all children are born artists. The problem is to remain an artist as we grow up. I believe this passionately, that we don't grow into creativity, we grow out of it. Or rather, we get educated out of it. So why is this?'

Sir Ken Robinson[100]

'We do not need just a renaissance of culture as occurred at the beginning of the modern era, we need a new formation, a new creation, of culture. We must become aware that we are standing before the task of re-creating cultural life.'

Rudolf Steiner[101]

'It is said now that the aim of the threefold order is to break up the unity of social life. In the future, however it will be said that the threefold social order truly lays the foundation for that unity.'

Rudolf Steiner[102]

Chapter 6

THE ECONOMIC SPHERE

The Economic Process and The Arising of Capital

In Chapter 2 an active imagination was developed of the threefold social organization, shaped within the polarity of spirit and matter. The cultural-spiritual realm is most closely related to the spirit, and closest to the matter pole is the economic sphere in which the Earth is transformed; this polarity is mediated by the political-rights sphere. Thus a start was made with a picture of the social whole as an archetypal threefold from which it is possible to illuminate all economic phenomena. We are thinking from the social whole into the parts in the same way an artist shapes a work of art.

Even just this preliminary step into an imaginative way of thinking economics represents something significant for social renewal in our time. To conventional thinking the widest possible gulf separates the artistic sensibility and the study of economics. What this outward cultural separation implies is a profound rift within the human sentient life, the alienation of thinking from feeling and willing. The Goethean form of economic research opens the way directly into an artistic penetration of economics in which every element is 'resurrected' from its purely intellectual form. Production, money, capital, price, the nature of taxation and loans—each and every element and process of the economic sphere can be re-enlivened in this way. Everything which follows in this chapter needs to be perceived with the eye of the imagination if it is to bear fruit. For what we are dealing with in the realm of economics are living processes of metamorphosis and intensification which demand of us the same kind of thinking as our study of plant metamorphosis and intensification in Chapter 4.

Spirit is mind; it is the non-material dimension of reality. Spirit is at work in human life in an individual way—as inspirations, insights or concepts; whatever name we give to a mental arising, these can only be considered as individual, as experiences and activities of the human 'I'. We could say: Spirit enters into human social life, not through a communality, but through the free activity of a human consciousness—through thinking—and the way these individually-derived thoughts are expressed and shared constitutes the cultural and spiritual life of a community. To be sure, it is possible for individuals to gather together in freedom and in a meaningful way that is receptive to the spirit, and for them to be raised together into a higher spirit. Jesus Christ spoke these words: 'Where two or three are gathered together in my name . . .'. Yet, notwithstanding, reception of the spirit is always an individual matter; no one can be inspired cooperatively or collaboratively. Cooperation belongs most essentially to the opposite pole, to the sphere of economic life.

The opposite pole is what is included in the traditional element Earth. It includes everything of a physically substantial nature and this means liquid and gaseous forms as well as the beings built up out of these elements, the plants and animals. Today we call this 'nature' but in traditional economics it is called 'land', an inadequate term because the waters and gaseous formations of the Earth definitely come within the scope of economic interest and activity.

Nothing of nature—minerals, water, gases, plants and animals—enters into economic life by virtue of the activity of a single human individual working for her or himself. Home gardening for example—working the soil and growing food for oneself or to feed one's family—is not an economic event. An economic activity starts where some kind of exchange takes place between those working on different tasks or aspects of production; in other words, when division of labour arises. Barter was the first kind of exchange involving a transaction between individuals who specialized in the production of different commodities and who belonged to different groups or tribes. The division of labour—and that might have only involved two or three people working cooperatively—meant that goods could be made more rapidly for trading purposes. A great and complex economic life has developed from the first forms of exchange but the important point is that any economic event is a cooperative, not a self-subsistent activity.

The fraternal aspect of human nature is awakened and drawn out in the way we engage with the Earth economically and allow it to be transformed and enter into social life. Most essentially, we strive for cooperation so that all aspects of economic activity take place as efficiently and productively as possible. The economic sphere, in the pure sense, is motivated by the ideal of brotherhood, with working with others in ways which will serve the needs of others. When we comprehensively picture the production of even a simple hammer, what becomes evident is the extensive division of labour involved in the many different facets of production, including the growth and harvesting of timber and the smelting of iron ore. If it is a finely made, beautiful product, we must consider this to be the outcome of shared intention on the part of a large number of people. It is an inner task of significance to apply one's imagination to an example such as the manufacture of a computer in which many thousands of people are involved, working cooperatively for that product to arrive at the point of distribution, purchase, and consumption, as something good and useful.

When we speak of 'raw materials' which can be further worked on to produce commodities which have a use value, we mean that nature has come within the economic purview and is being viewed in terms of a specific human need. It's important to note here that nature does not just exist as an economic resource; every mineral, plant and animal has a natural value, not merely an economic value. Very large tracts of nature have been set aside as national parks. Further, in relation to raw materials: many aspects of the beauty and perfection of nature are incorporated as such into human works; for example, flowing formations in stone and wood, complex biochemical substances from plants which may serve unaltered as medicaments. Here we must speak of cooperation with the wisdom and diversity of nature, the products of 'spirit-in-nature', not of reducing everything in nature to 'raw material'. Nevertheless, whether it is existing natural formations or actual raw materials, the economic mind perceives in the products of nature the potential for meeting needs in the human community.

A transformative process takes place, from nature as such, to nature as raw materials (say, felled timber and extracted iron ore), to a good such as a hammer. Spirit (mind) works on nature as conscious intention, transforming it into commodities. Mind spiritualizes nature in the sense of converting it into forms with specific meanings, exactly as painters do when they transform pigments into works of art. When we look at felled timber and extracted iron ore, nature still 'shines out' to a large extent. When we look at a completed hammer we perceive that nature has receded and the 'idea' shines out; this is the hammer's value or meaning. We observe a hammer's precise metallic shape, we feel its weight which is necessary for driving home nails, we grasp its wooden handle, and what we understand is its very specific function in the human world—this is its 'idea'. As a good—such as a foodstuff—is consumed and its purpose realized, its value decreases and its substance returns to Earth; but unlike a foodstuff we call a hammer a *capital good* because it holds its potential for ongoing constructive activities. The hammer can be used to build up other social formations which have an even greater capital value—for example, a house.

The thinking necessary to think the wholeness of the circle of colours as discovered by Goethe, is also the thinking required to think the wholeness of the economic realm. The colour cycle is a way of cultivating a living economic thinking. Colours have particular gestures which together form the whole. As explored in Chapter 4, the gesture of yellow is that it radiates out in all directions; in this it is closest to light. Blue, its polarity, is an 'inward radiation'—it retreats into itself and in this is closest to darkness. The polarity of yellow and blue harmonizes in green and the gesture of green is one of balance, neither outward nor inward. Magenta, green's polarity, is the intensification of yellow and blue and carries both their gestures in a heightened form. It has a gesture of depth and inner power which it 'gives forth' outwardly; it is for this reason considered a 'royal' colour. Such is the archetypal integrity of the circle of colours (see Fig. 24).

Just so, the key moments in the economic cycle have particular gestures or dynamic qualities and the economic cycle also expresses a wholeness and inner completeness. In the outward, radiating gesture of yellow we experience something of the outwardly radiating 'for others' of the production process in which Earth is raised towards spirit. Consumption is its polarity; the good (which is embodied spirit) is annihilated through being used up and returns to Earth—rapidly in the case of foodstuffs, slowly but inevitably in the case of a good like a hammer. Consumption is individual; one cannot consume for others; it relates to self and carries something of the inward gesture of blue. It is possible to view production and consumption from other points of view but a polarity they always remain.

At the moment of exchange (the exchange of money for a good or service) there is a balancing of these polarities. The value of one should balance the value of the other and this is represented by the harmonious gesture of green. But in the economic life the polarities of production and consumption can be unified in another way—through an intensification or enhancement. This is the production of capital which can be called the highest spiritualization of Earth connected with the economic process; capital has something of the magenta gesture, an inner power which is given forth.

The economic process in these four gestures expresses a wholeness or inner completeness. But in its intensified state, in the potential of capital-magenta, it tends beyond itself. In the economy of barter this

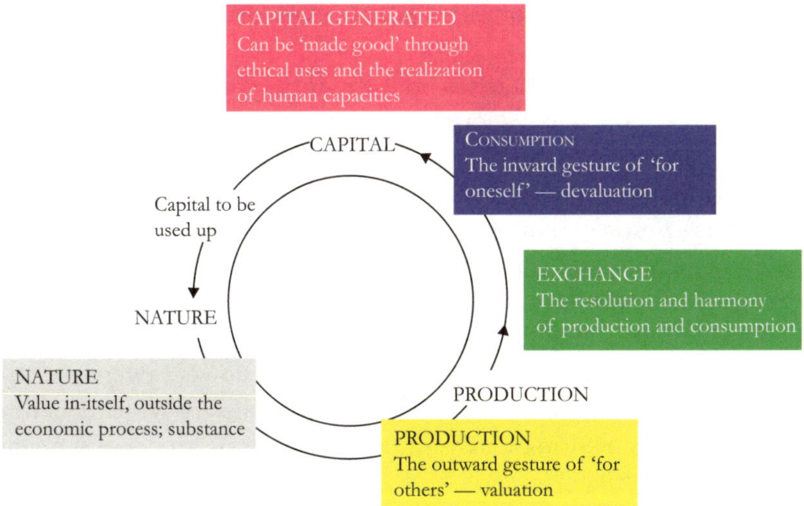

Figure 37

reaching-beyond does not happen; in the bartering event there is only the green of harmonious exchange. Barter was an aspect of the most ancient form of consciousness in which human beings were in tune with the cycles of Earth, the coming and going of seasons, the instinctive rhythms of production and consumption. By contrast, the appearance and experience of capital belongs to the evolution of human individuality.

Firstly, there was the production of *capital goods*; we have seen that a tool such as a hammer has a very specific potential for forming something else and so realizing a greater creative potential. The tool is made from Earth substance and nature still 'shines out' from it to some extent. Capital in the form of money is non-specific, indefinite potential for it has no fixed function or purpose; but this has stages of metamorphosis too. Capital as physical money is first tied to the substance of the Earth, the gold standard. Then money becomes fiat money, paper money—nature has almost entirely receded but the money is still bound up with a local geographical economy and is the legal tender of a country. Capital as digital money is pure potentiality, belonging to no particular country or legal tender; through its more or less instant electronic transmission it has come to belong to human life globally. It is the potential for human individuals to satisfy their needs and to realize their unique capacities in any number of different ways, depending on their inspirations and intentions. As Christopher Houghton-Budd writes: 'Capital belongs to and gravitates to the spirit in us . . . And the spirit is at work in everyone.

To the degree that this becomes conscious, everyone will realise the need for capital'.[103]

Just as nourishing fruit arises on the plant as the interaction of Earth and Sun, where the Sun's energy distils mineral substance into energy substance (sugar), so capital arises as the interaction of spirit and matter, from the transformation of Earth by intelligence—that is to say, from the spiritualization of matter. Through this process pure actuality—that is, mineral, liquid and gaseous nature, plants and animals which are complete unto themselves and in a sense 'finished works of nature'—is transformed into a state of potentiality. Capital is the flowering of the transformative economic process and, like the flower, awaits fructification. In one way or the other it is human creativity which fructifies capital. Spirit transforms Earth into the form of Spirit for the further realization of Spirit.

Thus we have before us in the modern economic realm an immense metamorphosis, effected through human creative intention and human labour. Imaginative thinking can participate in this process—in cognitive feeling we accommodate ourselves to the qualities and gestures of each step in the process; in cognitive will we inwardly *experience* the entire creative movement. Driving this metamorphosis, we could say, is an intensification—the intensification of matter into spirit. Spirit, 'hidden' in nature, is intensified into conscious spiritual potential, which is capital. The key point of this exposition of the economic realm is only to work with analogies to colour process and plant growth in order to cultivate living economic imaginations. It is without value for a new economics to merely declare: 'the formation of capital is like the production of magenta'; this is not economics re-imagined. In the intensification of yellow and blue into magenta there is an archetypal formative force at work and *this* is the formative force which can also be experienced (through cognitive feeling and cognitive will) in the economic realm. The following diagram can be interpreted in that light (see Fig. 38).

The Economic Sphere and The Social Whole

Everything developed on these pages is intended to show that forces in the evolution of human civilization have tended toward the differentiation of three spheres of social life but that these three spheres are still by no means consciously ordered as such. Modern economic activity is no longer governed by a theocratic or aristocratic social principle yet the influence of the political is still very great. The economic realm today is

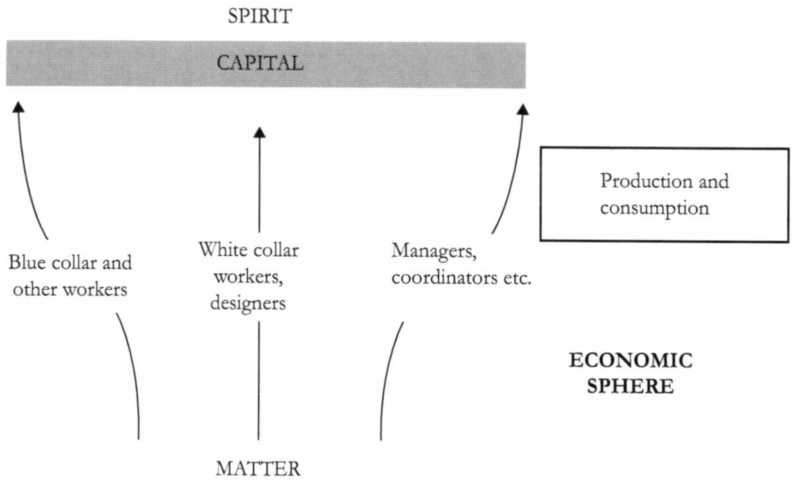

Figure 38

only in a primitive sense an emancipated, consciously-created sphere of social life.

Capital, as it is gradually distilled from the substance of Earth, reaches beyond the economic life and reveals itself as belonging to other spheres. Consider again the growth of a plant; in its seed stage the plant belongs primarily to the Earth and its dark enclosing spaces; in the vegetative stage with its sprouting, spreading, and spiralling rhythms of leaf forms it belongs primarily to the realm of water, air, and light. With the flower the plant is given over to the greatest degree to light and warmth of the Sun and this is revealed in the flower's colours and fragrance, the sweetness of the nectar, the cup-like receptive space of the blossom into which an insect or golden pollen descends from light-filled heights. The flower belongs primarily to the sphere of the Sun.

Likewise with the economic process: at the stage of *commodity* it still belongs primarily to the Earth and to the economic sphere of the social organism; as *capital good* it is still an economic product but also expresses an orientation to the cultural-spiritual sphere, for the potential of any capital good (say, a hammer, a paintbrush, or a computer) is that it can be fructified by a creative impulse (in this case, the will to build, to paint or to plan an initiative). In its most distilled form as pure capital it expresses indeterminate potential, and in this state it belongs primarily to the rights sphere, orientated towards the cultural-spiritual sphere. This is because capital 'speaks' principally to the human creative spirit, the individual capacities and creative intentions which can be realized through capital's potential. Capital is not an economic phenomenon (that is, a commodity) but primarily a rights phenomenon—it is born in the economic sphere, flowers in the rights-legal sphere and is used up (in a sense 'dies') in the cultural-spiritual sphere. This is why the German social artist Joseph Beuys called money or financial capital a 'rights document'.[104]

Every individual human being has the right to capital, for it is distilled from the common Earth, from the minerals, plants and animals, through the labour of countless individual workers; it is thus a community asset. No matter how ingrained the idea is that capital is an economic phenomenon, it is not. Also ingrained is the idea that rights are *granted* to us by the government—but this is not so at all. I have the right to life and equally do I have the right to be supported by capital. In connection with the worldwide and highly topical debate concerning a 'universal basic income' we see, although inchoate, the dawning recognition at the level of political and legal thought that capital is indeed a human right. Having said this, it is important to distinguish a universal income in the sense of a *right*—the right to live with dignity and to be able to fully participate in the cultural-spiritual life of society—from any kind of minimal social payment provided by the government with conditions attached, as a means of controlling and organizing the community. A universal income in the true sense is a large step toward a threefold social order and, as such, has nothing to do with a government's administration of the economic realm. In the realized threefold social life the whole way of conceiving and experiencing capital will be completely transformed, just as much as the experience of freedom has transformed, from life under the pharaoh in ancient Egypt to life in a modern democracy.

To say that capital is the asset of the whole community means something entirely different from saying that the whole community of individuals *owns* this capital. According to Marxist thought, the aim of socialism and eventually communism is to remove capital—meaning capital goods (the means of production), land and financial capital—from the hands of the few and place it into the hands of the many in order that they can control it for their mutual benefit. Marxism, just like capitalism, conceives capital only economically, fraternally, treating it as a commodity which can be possessed—either by a few or a many. But capital, as we have seen, is not primarily an economic phenomenon at all; it arises in the economic sphere but comes in its most heightened form to belong to the rights sphere where it pertains to the cultural-spiritual sphere. Only a vivid imagination of the dynamic social whole will bring understanding to the way capital relates to the social whole through its development. Capital comes to fruition in the cultural-spiritual sphere and what ensures that this coming-to-fruit will take place is the mediator of spirit and matter, the political-rights sphere. It is right and good that the whole of capital is made available to the spiritual-cultural life of society because that is the *meaning* of capital in human social life, as we have seen. A narrow, constricted sense of capital can only result in a constricted, diseased social condition.

Every single human being has the equal right to the capital which is distilled from the common Earth. No person has to do anything to win that right; capital cannot be the compensation for labour in the economic sphere as if that labour could be purchased like one purchases a work-producing machine such as a motor or a robot ('wage' is the name we have for that purchase). Capital is a right, meaning—like every right—it is accorded to a person simply by virtue of them being a human being. And it is the task of the political-rights sphere to ensure this right is accorded.

Every person has the equal right of *access* to capital but that doesn't imply that every person has to receive an equal *amount* of capital; every person has different needs and different capacities. Capital is formed by the human spirit for the realization of the human spirit and the criteria and method of judgement about how capital is to be distributed and used must therefore be a determination of the cultural-spiritual sphere, by those who actually work within that sphere. Steiner writes:

> When [an] individual is no longer willing or able to direct his abilities to the use of capital [at the service of the community], this use must be transferred to another person of similar abilities. It will not be transferred by state prerogative or by economic power, but by finding out, on the strength of the training acquired under the free spiritual life, which person will make the most suitable successor from the social point of view.[105]

Those who live and understand human freedom and the requirements of free individuality must surely be those whose task is to administer this aspect of social life.[106] Let us consider the situation where an entrepreneur wishes to revive a disused car factory. An entrepreneur is a cultural-spiritual worker, who has vision and inspiration and who understands the potentiality of financial capital. Of course, in such a project, the entrepreneur will work with those who have specific economic knowledge of car production. Community banks, as we shall see, have a vital role to play in the distribution of capital because such banks are 'rights organs', mediators between the economic and cultural-spiritual life. Loans and gifts are matters of rights.

But banks themselves are not the determiners of how the potential of capital is to be realized—or, at least, they are so only through the guiding influence of those in the cultural-spiritual sphere who are directly involved with the needs and creative capacities of free human individuals.

In Figure 39 (below) we see the 'flower' of capital opened in the rights sphere, yielding itself to the intentions, ideas, and visions given birth to freely in the cultural-spiritual sphere. The problem with such a diagram is that it gives the impression that capital passes outside the economic realm in a spatial sense and that rights and spiritual matters in relation to capital and labour are dealt with in a bureaucratic arena somewhere beyond the economic. That is far from the truth; in the actual living reality of the social organism the three spheres are independent yet interpenetrated. In every workplace in the economic realm the right of access to capital and the right to work can be exercised. Every workplace has a primary economic context (the production of goods or the provision of services) but as well, to a lesser degree of significance, legal-administrative and cultural-spiritual dimensions where individual rights and freedoms are exercised. In free, non-bureaucratic collaboration and negotiation between workers, managers, and administrators, the issues of capital and labour are worked out creatively.

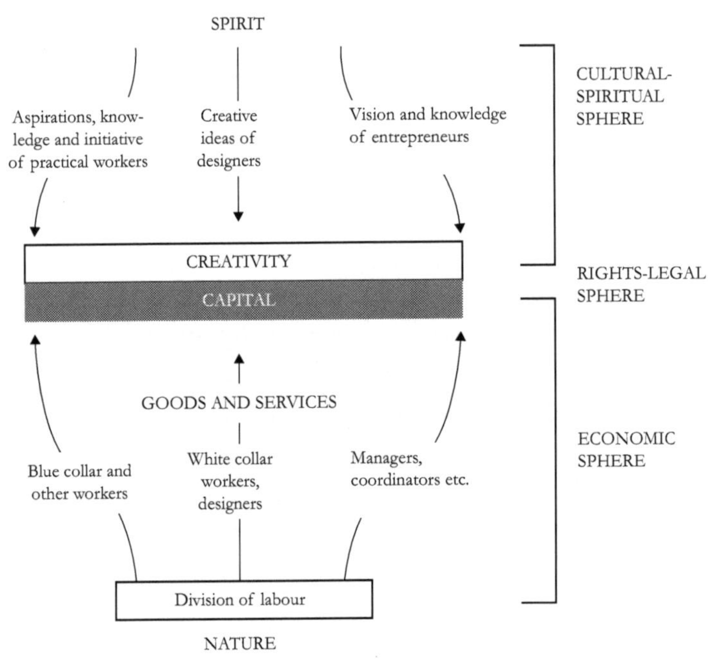

Figure 39

The Liberation of Work

The human creativity which comes forth within the cultural-spiritual sphere 'meets' capital in the rights sphere. This is practical creativity or what could be called 'spirit-in-action'. Just as capital arises through the processes of the economic realm, so creativity undergoes a distilling and refining process in the cultural-spiritual sphere—from conception, the intuition of an idea or possibility, an insight or inspiration, to where it can be put into action and may require capital to becomes something actual.

Creativity is a form of work, which is why we speak of a 'work of art'. However, to speak of creativity only in this way makes it seem to be a very limited or specialized human activity. In fact every kind of human work is creative in some sense; the world is being transformed, recreated, through an action of the will, through a doing or making process. Work cannot be considered something which is just intuited or felt (although thinking and feeling, under circumstances in which they are consciously directed and applied, *are* a form of work).[107] Our concern here is specifically with economic work which is normally called labour. Economic work which creates goods comes about through the recognition that the Earth must be transformed to provide for the needs of people. This is the economic process we have traced above, leading to the formation of capital.

People need to live and need to work. However, if we must work *just in order to* live then we are most assuredly shackled to the wage system which has enslaved the larger part of human populations for centuries. The question of work and income needs to be clearly perceived: we do not actually live through money at all, even in a normally functioning capitalist economy. Each person lives through the work of others, through all the producers of food and other goods and through all the services people provide. And other people live through our work. In the economic sphere all work done must of necessity be for others, even if we think we are doing it for ourselves in order to receive money to be able to live.

Only the most jaundiced view of human nature could assert that people wouldn't work if they were not being compensated for it through money. And even if, for one reason or another, they do not wish to work or are not able to, then they still have the right to receive a universal income. If they are free and healthy then they will love to work, out of themselves and their sense of their own capacities and potentials; this is something specifically cultivated in the Mondragon Corporation in Spain.[108] The free human individual has a *right* to work and fulfil themselves, just as they have a right to live in freedom and obtain the support of capital. Steiner indicates that for a truly free, autonomous economic sphere to come into existence, work must come more and more into the sphere of rights where capital is received according to needs. If work is considered economically it means that the economic sphere is still entangled with the spheres of rights and culture. In a society ordered in a threefold way there can never be any question that a person has to work to be able to eat, to be sheltered, clothed, and educated. To be sure this is a development of society still to come and much depends on a re-imagined social science which, by degrees, will inspire people with true social will, the will to work for others out of love and the wish to fulfil oneself through one's work. Nevertheless, we can see in the world today certain examples of enterprises—notably Sekem in Egypt—where such an 'economics of love' takes place successfully and as a matter of course.[109]

In truth, work (labour) is not fundamentally an economic phenomenon. The economy is only about the production, distribution and consumption of goods and the provision of services. Labour *allows* these economic processes to take place, just as money does. However, neither labour nor financial capital *belong* to the economic sphere as such. If we treat work economically and thus a human being and their time as a commodity which can be purchased or hired—then it must be considered a form of modern-day slavery as Marx rightly observed.[110] Every right has a history which begins, at some point, with the urgings of conscience in a population and only gradually reaches the stage of a social imperative and a law. The question is: How far along the path are we toward the point of accepting that for a person's time and labour to be permanently or temporarily owned by another is an immorality and an impossibility?

At the moment work is liberated from its traditional shackling to the economic realm then it reveals its true nature as a fundamentally cultural-spiritual deed. How a free cultural-spiritual life can inculcate a love for society and love of work is looked at in Chapter 8 on the cultural-spiritual sphere, and in Chapters 10 and 11 on school and university education. When such a liberation of work takes place—and for modern society that will be the fruit of a great and sustained social striving—then the possibility comes about of what Steiner calls an *associative economy,* which is already present today in germinal forms.[111]

The Associative Economy

As social artists we try to form an exact imagination of what belongs to the economic sphere and what does not; we perceive how any aspect of the economic sphere is meaningful within the context of the whole. That is the way of the artist—always to sense the whole in the parts in the shaping of the work. Thus we see the three moments of economic process—production, distribution (trading), and consumption—in relation to the polarity of matter and spirit and as related gestures within the economic cycle.

In a choir what is necessary is a highly developed listening in order for a many to sound together as a one. In the movement arts this 'listening' takes the form of a coordinated moving-together, through each performer being intensely aware of every other. These are social arts and many of the skills also pertain to the economic sculptural art. In the economic process, which is the way the elements of the economic sphere associate and develop in relation to each other, equally necessary is the kind of attentiveness which we could call an *economic listening* (see Fig. 40). Such attention to the needs of others is the vital element in what Steiner called 'economic association'.

Economic attentiveness takes place when those involved in the production, distribution, consumption and management of goods open and respond to each other and thereby cooperatively create and maintain the economic whole as something balanced and healthy. It might be asked sceptically: What could possibly motivate such a 'listening', given the normal view that the personal-profit motive reigns supreme in economic matters? The answer can only be that through fraternity, through care and interest one with another, such mutual awareness arises. As Victor Hugo expressed it: 'The protection of all men by every man is Fraternity.'[112] Care for every particular aspect of the work naturally arises when there is understanding and responsibility for the sphere of activity in its wholeness. In contradistinction to any kind of socialist theory or programme which *compels* people to work together communally through a government-orchestrated economics, the activity and processes of economic association function through a love of society and a truly liberated work.

Such care-filled 'listening' actually already takes place and always has taken place in the economic life of society. Barter is a form of caring, fraternal exchange where the value and quality of 'my' goods should meet and balance the value and quality of 'yours'. In any division-of-labour production there needs to be a careful and caring coordinated activity in order to shape the whole product as something good—for example the production of a table lamp, where some make the glass base, others the shade, others the special metal fittings. Individuals working within a modern corporation—at all levels—may conduct themselves with enormous responsibility and cooperativeness in relation to co-workers, the customers and producers, even while the aims of that corporation may be utterly self-serving.

Thus, at the level of the individual, we already have the fundamental qualities of the economic association. In terms of modern economic organizations the picture is different; care and cooperation aren't the principal motivating and regulating factors because at this level of the economy the main determinations are governed by 'the market'. The market is like a large hiatus in the total economic listening, a kind of blank in consciousness. 'The market' is not part of any economic conversation; it is anxiously or greedily watched as if it had its own life, an almost non-human, instinctive life. It is 'the market' which determines price, profit, supply and, through market manipulation—depending on which supplier is most capitalized—demand as well. In a true associative economy 'the market' is an impossibility.

The reality of the market in modern economic life, this hiatus in economic listening, points to a lack of understanding of the meaning and role of capital in the economic whole and in human social life altogether. In the economic cycle the need to balance supply and demand has been long understood; this is the green gesture of harmonizing the polarity of production and consumption. We have seen above that this balancing of supply and demand results in the economic manifestation called *exchange*—the moment when a good is purchased by a consumer.

However, the gesture of economic intensification, the magenta gesture, is a relatively recent coming-to-consciousness. Capitalism represents just the beginning of this coming-to-consciousness of capital; but the fulcrum on which capitalism turns is still the unconscious 'market'. The economics of Steiner point to how the representatives of capital can and must be part of the whole economic conversation and in the shaping of a conscious associative economy.

In terms of the actual lived reality of associative life, the economic conversation can never be healthy and whole while the magenta element is not represented. The unconsciousness of 'the market' distorts and skews this conversation so that we have the situation where

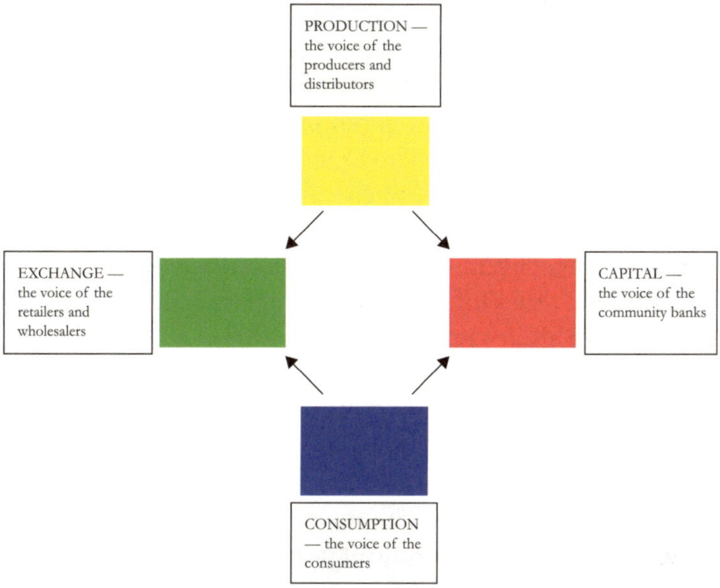

Figure 40

producers may form cartels or monopolies in an effort to game the market in their favour, play the stock exchange, aided and abetted by banks. Increasingly today producers also own and control the situations of exchange so that the monopoly is complete—while consumers have the most meagre voice or are not heard at all. While there is no artistic sense of economic wholeness there can be no true meeting of producers in order to listen to the real needs of consumers. And when price is determined by 'the market' there can be no associative conversation where *true price* is worked out in the kind of conscious, caring way which Steiner pointed to.[113] In relation to the profit and the production of capital through the economic process, the key participant in the conversation must be those who speak for the magenta intensification of capital—namely, the banks. These are not the banks as representatives of the unconscious market but the conscious and caring ethical bank, the kind of community bank which has developed out of Steiner's economic indications.[114] Through the agency of such banks capital is created through strictly-controlled investments which are deemed sustainable, healthy for the Earth and for human society.

'The market' is superseded by the economic association—superseded in the sense of becoming outmoded. Capitalism is superseded by the associative economy which doesn't mean that the valuable achievements of capitalism are simply negated. Capital comes to a developed consciousness in human social life when it is understood as the 'unity through intensification' of the economic cycle, as the refinement and intensification of the Earth by and for the human spirit. The community bank accordingly is not an organ of the economic life—it belongs primarily to the legal-rights sphere as mediator. One face of this bank is oriented toward the economic sphere and is an intimate participant in the economic conversation and in economic listening. Its other face is orientated towards the cultural-spiritual sphere where it serves—through loans and gifts and other forms of monetary transaction—the realization of the capacities of all free human individualities.

This is why the corporation has no place in the realized associative economy. During the twentieth century the corporation became the supreme economic manifestation, many inordinately profitable due to their global reach and market dominance through monopolization. Like everything else in the social world, the corporation has had a history of development and it will have a time of passing away if the forces of social renewal render it unnecessary and even morally bankrupt. While the corporatized economic life appears to be self-sufficient and independent of government, the corporate model is actually a hierarchical, semi-political formation. It has a governing body, elected by shareholders as their 'representatives', and a commander-in-chief which is the CEO controlling the ranks of employees below. In Chapter 9 we shall see that the form of governance appropriate to the economic life in the realized threefold social order is simply the associations themselves, the webs of economic relationships guided by economic expertise.

Chapter 7

THE POLITICAL-RIGHTS SPHERE

The Bestowal of Right and The Democratic Striving

We have already developed an artistic picture of the political-rights sphere as the copula, the mediator in the threefold archetypal social order, forming the link between the cultural-spiritual and the economic spheres. Just the imaginative study of the magnet is enough to bring real insight into the nature of this mediatory aspect of society. This exercise is certainly not to be underestimated; it requires penetrating, flexible imaginative perception. Other manifestations of the archetypal threefold in nature were also looked at—in the plant and the human being. Here a 'third thing' is formed as an intensification, not just a neutralization of the poles, and the political-rights sphere is such an intensification of the two other polar social spheres. We must picture the political-rights sphere as having existence only in relationship, as an 'in between' the economic and cultural-spiritual, belonging to neither one pole nor the other but pertaining to both.

The rulers of society, monarchs and emperors, going right back to the theocrats of the ancient world, are all-powerful yet essentially only mediators. A ruler cannot personally, as a single 'mere' human being, wield the power necessary to keep the kingdom under control. The power doesn't stream out of the autocrat like a kind of superforce. Autocratic rulers obtain this power by mediating between the military, the religious leaders, those involved in finance, administration, and the general populace. If we go back to the ancient Egyptian theocrats the ruler is mediator between his earthly subjects and the realm of the gods. In these early social structures the mediator-figure was all-important because the role was absolutely unique and unassailable. The theocrat had a *right* which no other person was considered to have—a divine right—which seventeenth-century European monarchs such as Charles 1 of England still claimed as the basis of their legitimacy.

Anything we now call a 'human right' derives from this original mediation of matter and spirit, humanity and divinity. In and through the act of divine mediation the first human right was bestowed. The moment of that bestowal is expressed to perfection in the image of Pharaoh Chefren, when spirit in the form of the falcon-god Horus embraces the consciousness of the god-man (see Fig. 10). No one in that society could be equal to the pharaoh for no one else was recognized as enspirited in this way. In a sense the pharaoh is *receiving* the bestowal—but the falcon is directly behind his head, embracing it, and the pharaoh's consciousness is evidently equal to spirit, on the level of spirit. He is enspirited and it is that which makes him an individual. As we have seen in Chapter 3, the theocrat was the only true individual at that stage of human civilization; every other person in society was merely a 'subject' and to that extent not a full human being. The spirit-creation of human individuality is the key to that first right and every other right which has since been conceived.

That first moment of bestowal is also, we could say, the moment when the ineluctable longing for democracy first arose. Humanity has gradually come to realize that a right cannot belong to one human being, or one class of human beings. We all have different physical forms and capacities and in this respect we are not all equal; one person may have more physical possessions than another. But spirit approaches and touches every human being equally, man or woman, aristocrat or plebeian; that is the Christian message which brought revolution to the Roman world with its emperors and aristocrats claiming privileged rights. It is the dawning realization that every person is equally an 'I', a self, which means a right belongs to every self equally. Selfhood, egohood, is the same for every human being and constitutes the spirit pole of the human being.

As we live and experience our 'I' nature in our body and our soul (our thoughts and feelings), we know ourselves to be independent beings, separate from everything and everyone else, with unique aspirations in life, unique joys, unique desires. This is the experience of freedom which grows in us as we develop within the cultural and spiritual life of our community. But our mature sense of freedom *relates* us to every other person, because we see that if I have a right to be free, then everyone else does too, because each person is equally a self, an 'I'. This means that the cultural-spiritual sphere of society matures and differentiates itself concomitantly with the political-rights sphere. In the Western stream of civilization, human individuation evolved from the ancient Egyptian worlds, through the ancient Greek and Roman worlds, and that evolution is characterized by the growth of understanding and recognition of human rights. The sense of rights develops in the first place within particular cultural milieux—for example, European Christian culture. It took until the world wars of the twentieth century for certain *universal* human rights to be declared—including the rights to life and liberty.

The evolution of the sense of rights was slow and largely beneath the surface of cultural life. From the ancient theocracies right through European history until around the eighteenth century, the idea persisted that rulers have a privileged divine right—but through the layers of the social fabric the democratic longing was rising. It burst to the surface in the French Revolution with its declaration of the ideals of liberty, equality, and fraternity. As Victor Hugo expressed it in relation to the strivings of that revolution, sovereignty can now only mean 'the sovereignty of man over himself' which is the principle of individuality and liberty. Each sovereign individual can claim the same right. Writes Hugo: 'The common law is nothing but the protection of all men based on the rights of each, and the equivalent sacrifice that all men make is called Equality.'[115]

Curtailing the all-controlling power of the state represents a real desire and hope for many people in the modern world. Yet, what we are actually witnessing today is an *increase* in this power, on many different levels but especially through the coming about of the 'surveillance state' in countries the world over. The modern state is never going to limit itself and, being the executive and in control of the armed forces, it is unlikely to be overthrown by any kind of revolutionary countermovement even if that is still the aim of some socialist loyalists. Yet the democratic spirit rises ever anew on the wings of the unassailable knowledge that every individual has the equal right to be free and self-determining. Democracy is founded on the understanding of what it means to be a free individual, and that understanding ever seeks the way to transform society to make possible the ever-more-perfect realization of human liberty.

Rights and The Making of Laws

A right is nothing abstract, something merely thought-out like a political theory or philosophical category. There has been a concerted effort by social theorists over the last few centuries to 'work out' rights—notably, John Locke, Immanuel Kant, Carl von Rotteck and G.W.F. Hegel. If rights can be so fashioned intellectually, governments of course can then 'work out' whether they should or should not be accorded to the populace, according to different political criteria. Marx and Engels discussed the question of human rights in their writings.[116] Here rights are theorized to be social constructions, a function of economic conditions in any particular age, promoting the interests of a certain class and having nothing to do with what people actually themselves grasp out of their conscience, care and understanding. On this subject Steiner makes the following remark:

> [The democratic feeling] declares that there is no such thing as an all-embracing abstract definition of human rights, but only the possibility for human beings within any kind of social community mutually to understand one another . . . Human rights arise purely out of the reality of what human beings desire mutually from one another . . . there cannot be any rational rights . . .[117]

Such a statement could only be made by someone who perceives the dignity and potentiality of every human individual. Democracy has its origin in the way people experience themselves as individuals and the way they experience their relationships with others. What is democratic is how people decide what they want mutually, not through any politically or economically motivated strategies of the 'common good' or abstract 'social constructions'. Steiner is speaking about the mature form of democracy which will find its expression in a realized threefold social order.

Today we think democracy is just a matter of electing representatives who then proceed to decide—to a large extent independent of those who voted for them—what rights we have, then form them into laws and impose them on the population from above down. In that sense a democracy works in precisely the same way as an autocracy; both elected leaders and the autocrat dictate what rights people have and what they can or cannot do. The fact that our highly prized democratic states are but a juvenile form of democracy couldn't be made more evident than by what occurred very rapidly through the coronavirus crisis which began in 2020. Citizens in 'democratic' states, during the course of just a year, saw their rights begin to evaporate. Whether countries have Constitutions as their supreme law (like Australia), or a Bill of Rights (like New Zealand and the United States of America) has made only a negligible difference; declared 'states of emergency' have allowed extra-parliamentary groups, composed of a health official and a few politicians, to make laws dictatorially. These states of emergency have in many countries been extended indefinitely and as that happened certain rights have faded away, rights which have been taken for granted in democracies for centuries.

Actually the coronavirus crisis has brought to a head tendencies in Western democracies which have long been in play. The elected representatives in a parliament introduce a bill which may only to a minimal degree reflect 'the will of the people'. The bill is then debated and may or may not be rejected; because members of parliament for the most part vote along party lines, the diversity of points made in such debates can be most constricted. In many countries to become law the bill will have to pass through an upper house, a 'house of review' where party blocs can again dominate. Laws created in this way relate to all aspects of both the economic and cultural-spiritual spheres of society. An example relating to the cultural-spiritual sphere is a law enacted in the state of Victoria, Australia, in 2020, outlawing certain kinds of prayer and even advisory conversations within a family, with penalties of up to ten years in jail.[118] Other examples are laws which determine the make-up of every school's curriculum.[119]

In the realized threefold social order anything to do with family life, education, religion, medicine belong to the cultural-spiritual sphere and are a matter of freedom. In a free society people come to conclusions about what they 'desire mutually from one another' and this has nothing to do with laws imposed on them from above down. People decide themselves—perhaps in consultation with others whom they choose to consult—what they want to say to one another, to pray about, which school they want to attend and what they want for their child, what medical procedures they want and require.

In a society of free individual wills there are many ways people can, and do, work out what they desire mutually from one another. Such ways have diversified greatly in recent years through the growth of social media and other Internet-based methods of communication. In the time of the coronavirus crisis, when the mainstream media appeared more and more to be the propaganda wing of the government and in spite of attempts at censorship, an immense exchange of thoughts and observations took place which couldn't have happened even thirty years earlier. The breadth and diversity of the conversations mean it has become far more realistic that issues of all kinds can be decided by referendum; people are no longer hearing just one point of view delivered through the mainstream media. Besides, we are now at the point where information technology can enormously facilitate the dissemination of necessary information and the cumbersome process of holding referenda through attending polling stations. The opportunity for a far more participatory democratic involvement in the making of laws is directly before us.

The Mediatory Role of The Political-Rights Sphere

The right to life, the right to education, the right to free movement and free speech are rights which have, over a long period of human development, emerged in human consciousness as 'what human beings desire mutually from one another'. This is the basis on which they have been included in the United Nations Declaration of Human Rights; they haven't been 'worked out' by social philosophers although philosophers, as citizens, have had a role in their formulation. Although they are stated in the Declaration as if they exist abstractly, they are actually meaningless if seen outside the context of concrete social relationships and in isolation from one another. The right to life, one could say, is primary—but one could be alive in the most inhumanely incarcerated, limited circumstances. It means the right to live in freedom, so that the right to life belongs inseparably to the rights to an education, to a good standard of living, to free speech and free movement. In their primary orientation this cluster of rights pertains to the cultural-spiritual sphere because they are all inspired by the ideal of freedom.

But to live and be educated in freedom, every person must be met with capital from the economic sphere and, as we have seen in the previous chapter, capital is the right of each individual equally. Rights are mediatory because they are the entitlement bestowed on every individual to participate within and be protected by the threefold social wholeness in which the economic and cultural-spiritual spheres are intimately united. Thus we develop a picture of the political-rights sphere as the copula between the poles of the economic and cultural-spiritual realms. It is Janus-faced, looking each way simultaneously, sensing the relationship between the poles and acting to bring about a unity and balance. This kind of perception requires the kind of dynamic, imaginative form of thinking we have been considering in previous chapters. Workers in the political-rights sphere—the politicians, lawyers, and police along with those involved in ancillary and administrative tasks—will need to comprehend their role in this way if there is to come into being this wholesome relatedness of the economic and the cultural.

The role of the parliament remains and, indeed, is strengthened although greatly transformed in a society ordered in a threefold way.

Democratically elected members of parliament debate the issues at hand; but in the realized threefold social order the idea of parties is redundant, an eventuality long sought. The well-recognized problem is that a constituency elects someone to represent them but in the end that representative has to toe the party line. The issues which arise go far beyond the limited number of party policies presented to the constituents at an election so it stands to reason that a member of parliament must have a truly independent voice. The important thing is that the representatives can truly be the voice of the constituents, a true public servant rather the sham which humanity has endured for so long. Like other aspects of the threefold social outlook, the idea of moving beyond party politics may sound utopian. This future of political life must be ventured in spirit and then the ways will be found to make it a reality in practice.

What, then, is the work of the parliament in the light of everything said above—namely, that laws cannot be imposed on the people from above down? We know that the role of parliament (legislature) is to create laws; but these laws will be what civil society wants and considers right, what people 'desire mutually from one another'. How this can happen is something for which much preparation has already taken place; there are various kinds of forums—including people's assemblies and social media networks—along with referenda, where what civil society wants can be brought to focalized expression. Only then, through listening to the will of the people, can parliament act; only, and exactly, from what society collectively wants and considers right, can laws be fashioned.

But every law, concretizing every right, must express a mediation between the cultural-spiritual and economic spheres. So the work of the parliamentarians goes beyond listening to the cultural-spiritual sphere; Janus-faced, they must equally be listening to the economic realm, partly through the 'ear' of the community banks and other political-rights 'sense organs'. They are listening to the multifarious economic associations and taking part in conversations with them, on many different levels. For example, taxation can be made a much more conscious process; there is no reason why the population cannot be accorded the right to choose to what use all or most of their taxed money will be put. This right, like every other, is something that will need to be initiated as a possibility and nurtured within the cultural-spiritual life; it cannot be some kind of political determination. The principal task of every parliamentary representative is to ensure that the mediation of the economic and the cultural-spiritual takes place and *that* is where parliamentary debate has a vital role. For example, let us imagine that numbers of people, in one or more constituency, may put forward their desire for certain kinds of alternative medical treatments to become available in hospitals. The task of the representatives is not just to present the views of the constituents but to ensure that finance which flows from the economic sphere towards such an initiative (in the form of gifts or taxation money), is equitable. Every mediatory decision is likely to be complex and difficult and great challenges of integrity and perceptiveness will undoubtedly be involved.

In every workplace in the economic realm there must be some kind of rights-legal forum where questions of rights are negotiated, where what is lawful for a group comes into relationship and possible conflict with what is right for an individual. Such interactions might be concerning distribution of profit or workplace conditions. Unions have for a long time played this role in the situation where workers are pitted against their bosses; with the liberation of work and with labour moving more into the sphere of rights, it becomes more of a question of creative negotiation between workers and managers. Every community bank, as discussed in the previous chapter, is a key social organ, pertaining to the economic but mediating the cultural life through the handling of loan and gift money. Every school is a threefold organization in which the legal or rights dimension must mediate in all matters of fairness such as school fees and disciplinary action. In our complex modern society all matters involving the activity of the political-rights organization are complex and multidimensional; but in the realized threefold social unity all complexity is governed by the simplicity of the archetypal threefold—the poles of individuality and communality and the mediatory principle which both separates and unites these poles.

Justice and A New Jurisprudence

It is said: the rule of law must be in force if society is not to fall into a state of chaos. But laws can be made by tyrants to serve their dictatorial ends. Laws can be utterly unjust. What must be alive and burning like an eternal flame in the heart of the social organism is the power and experience of *justice*. Only through justice can good laws and good legal judgements be made (the words 'justice' and 'judgement' both derive from the Latin *jus* meaning 'law'). Good laws are those which the people have decided, between themselves, are good and right. Of course this may seem to be turning society on its head; 'surely it is only the legal experts, the theoreticians, the jurisprudicians, who know what justice is', it might be insisted. But this is not the case! Justice is a quality and virtue close to love; both can be cultivated and both are the possibility of every human being.

The realization of the threefold social unity is not merely an economic or political transformation. It is the transformation of society in its every aspect. New laws will always be required, laws which express what people 'desire mutually from one another'. But just as important—and perhaps more important—is the transformation of the *way* laws are made, the kind of thinking which leads to the formation of just laws. What is necessary is a way of engaging in the practice of law entirely different from what has held sway for centuries. Since the eighteenth century jurisprudence had meant the study or science of the law and principles upon which law is based. But 'science' or 'study' is only a secondary meaning of prudence; prudence is actually a form of wisdom, the wisdom which guides our doing or willing, the way we act in the world and allow others to act. We can find our way to a new jurisprudence through understanding how justice is developed in the human being and how the experience of justice allows every person to shape the world around them.

Coming to us from the dawn of Western civilization, Plato in his *The Republic* speaks about justice as the key to an ordered society. If the human soul can become ordered and just, then society in its wholeness will also be just and good. Plato is well-known for valuing the truth-seeking intellect far above 'mere opinion'. But justice, he says, comes about, not merely through the intellect, but through the harmonization of the three parts of the soul—the thinking, feeling, and willing. In *The Republic* he writes:

> The very forms and dispositions as are in the city [are] in the soul of each one severally and that their number is equal . . . [a just man] really sets his own house in good order and rules himself; he arranges himself, becomes his own friend and harmonises the three parts, exactly like three notes in a harmonic scale, lowest, highest and middle.[120]

Plato is saying that members of society need to become the *rulers of themselves* for justice to prevail in society as a whole. Here, in this rather esoteric statement with its musical allusion, we find the seed of a mature democratic social life.

The Republic is an ancient text and relates to a form of society very different from our own. But it would be unwise to assume that what

Plato means by justice, and how it comes about, has no relevance to us. The fact that jurisprudence became a highly sophisticated form of academic study takes nothing away from the fact that justice actually cannot be 'worked out' intellectually, any more than rights can be. When we make judgements in social matters, we want our judgement to be equitable and just, exactly as we would want the judgement of others to be. We want this to be the way all people in society make judgements and we want it to be the way the judiciary come to their judgements in all legal determinations.

For the realization of the threefold social order we are reaching toward a justice which is not merely rational and philosophical but which belongs to a thinking of the whole human being. Justice, equity, is not just a theory but an inward *experience*, an existential act, and that, as we have discussed in previous chapters, calls upon both the artist and the scientist in the human being. We cannot cultivate justice through the philosophical study of ethics. Justice calls upon the human power of feeling, but not just *feelings* in the sense of antipathies or sympathies; it requires the heightening of feeling into a thinking function, or what we have been calling cognitive feeling, leading to cognitive will. Steiner comments:

> . . . conditions of justice can develop in a community of human beings only in accordance with feelings that have been trained and refined. As people feel toward one another in their mutual exchanges, likewise will be the system of public law. Moreover, by omitting this vital element of feeling when considering the social question, the problem of justice was necessarily lost from view . . . out of the interchange of human feelings in public life the desire for law is kindled.[121]

This is a significant statement. It is the people, civil society, who generate the requirement and will for law, not the theoreticians and scholars at work in the field of jurisprudence. He is speaking of the evolved and refined democratic spirit which is at the heart of the consciously-realized threefold social organism.

The developed sense of justice—through feelings which have been 'trained and refined'—stands behind all acts of judgement, in all social deeds; it becomes especially significant in civil society in people's assemblies, in enacting referenda, and in all judicial processes. Such 'training and refining' must of course take place in education and here we are specifically concerned with the social science of jurisprudence, with the education of a living, legal imagination. Today it may seem strange to suggest that colour, plant and animal studies will be preliminary to the development of a tertiary education in jurisprudence and legal practice. However, this Goetheanistic, natural scientific training could form the basis of an orientation course of study. The whole human being must become involved in the thinking process—the clear, logical apprehension of facts deepening to cognitive feeling and cognitive will.

Now we can consider the pathway from judgement to conclusion in terms of a judicial determination. Any case—criminal, civil or otherwise—is built up on evidence which needs to be comprehensive, objective, and accurate. The same thing applies to any act of legislation. Through unbiased, rational thinking we bring the details of any situation or case, its pros and cons, into the light of clear, objective consciousness.

Steiner explains how judging takes place in the 'middle human being' which has its primary expression in the life of feeling. We most certainly do not judge 'in the head'. It is the nature of *cognitive feeling* to be able to enter into all the facts and observations which constitute the evidence in any legal case, to permeate them selflessly; feeling moves between opposing facts, testing them against each other, weighing them up, discovering what predominates and where the balance lies. This is the *exact imagination* which Goethe spoke of. Certain elements of evidence may have a similar or perhaps a quite opposed quality. In cognitive feeling we hold them together inwardly and let them 'speak' to each other and balance each other, in the same way we do in our Goethean studies of colour in the circle of colours. At this point we have still not reached the stage of conclusion and need to consciously hold back from coming to conclusions prematurely.

The judging power thus has its seat in the rhythmic organization of the human being which is mediatory, moving between poles of the nerve-sense and the metabolic-limb organizations. Judging, and the coming about of justice, is such a mediatory function which reflects in the mediatory role of the political-rights sphere as a whole. We find this symbolized in the 'scales

Figure 41: Maat, the ancient Egyptian goddess of justice and fairness.

of justice' which goes back to Maat, the Egyptian goddess of justice and fairness. The upper limbs which hold the scales are extension of the middle human being. Steiner explains:

> The arms, although in harmony with the rhythmic organism, are at the same time liberated from it. In this physical connection of the rhythmical organism with the liberated organism of the arms, we can see a physical, sense-perceptible expression of the relation between feelings and judgments.[122]

We make all judgement in the middle human being and these are reflected in the head as mental images or concepts.

Through judgement we come to conclusions, we *make a stand* in the world. Another way of saying this is that through the process of weighing up a situation we form a resolve. Again, we certainly do not come to conclusions 'in the head'; Steiner goes on to explain that we actually draw conclusions *in the lower limbs*, the most outward expression in the body of the will. Our resolve is reflected in our thinking as a conception or mental image but the conclusion itself is a will process. This is when we can speak of concluding in the legal sense, of arriving at some form of enactment. It is 'taking a stand' which means, outwardly, placing ourselves in the world so that a firm position can be adopted.

THE PROCESS OF JUSTICE

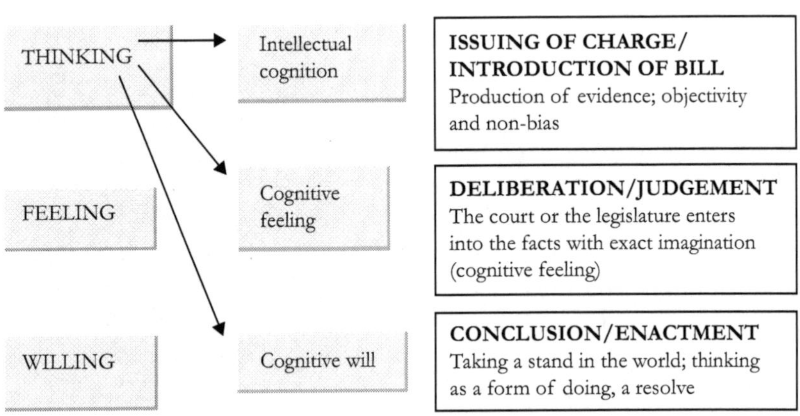

Figure 42

Beyond Roman Law

We must go beyond Roman law which is like a ligature, tying us to the past. The present coronavirus crisis, more than any situation in world history since the Roman era, is compelling us in the direction of such a decisive social transformation. This is because, far from being merely a medical emergency, the coronavirus crisis is eating at the heart of our political-legal system, not just in Western civilization but in every country where the political and legal systems of European origin have spread.

What in earlier periods of civilization took the form of an overt figure of absolute authority—and here we can think again of the pharaoh of ancient Egypt—transformed over millennia and became a *legal framework.* In terms of Western civilization, we saw in Chapter 3 how in the Graeco-Roman period the kind of abstract mentality developed such that the aristocratic principle of authority could become transmogrified and codified into a system of justice—specifically, the Justinian Code, which became the basis of modern Western civil law. In Plato's *The Republic*, the character Thrasymachus claims that 'justice is the advantage of the stronger'.[123] For modern-day libertarians and anarchists, the state's legal apparatus represents nothing other than a means of oppression and control, the aristocratic few determining what the many can and can't do.

The practice of the law is still very much under the spell of the ordering, codifying mentality with which the Romans first developed their systems of law. Roman-style legal thinking was consolidated and fostered in medieval times in the new universities, particularly after the rediscovery of the *Digest*, Justinian's compilation of Roman law, which had been lost to scholars for five centuries and then became the basis for the study of law at the new university at Bologna. The Romans developed their law as a *power* structure, an expression of their characteristic conquering, organizing mentality. Apart from their governmental legal structures, their senates, magistrates, assemblies and so on, they instituted the registration of a person's birth which was all-important for determining citizenship. The Romans carried out a thoroughgoing census of all persons in all conquered lands, in which names and associated property were registered in lists which were kept in temples (*Tabulae Censoriae*).[124] Roman law was about controlling the citizens and non-citizens through according different forms of rights and privileges, and this is the form of law which has passed down to us. Today information surveillance technology and artificial intelligence have gone far beyond what the Romans were able to achieve in order to control a population and what information they could collect and store in their temples! Given this fact, it is understandable that in our time of individualized consciousness there is a counter-movement of people seeking a way of standing outside the law, of asserting themselves only as their natural, sovereign human self.[125]

Steiner makes the point that we don't need a re-birth of the old, like the European Renaissance, but an altogether new creation of culture. He points the way toward a renewed legal *form* of thinking:

> Until now we have been unable to create anything more in the area of rights than a renaissance of Roman law . . . if we remove the former basis for rights and culture from the social organism, then we must establish a new foundation . . . we need a new birth of the state based upon the equality of the human being.[126]

The danger is that what has the appearance of the new may in fact be only another refinement of Graeco-Roman thought structures. Our society continues to be fundamentally aristocratic because alive within its heart is an aristocratic conception of the human soul nature. A truly new culture can develop from a thinking in which the whole human being is active—thinking, feeling, and willing as an organic whole—without one aspect 'higher' or 'more true' than the other. Everything about Steiner's conception of a threefold social order turns around this potential for a metamorphosis of thinking.

Turning again to Plato's *The Republic*, we find expressed in this work the educational aim of cultivating the thinking function which is the aristocratic principle, outwardly the guardians or rulers of society. Thinking—or 'the intellect'—represents the way to the truth which Plato calls the intellectual realm; as such it has supremacy over the feelings and will which represent outwardly the lower strata of society—rather like the human head carried aloft by the body, a monarch in a carriage, carried along and presiding over all. That is the exoteric aim of this work. However, as we have seen above in relation to justice, Plato speaks only of the *harmonization* of the thinking, feeling, and willing; this is the more esoteric aspect and represents a seed-image for the future. So when we speak of going beyond the power-principles of Roman law, at bottom what is required is to break free from the Graeco-Roman aristocratic *conception of thinking* which was expressed in the exoteric aspect of Plato's work and developed in the Roman legalistic mentality.

There has been a profound mission in the aristocratic order for human evolution and for the accentuated development of the thinking function. We see it, for example, in the powerful growth of scientific rationality through European history and its resultant technologies and medicines.

It can only be considered as something negative when it becomes an impediment to cultural transformation. The development of objective rationality has liberated humanity from the more unconscious, instinctive forms of consciousness which characterized archaic stages of human development. Thinking's rulership has gradually elevated the lower 'classes' of the soul towards the spirit and towards freedom—just as through spiritual communion the theocrat became the first truly human individual and exemplar for the whole of society. In our age of individualized consciousness it is not a question of asserting the value of feeling and will *against* thinking's dominion. Thinking itself needs to serve the human sentient life in a new way and this is by transforming feeling and will into powers of cognition in their own right; feeling becomes *cognitive feeling* and willing becomes *cognitive will*. What thereby takes shape is a thinking of the whole human being; it is in effect a 'democratization' of the soul.

The thinking of the whole human being translates into a new legal outlook, into the altogether new culture which Steiner says is so necessary. The principle of rulership is obviated, not overcome; it becomes without relevance for a society of individual wills. Individual wills are human beings who are free, who are working and developing their lives from out of themselves, not according to the dictates of a ruling elite or ruling principle which stand over them—elected or otherwise. The individual will doesn't need to be ruled. In Steiner's words:

> The kind of spirit that does not develop in freedom out of the life of the spirit itself but rather out of an external organisation simply does not know what are the spirit's potentials. It looks about for something to guide and manage it, not knowing how the spirit guides and manages itself if it can but draw its strength from its own sources.[127]

Any kind of stricture or imposition on the free life of the spirit, any kind of general system of law imposed from above to which the individual will is required to conform, limits spirit's creative potential. To speak of spirit and spirit's potential no longer refers merely to the thinking principle which can rise into a world of abstract forms or theories. Spirit pertains to the whole human being; individual wills experience spirit's potential in *themselves*, not in what is 'higher', controlling them, ordering them. To go further into the potential of the individual will we need to take up a consideration of the cultural-spiritual sphere of the threefold social organism, the theme of the next chapter.

Steiner's indications for the way beyond Roman law are radical, as is everything else in connection with the threefold social conception. The pathway he presents is radical, yet it is precisely in tune with the needs and aspirations of the modern individual. We have already discussed some ways in which parliament needs to transform in order to truly reflect human rights as mediating between the realms of culture and economy. To step decisively beyond Roman law is to bring about a profound change in the whole administration and functioning of the political-rights sphere of society.

Chapter 8

THE CULTURAL-SPIRITUAL SPHERE

Freedom

The great Dutch philosopher Spinoza declared that 'the purpose of the state is, in reality, freedom'.[128] Notwithstanding the stature of Spinoza as a philosopher this view remains remarkably limited; socially speaking, freedom is no more fundamental a human ideal than is fraternity and equality. In truth, the ideal of freedom stands as the primary driving force behind one particular dimension of society: the cultural-spiritual sphere. It works there to inspire all its forms and all activities—the arts, education, the sciences and all varieties of spiritual life. Just through this single declaration Spinoza brings clearly into relief the problem of conceiving of society as a unitary entity of absolute significance, driven by a single aim or ideal.

At the dawn of the twentieth century Friedrich Nietzsche wrote a statement which defines the essential striving of the cultural-spiritual sphere: 'Freedom is the will to be responsible for ourselves.'[129] The quest for freedom is radically individual and individuality is the essence of this pole of the threefold social order. Manifestations of free spiritual activity—like works of art—may be influential throughout the social fabric but they always begin with an individually willed deed. Nietzsche brought the idea of freedom from the philosophically abstract into the domain of the existential, to the consideration of how freedom actually comes about concretely. The general philosophical notion of human free-will he calls 'boorish simplicity, a long folly, owing to our extravagant pride'.[130] In reality we struggle towards freedom, we forge our lives creatively and through creative engagement we may find a path to freedom. This act of forging one's life through the struggle with doubts and difficulties Nietzsche conceives through the model of the artistic process.[131] Nietzsche's way of thinking made an extraordinarily great impact on European culture of the new century because it spoke to the lived experience of people. It brought a new consciousness to how we all stand as individuals in the world, serving the voice of conscience which asks us to be responsible for ourselves.

At the very time when Nietzsche penned these words a counterforce to cultural and spiritual freedom was coming into being in Western civilization: communism. The communist conceptions of Marx, Lenin and Engels were taking hold of the hearts and minds of Europeans as an apparent call to liberation. Yet, this was not at all about freedom in Nietzsche's sense of 'the will to be responsible for oneself'; it was actually more a call to equality and fraternity with the aim of liberating workers from the tyranny of class structure. Freedom in the sense of individual freedom was considered bourgeois, the privilege of the ruling economic class. According to the *Communist Manifesto* of Marx and Lenin, this individual sort of freedom had to be abolished, 'swept out of the way, and made impossible'.[132] The appeal was being made to the ideal of fraternity or brotherhood and this is because the whole thrust of Marxist socialism took place within the economic realm. Freedom in the sense of the ideal of the cultural-spiritual sphere of society—this freedom, in Marxist thought, is considered merely 'ideological superstructure', abstract and lacking revolutionary efficacy.

Stirred by the ideal of true universal brotherhood, early twentieth-century communist uprisings sought the transformation of the economic sphere of society and the collectivization of the proletariat workers. This revolutionary agenda relied on the political realm's brute power of coercion; there was no conception that the true liberating power may reside in the individual and in everything which supports the unfoldment of the individual. Steiner writes:

> Marx and Engels were right to demand a new economic order—right, but one-sided. They did not perceive that economic life can only become free when a free sphere of rights and free cultivation of the spirit are allowed to arise alongside it. [133]

What he is saying here is that the sphere of economics and the sphere of culture and spirit must be entirely independent of the political life: this is the threefold organization of society. It means, with respect to the cultural-spiritual sphere, that religious life, education, science and art, medicine and the media, must be organized, regulated, administered, and governed in a way which is completely autonomous and free from political and economic dominion.

Marxist ideas undoubtedly had a strong influence on Steiner, in particular when he was a young man in Berlin and was mixing with many who were striving toward socialist reform. It influenced him mainly by impelling him to set an entirely different course in his thinking about social renewal. When over a four-year period he was delivering lectures at a college for the proletariat, which was founded on socialist principles, he chose not to inculcate these workers with Marxist notions of economic determinism.[134] What he wanted was to set his listeners' hearts on fire with the potential for individual freedom, recognizing that the proletariat had little access to bourgeois culture and spiritual life which might otherwise have stimulated a quest for individuality and self-determination.

Steiner insists that only an independent cultural and spiritual life can 'supply the economic life with the human spiritual impulses that can fructify it ever and again . . .'[135] Notwithstanding its one-sided emphasis on economic transformation effected through political might, the social impulse which communism represents has been highly significant in the movement towards a conscious threefolding of the social organism. The communist revolutions in the twentieth century—both those which failed and those which have lived on into the present—through their attack on individual freedoms and individual rights, have served to bring clarity to a more healthy way of shaping the social organism. They have demonstrated the need for *all three* spheres of the social organism to come into their own, to achieve a high level of independence from each other such that they can work together as an integrated unity.

The Pathway of Free Creative Origination

Every free creative action is a deed of the cultural-spiritual sphere. Creative freedom is always related to an individual's need to bring something to expression; as such it can take the form of thoughts, insights, creative impulses, the realization of one's individual mission or capacities. In Chapter 2 it was shown that the essential 'for self' of the creative act is polar to the essential 'for others' gesture of the economic sphere. It is this very gesture of 'for self' which allows the individual work of the cultural-spiritual sphere to act positively on the other two, to fructify the economic sphere 'ever and again'. Paradoxically, only what is educated to be creative, individual and original (and in that sense separate and anti-social) can ultimately renew, inspire and uplift the social whole. There can never be consciousness if we are immersed in a semi-instinctive oneness with life, like drops of water merged in an ocean. For consciousness and for freedom there must be separation, difference, individuality; yet through that separation a new order of wholeness may come about—through conscious, individual will.

To be free is to be able to act without restriction or compulsion so that what exists only in potential can evolve and become actual. In general terms we can characterize the cultural-spiritual pole as the striving for the actualization of spirit. The creator experiences a powerful necessity to actualize what it intuited but not because of an external, enforced moral imperative. It is because the creator loves the intuition of what can be, and wants to ensure that it comes to pass. It is entirely individual; no other person can be involved in such a creative intuition. An insight or inspiration can never come about cooperatively. The shaping of a creative intuition is a matter of individual will but the way this intuition works out into the social body may involve many others—for example, the musicians in an orchestra or a choir performing an individual's work or a team of researchers elaborating and putting into practice the insights of one scientist into a particular phenomenon of nature.

What Steiner means by 'human spiritual impulses' are deeds of the free individual creative spirit and they may take any number of different forms. Such impulses are epitomized by the creative artist who abides perhaps most purely in the creative process; but in truth creativity is an all-human capacity. For, *every* person participates to a greater or lesser extent in the cultural-spiritual sphere by virtue of the ideal of creative freedom working in them. It refers to the creative-spiritual work of the teacher who is shaping every moment of learning in a classroom; to the mother who is forming the womb of family life for the nurture and upbringing of children. Every social deed can be touched by the spirit of free creation or can remain a mechanical, habitual affair, governed more by convention and fear than by individuality. We learn from the act of artistic creation how the creative process proceeds by a lawfulness, from intuition to manifestation—through the research, incubation, illumination, manifestation and verification stages.[136] The avant-garde artist who revels in their creative freedom, who breaks open the crust of tradition and makes an expressive statement which springs directly from their individual will—this takes on a significance far beyond the world of art as such. Artistic creation and the world of art altogether become the vanguard for what Steiner calls 'a society of individual wills'.

A Society of Individual Wills

The expression 'society of individual wills' might sound dangerously anarchical, for it may be asked, logically and practically speaking: How could such a society possibly hold together and not dissolve into a chaos of conflicting views and egotistical ambitions? Notwithstanding, the society of individual wills is what Rudolf Steiner considered as the only possible healthy society of a future humanity. Victor Hugo had already said it in his evocation of the aims of the French Revolution:

> In terms of policy, there is only one principle, the sovereignty of man over himself, and this sovereignty of me over me is called Liberty.[137]

Such a picture of society cannot be brushed aside as 'merely utopian'; it is the form of society which belongs to the inmost striving of the modern human being. Such a striving is evident in the whole tendency towards individual expression in twentieth-century modernist culture.

We should not underestimate the tenacity of the mindset which insists that a 'society of individual wills' is an impossibility. Steiner certainly recognized this resistance in the society around him:

> Most people today still lack faith in the possibility of establishing a social order based on individuals wills. They have no faith in it because such a faith cannot come from a cultural life that has developed in dependence on the state and the economy.[138]

Today it still may seem nonsensical to suggest that any other social organization is possible other than that which takes place under the auspices of a centralized government. There is a strange contradiction between our consciousness of self and our political expectations. But this lack of faith is not without reason: no civilization on this planet has yet seen a culture of individual wills and understandably there are doubts as to whether it will produce something which is secure and lasting. The society of individual wills is going to have to be ventured from out of our authenticity of spirit and unyielding sense of spirit's potential, for only this will ever provide the necessary courage and resoluteness to bring it about.

Steiner spoke about a society of individual wills in order to draw attention to a powerful and what he considered dangerous tendency of socialist thought in his time: this was the social conception of Marx and Engels which emphasized the idea of a common will imposed through economic determinism. But we know, from everything already developed on these pages, that when Steiner was opposing socialism he wasn't thereby promoting capitalism as the 'right model'.[139] The society of individual wills is what is educated, nurtured and promoted in the cultural-spiritual sphere of a threefold ordering of society. Here the individual human spirit can come into its own. And of course there is, by contrast, a sphere of society—the economic sphere—in which there reigns the common will or what we could also call the fraternal will. But in a truly emancipated society this common, fraternal will is formed *through the volition of individual wills*. People work together in the associative economy because they *choose* to do so, because they *wish* to serve each other through their labour (more than that, they wish to work for the whole community of life on Earth). Individual wills together *create* the common will. What so concerned Steiner was the idea, coming from the socialist thinkers, that the common will would occur through eliminating the individual will. But he was equally concerned that the individual will does not come into its own in capitalist society, because, rather than achieving the fraternal will through volition, and because individuals are mostly enslaved by the wage nexus, they are as compelled and governed as through Marxism's economic imperative.

In the second decade of the twenty-first century the whole of humanity has been engulfed by a state of crisis which has superficially been classified as 'medical'. It would better be referred to as 'a crisis of the individual will'. The attack on the individual will has the character of an onslaught; any suggestion of 'my rights', 'what I wish' is met with condemnation and is judged selfish. To an increasing extent nothing is considered important and virtuous except the 'common will' and the 'common good'. The important thing to note is that this 'common will' doesn't arise of itself but only through strategies of coercion. Part of the attack on the individual will has involved taking 'medical measures'—lockdowns, curfews and social distancing—which most directly impacted the organizations, venues and activities of cultural and spiritual life where the ideal of freedom is paramount and is the guiding light. This includes concert halls and theatres, churches, pubs, festivals, cafes, cinemas, clubs—all situations where ideas and insights are exchanged, creative visions shared or realized. The medical measures deem all such activities non-essential. Many educational institutions have gone online, making free, creative interpersonal interaction minimal or impossible.

The coronavirus crisis is being married in a most deliberate and carefully thought-through way with the area of social life where a medical issue normally would be thought to have no relevance whatsoever—namely, environmentalism, or at least, environmentalism seen from a certain perspective. This is the perspective that declares that 'individual wills' are a blight on the planetary biosystem and the cause of environmental destruction, through over-population, consumerism, private transport, and other such 'selfish' activities. Those who see the world from this perspective believe the only option is to radically control and regulate the activities of individual wills, and a digital social credit system is undoubtedly an aspect of this plan.[140] As with all socialist revolutions, the common will is not what is agreed on among people mutually; it is what is *decided* to be important and good by a political-economic elite. In the socialist revolutions in Steiner's time 'brotherhood' was the catchcry; now it is 'social justice'—*but not freedom*.[141] If a crisis of the individual will was developing in Steiner's time, it is now vastly magnified and has entered a particularly dangerous phase.

For it is ignored, or simply not understood—now, just as in Steiner's time—that a truly free cultural-spiritual life engenders responsibility, creative possibility, vitality and hope, care and authentic engagement. Every genuine artist knows that creative liberty means responsibility for what is being created and brings about the kind of care which could never possibly be enforced through the dictates of the communality or the imperative of an 'absolute' or 'higher' principle—whether you call it 'the common good', or 'the transcendence of the proletariat', or any other such theoretical construction. There is nothing to say that, in a society of individual wills, individuals cannot find themselves in agreement with others, that they cannot work out what is equally right and good for themselves and each other. This in fact happens through shared participation in the processes of life, in mutual observation of forms of nature and of society, in workplaces of every kind, even if at times there is conflict which needs to be taken as part of a creative process. Order arises in this society out of what free individuals create mutually.

It was Hegel who declared: 'Real freedom presupposed others who are free.'[142] An individual who is unfolding his or her life according to a need which they individually intuit, thereby gains a capacity to imagine the same need for the creative unfoldment of others. Through this they discover a love for the entire free spiritual formation of the cultural-spiritual sphere. A society of individual wills requires a certain kind of cultivation within the cultural-spiritual life, in particular through education, in order to come to an ever-higher state of realization. In this regard Steiner provides a guiding thought:

> If men are no longer to 'govern' their fellows in the old way, then it must be made possible for the free spirit in every human soul . . . to make itself the guide in life. This spirit will not allow itself to be suppressed.[143]

The aim of education—both school and tertiary—is essentially this: to provide the pathway whereby every human individual can come forth in freedom, sovereign over themselves, their own guide in life. For this reason the last two chapters of this book are devoted to the topic of education and the threefold social order.

Cultivating The Will to Work

As adults we work because we wish to realize our own potential, to follow the guidance of our own free spirit, to bring forth in our activities what we know to be our innate capacities and gifts. We could call this a person's true vocation. It is not in the least utopian to make such a statement; to say anything other is to advocate compulsion to work which has to be slavery in some shape or form. Certainly it is an ideal which involves great creative challenges in order to be realized—but it is an ideal which belongs to a healthy social order, to a true society of individual wills. And the task of assisting individuals to achieve this end belongs centrally to the cultural-spiritual sphere.

Those currently advocating a large-scale reorganization of social life speak of a Fourth Industrial Revolution, this being an advanced-stage digitization and robotization of industry and commence. It seems to some of those promoting the notion of a Great Reset (and this is already happening, through artificial intelligence and rapid development of robots) that many jobs will disappear and people will have much more leisure, which is presented as an eventuality greatly to be desired.[144] This is the opposite of what needs to come about through a society of individual wills. Certainly many forms of employment will be no more, through artificial intelligence; but this will provide the opportunity for people to create their means and form of work out of their own resources. This is what has always happened in earlier stages of history when different forms of mechanization came to prominence; the society of individual wills is only enhancing an existing tendency and characteristic of the development of human individualization. But if a Fourth Industrial Revolution is promoted without an equal emphasis on the cultivation of the free will to work then a grotesque one-sidedness and curtailing of the human spirit is going to gain ascendency in the future course of civilization.

In truth—given the right conditions—people love to work because they wish to serve and build the world through their work. Work in its multitude of forms, to a very large degree, gives purpose to human existence and it is for this reason that every resource and means within the cultural-spiritual realm should be pointed in this direction. In Chapter 6, under the heading *The Liberation of Work*, it was proposed that work is a *right*, not a commodity which can be purchased with a wage, not an economic phenomenon at all. It was in the context of this discussion that the idea was introduced—fundamental to Steiner's picture of a threefold social organism—that work comes about through love, as the artist loves and carefully creates the work of art in its totality. On this topic Steiner has the following to say:

> The threefold social order aims at establishing within an independent, self-sustaining cultural life a realm where one learns in a living way to understand this human society for which one is called upon to work; a realm where one learns to see what each single piece of work means for the combined fabric of the social order, to see it in such a light that one will learn to *love* it because of its value for the whole. It aims at creating in this free life of spirit the profounder principles that can replace the motive of personal gain. Only in a free spiritual life can a love for the human social order spring up that is comparable to the love an artist has for the creation of his works.[145]

The key point in this passage is that we must learn to understand human society *in a living way*, through an authentic education for freedom, if we are to develop a will to work out of ourselves. This statement will make sense in the light of everything presented on these pages—that one must call upon an artistic, imaginative intelligence to understand the living being of society. We come to love society when we have entered into it with a thinking which recreates its forms and processes in our feeling and will; in this way we come to know the social organism intimately and creatively, in exactly the way artists know their own creations. Society conceived abstractly, merely theoretically, can never engender the kind of love and will to work which Steiner is speaking of.

A truly free will to work will not come about through a concession, strategy or dispensation of the state, through any neo-Maoist 'great leap forward', 'incentivization programme' or the like. It can only come about through the cultural-spiritual life itself. Of course a great deal of human work in modern society takes place in the economic sphere, but that doesn't mean work is *fundamentally* an economic phenomenon. Forms of work such as that of the scientific researcher, the teacher, the artist, are much more clearly cultural-spiritual activities, although these all may have an economic aspect. What *all* forms of work have in common is that they have to do with unfolding one's self in the world, with realizing one's own capacities. Going back to Nietzsche's definition of freedom as 'the will to be responsible for oneself', we can now say that this is exactly what the will to work essentially is. When we are working in this conscious way we are the creators of the threefold social order. Work then becomes a social art.

Chapter 9

THE QUESTION OF GOVERNANCE

Threefold Governance

Steiner's presentation of his radical and widely-studied views on social renewal in the immediate aftermath of World War 1 was extremely challenging and he faced numerous logical objections—in particular, the idea that doing away with a central bureaucratic form of governance was going to lead to social dissolution. It appeared to some commentators in his time that advocating the separation of three spheres was fragmenting society, violently dismembering it rather than healing and unifying it.[146] It is possible that such objections may still be heard today.

Firstly, we need to consider the fundamentals of the kind of centralized, bureaucratic governance which is so familiar to us that we tend to think it is the only way things can be. The noun 'government' cannot be narrowly defined but it basically means the organ of society which establishes legal structures and ensures that structures are adhered to. Centralized forms of governance have a long and chequered history; all traditional monarchies exercised sovereign and absolute authority over a people or country. This tradition lingers on; the King of the UK, according to the constitution of Australia, is officially the sovereign authority and supreme governor even if, effectively, Australia is a functioning democracy. The meaning and gesture of representational democratic governance is 'softer' than the governance of absolutist, dictatorial states. Whether and to what extent representational democracies actually serve the wishes of the people is another matter and the well-known statement by eminent social theorist Herbert Marcuse from the 1960s is arguably no less true with the passing of a half-century: 'Free election of masters does not abolish the masters or the slaves.'[147]

Whether it be an absolutist government or a representative democracy, what both have in common is statehood. Into the notion of state a great deal has been pressed; it basically signifies a centralized political organization but it can include everything implied by the word 'nation'—that is, a social unity based on ethnicity or shared cultural values (hence 'nation states'). Marxist socialism aims to take revolutionary control of the state;

anarchism seeks to dismantle it, considering it to be unnecessary for an ordered social life. Woodrow Wilson spoke of the *will* of the state, meaning the all-commanding authority of the state over a society in its entirety.[148] In Steiner's picture of the threefold social organism state only refers to the political-rights sphere which, as we shall see, has no absolute authority or controlling power.

The modern state is founded on the conception of a unity and the fear of any government is separatism; if a people is divided within itself it is said to be in an ungovernable social condition. Strong governance is considered to be measured by the degree of social unity. Given the strength and dedication with which this view is held, it is not surprising that Steiner's concept of the threefold social organism was vigorously criticized for *apparently* wanting to pull society apart. Actually Steiner was intending no such thing with his conception of a tri-articulated social unity.

When we have worked through to the point of seeing—that is, actually *perceiving* with the eye of the imagination—that society is a threefold unity, then a very simple and straightforward thought follows: each of the three spheres must be self-governing, because all the expertise which is required to govern each sphere is inherent in that sphere itself. Each of the spheres has its own integrity, its particular lawfulness and requirements which relate to its archetypal constitution and the primary ideal which inspires it—freedom, equality, or fraternity. How can everything which pertains to human freedom and individuality pretend to govern that sphere of life which relates essentially to human cooperative, economic life—and likewise the other way round? The same thing applies to the sphere of politics and rights, where equality stands as the ideal, in relation to the other two. When one enters into each sphere with an exact moral imagination it appears even grotesque in our day and age that it could be any other way—that there could be an encompassing government responsible for science, responsible for education and medicine, responsible for rights, responsible for anything to do with the economy, responsible even for the arts and spiritual life.[149]

The key is grasping that this threefold membering is a threefold *unity*, meaning that the three governances are related as intimately as the nervous system, vascular, and metabolic systems are in the unitary human body, without any all-embracing 'control centre' unifying them. The difference of course is that the social threefold unity is something that we ourselves create—or we could say, socially sculpt. A healthily functioning integrated threefold governance *results* in this deliberately and carefully formed unity. The tenacious thought—which Steiner noted on numerous occasions—is that for society to be in a state of health or wholeness it must be one entity, a single unit, a monolith. This thought is remarkably atavistic—it harks back to the picture of ancient pharaonic society which fans out beneath the single point of absolute governance—the god-man or pharaoh. We still hold to this picture even though any number of examples in modern life tells us that social unity comes about in an entirely different way; for example, a modern family is not bound together by an absolute authority figure as was traditionally the case—a patriarch or matriarch. It achieves unity or wholeness through bonds of love, care, and responsibility.

In no living being does difference imply opposition or enmity. When a plant or animal grows from a single cell and gradually differentiates into a cell mass and then into discrete organs, what is coming about is not a breaking apart but an integration on a higher level, a new unity-in-multiplicity. In a society which has become a consciously ordered tri-unity the three spheres are brought into meaningful organic relationship *by virtue of their separateness*. In other words, the task is as much about integrating as it is about separating and distinguishing the three spheres. This is exactly what takes place in any artistically creative process: through the cognitive imagination of the artist the disparate elements are shaped into an aesthetic whole.

What is the necessary artistic disposition for governance in the threefold social order? Let us consider the American minimalist-abstract painter Mark Rothko whose work was often the juxtaposition of three large colour 'fields'. Everything about the meaning and significance of these compositions depends on the complete separation of the three colours—yet in that very separation the unity of the work is found. Each colour maintains its integrity; for example, a carefully separated blue does not 'swallow' a red and white and each gathers to itself what is true to itself.[150] Out of that independence of the colour fields the meaning of the whole arises. Rothko is working with archetypal relationships in all his paintings. The study of such artworks can be a starting point, an orientation for the eye of the imagination to then be able to perceive threefold wholeness in living form. However, with an organism the three separate spheres are not side-by-side as in a Rothko painting; they interpenetrate each other dynamically. So that, after such an orientation with works of art, it would be necessary to turn to the artistic perception of the threefold human organism as described in Chapter 4 under the headings *Human Physiology* and *Animal Physiology*.

Only through exercising this power of imaginative perception will it be possible to recognize that Steiner's proposal for threefold governance is not just another 'social system', a kind of idealist mental construction which has no relationship to the struggles of lived reality. On the contrary, he discerned the need for the threefold governing of society out of the social reality around him which became starkly problematic during and after the First World War. For example, he saw that when cultural entities like distinct language communities within a country's population (and there are many such in European countries) assert themselves politically, then strife often follows which can be inflammatory to the point of civil war. Language groups belong to the cultural-spirit sphere and risk losing the freedom native to that sphere if they allow themselves to be 'swallowed' by the political sphere. What is necessary is to *see* what element belongs to which of the three social spheres and to ensure that it remains within that sphere of governance.

The conscious creation of the threefold social order is artistic in the broad sense of social sculpture or social architecture. The artistic sense does not impose or dictate—it discovers and reveals. Everything in connection with governance and the threefold social order issues from this point: we *find* within each of the three spheres the forces and methods necessary for its own self-governance and for its relationship with the other two governances. As Steiner puts it: 'by separating them the impulse engendered within any one of these three spheres works in a harmonizing way on the others'.[151] There is no overarching, central controlling governance to bring about this harmonization which means that the idea of the national state is obviated. From this it does not follow that there is going to be a breakdown of law and order into anarchistic chaos because there remains a fully autonomous legal and rights sphere.

In the threefold social organism, Steiner indicates, the state will have become a 'shadow-image', exactly in the same sense as the Catholic Church is 'a relic, a shadow-image of what existed in the very first imperialism'.[152] In the great monarchical nations of pre-modern Europe the state was supreme and its power total; the Catholic Church was the central institution of the state at that time. In the realized threefold social order the state is equated only with the political-rights sphere; it is separate from and doesn't impinge upon the cultural-spiritual and economic spheres. But we can equally say that the latter two spheres must not impinge upon the state. In pre-modern Europe the cultural-spiritual life transmitted and inculcated by the Catholic Church certainly did 'swallow' the state. Today the main difficulty is the tendency of the economic life—in particular big business—to exert enormous influence on the political. Some effort is made to stem the flow of corporate capital to political parties, but this nevertheless goes on to a large extent with impunity. There is an immense entanglement of political and economic interests, in particular weapons manufacturers, the fossil fuels industry, industrial agriculture, and 'big pharma'. It almost goes without saying that the candidate with the largest budget will win the American presidential election. All of this is an impossibility in the consciously tri-articulated social organism.

One area of contemporary social life in which all three spheres are particularly entangled—one could almost say intractably so—is the media. This became glaringly obvious during the coronavirus crisis when the corporate-owned media went about censoring social media and curtailing broad debate in the mainstream media in order to serve the government's line on the issues surrounding the virus. Journalism is a cultural pursuit and as such should be independent of the political and economic spheres. When below we consider the governance of the cultural-spiritual sphere the question of the media can be taken as an example of cultural activity which needs to be entirely self-governing. The liberation of the media is going to come about partly through the strengthening of the rights life, in particular the right to freedom of speech. Breaking the connection of the economic and the media—namely, corporate ownership of the press, television and social media platforms—is plainly a more difficult task. But this, like everything else connected with realizing the threefold social unity, cannot be carried out in isolation. It becomes part of the total reshaping of the social order and, in particular, the realizing of capital as a right. For it is free capital becoming available to the cultural-spiritual sphere, for all forms of creative initiative, which will support the independent governance of the media.

Steiner's proposal remains as groundbreaking and challenging as it was when it was first presented to the world over a century ago. But could it be—in our world today rent asunder with racial conflict, abuse of political power, inequality and the imminent threat of a technocratic new world order—that the time is at hand for moving with decisive steps towards the creation of a tri-membered social governance?

The *Trias Politica* As Prophetic Form

Plato put forward an image of a republic in an early expression of the archetypal threefold social principle, with his three social 'estates' (the guardians, the soldiers, and the merchants) standing for the soul functions of thinking, feeling, and willing respectively.[153] This way of thinking belonged to ancient Greek consciousness and the estates were rigidly demarcated social classes or castes. A person in one estate was bound to that division and there was a ruling class—the guardians—who were the elect because they represented the thinking function. Plato's republic was not too far distant from the more ancient theocratic hierarchical principles of governance such as existed in ancient Egypt. Nonetheless, Plato had an artistic sense—specifically, a musical sense—of how these three functions could together form a unity by not interfering with each other's activity. 'Like three discrete tones of a chord', he writes, the three social estates of the guardians, soldiers and merchants 'sound together' harmoniously and create a unity-in-multiplicity.[154]

The archetypal threefold works beneath the surface of evolving social life as a germinal force; at different points it has emerged and taken a form entirely in keeping with the needs of the time. After the Graeco-Roman era, aristocratic-monarchical forms of autocratic governance dominated Western civilization for many centuries. Through this time society remained largely monolithic, still a reflection of the far more ancient theocratic form. Such was the social reality when, in the eighteenth century, the French social philosopher Montesquieu advocated that government should be divided into three branches: a legislature, a judiciary, and an executive. This *trias politica* is usually referred to as 'the separation of powers', the idea that the judiciary should not be under the control of an absolute ruler, that there should be no concentration in the sphere of the political or governmental life. A real need was being expressed here to emancipate different areas of political life and a separation of powers became fundamental to Westminster and American parliamentary systems and those countries which adopted these systems. It did something never conceived of in previous eras of civilization—namely, the limiting of the power of the ruling elite. This threefold differentiation of the political realm has become a reality in the majority of democracies today.

We rightly hold to social structures which have an enduring value and proven efficacy. The *trias politica* has been profoundly important in the development of government in the last two centuries even while constantly being put to the test. But enough turbulent water has passed under the bridge to see its limitations—or perhaps we should say, its further potentials. What was good and true in Montesquieu's time and for the setting up of the American Constitution and Westminster system of governance, is not sufficient for our time and for the human future. The key to social renewal does not now lie just in the threefold separation of the political sphere; such a separation must be enacted in society as a whole. The *trias politica* must become a *trias societa*.

The inner driving forces of differentiation and emancipation have led society to the condition today where we have three definite centres or functional hearts of activity as observed by Jürgen Habermas: the economic, the political, and the cultural. However, as Habermas notes, the centres of activity impinge on each other in such a socially destructive way that he questions the legitimacy of centralized government in modern capitalistic states.[155] What we need today is not just a separation of *political* powers but *a separation of societal powers*.

The *trias politica* principle of Montesquieu is in a sense the 'prophetic form' of the separation of governances fundamental to the threefold social order. Each of the three elements of the *trias politica* has a characteristic gesture which relates it to one of the spheres of the threefold social order.[156] Firstly, the legislature (the parliament) deals with the formulating of laws in which the ideal of *equality* works absolutely and unquestionably. No one is above the law in relation to the legislature—no freedom or selectivity is possible in this regard. However, when it comes to the judiciary, the interpreter of laws, what is called 'judicial discretion' comes into play whereby the judiciary exercises liberty within a range of options pertaining to a particular case, in the weighing up of the situation. Thus the ideal of *freedom* has a relationship with this aspect of the *trias politica* and freedom is the ideal of the cultural-spiritual sphere of the threefold social order. The judiciary is not *compelled* by the legislature. And, thirdly, in relation to the executive—what we usually call 'the government' and the law enforcement agencies, the police and the army—the fulfilment of executive tasks are by no means a mechanical, automatic affair. What is always required is an acute 'listening' to the surrounding context of the task and the situation and needs of the different people involved, in order to know how best to act in a practical way in regard to human relationships. Even in circumstances of criminal activity and war, the ability to work with people cooperatively and respectfully is vital in relation to this aspect of the *trias politica* in order to execute justice. In some cases members of the executive might even lose their lives in the service of others. The ideal of *fraternity* or brotherliness pertaining to the executive is an intimation of the quality of the economic sphere and its associative economy, where 'listening' and cooperative activity are paramount.

The citizens of today's democracies have a sense of the *trias politica* in their bones, as it were, in their feeling of social morality. It is shocking to the population of democratic nations when, for example, a political leader finds a way to appoint preferred judges; such happenings disturb the people's trust in democracy. In the future, as the trifold archetypal form transforms into the threefold organization of society altogether, we can anticipate a similar moral outrage will be felt if, for example, the political-legal sphere attempts to influence the independent cultural-spiritual life (something still entirely normal today). Currently we still feel it 'right' that, for example, the government controls education. In the realized threefold social order this control of education by the state could only be felt as a moral impossibility.

To perceive the seed-potential of the *trias politica*, to sense what it can and indeed *must* become, is to gaze directly with the eye of the imagination into the unique needs of the present age. Montesquieu was concerned with the separation of powers necessary in order to properly administer justice. The particular kind of social disintegrative tendency of our time means that the differentiating of the three social spheres needs to be equally a deed of integration. Steiner's notion of a new social order based on three separate governances is profoundly integrative and restorative in its impulse because within it works the creative striving which ever seeks the living social unity.

Governance of The Economic Sphere

The emancipated economic sphere will only ever maintain itself as a self-governing wholeness through its conscious relationship to the tri-membered unity of which it is a part. The threefold social order is a spiritual-organic wholeness and the order of each sphere is meaningless outside the unity of the whole. However, as we know, there is no all-embracing 'control centre' or governing body in the threefold social organization; the parts of a living whole simply order themselves in relation to each other because they belong to each other.

In the not so distant past all economic activity in Western civilization was carried out under the aegis of a monarchy. Today the business world looks after its own affairs to a far greater extent. However, as is common knowledge, that 'looking after its own affairs' is very often an utterly self-serving affair. This is the freedom of 'free enterprise' and the 'free market' which translates as the licence to monopolize the means of production, accumulate vast capital and so garner to oneself untold economic and political power. We have already considered the fact that the economy has emancipated itself in recent centuries and is on its way to autonomy. But unquestionably, we have a long way to go before we have achieved economic self-governance in terms of a healthy threefold social organism.

As different as the brain is from the liver, so the governing principle of the economic sphere of the threefold social order differs from that of the other two spheres. In the economic sphere this governing principle is the economic association; this association, as discussed in Chapter 6, is a fraternity of those involved in a particular dimension of production or service; the totality of such associations is what we call the 'associative economy'. The regulating principle of this economic governance is what people work out with each other through a sense of mutual concern. Of course it can be mixed with many different motivations, but at the core of the associative economy is the impulse of love for other human beings and of concern for their physical needs. When labour and capital are legally recognized for what they fundamentally are—rights, not economic issues—when the economic sphere is not driven by an immoral and inhuman survival-of-the-fittest struggle for capital, then a truly fraternal economic life has the possibility of coming into being. When we provide the right conditions of air, warmth, and nutrient for a plant then it is bound to flourish and give forth of its most fragrant essence.

We are considering here the need, in the realized threefold social organism, for the economic sphere to be independent from the political-rights sphere (the state), to be self-governing. But it also works the other way: the economic cannot impinge on the political by exerting pressure to get what it wants in terms of rights and laws—something still commonplace today. The political does not control or govern the economic; while its controlling power is curtailed its legal and rights authority is strengthened.

In Chapter 6 we spoke of an economic 'listening'; this, assuredly, is the key to the governing of the associative economy. It is a form of listening that those endowed with a business acumen already possess, even when it is exercised in the self-serving way meant when we use the expression 'a shrewd business person'. But, in the most positive sense, it is a vital part of what it is to have expertise in economic matters and expertise is what is required at every level, in every organization, of the associative economy. Everyone is not equal in terms of expertise. An expert producer requires more than knowledge of the processes and means of production; she or he just as much needs to be knowledgeable about consumer needs and the requirements of distribution. The same thing applies to those whose focal expertise is distribution or retail. The capacity for a profoundly intelligent listening is already there in the economic world; but again, our economic life currently does not provide the conditions where a healthy association of expertises can take place. Competing for capital means that the economic plant becomes etiolated and distorted in one direction or another.

Experts can represent different associations on different levels and for different purposes in relation to the coordinated running of the complex economic life. The modern international economy is a very large-scale operation involving millions of individuals in coordinated activities but that doesn't mean that the expertise and form of governance cannot be found within the economic sphere itself. How the whole economic operation is managed is a matter for economic expertise alone.

Governance in the economic sphere does not mean control 'from above'—there is no government in this sphere. Rather there is a governing principle which is expertise, and if we are to speak meaningfully of governance in relation to the associative economy we must speak of a vast 'cooperative of expertises'.

Governance of The Political-Rights Sphere

Traditionally governance means rulership, the exercising of control over a whole population or community. Following that tradition today we have the absolute head of state, supported by legal institutions and maintained by the military. In political and corporate structure—what in American-English is meant by the word 'administration'—this ruler is the chief executive officer or principal (president or prime minister) who in the 'free world' is democratically elected.

In Chapter 3 we explored how forms of centralized, hierarchical governance characterized all ancient cultures, at least from the age of theocracies forward. The paternal or maternal principle of divinity in even more ancient tribal life now took the form of an actual human being—the theocrat. The theocratic form of governance transformed into the aristocratic social system of ancient Greece, structured along bloodlines, and this aristocratic form was systematized in the Roman era as a power structure which the modern world inherited. As long as we retain our modern unitary state with its political elite and absolute head of state we remain in the thrall of Graeco-Roman ways of political thinking and acting.[157]

In the consciously-realized threefold social unity the role of the parliament is strengthened—strengthened in the sense of allowing a true democratic process to be realized by making the party system redundant. It specifically does not suggest 'strengthened' means heightening the degree of control over society as a whole. The entire parliamentary system with its focal procedure of debate between government and opposition is going to need to be radically revised. Such a revision of the august institution of parliament could only be made possible through something as all-inclusive and radical as a re-imagination of the form of society as a whole—and that is exactly what the impulse towards social threefoldness sets out to achieve. The legislative process is what is strengthened and this means the capacity to make laws which truly represent the will of the people.

The key point is that the political-rights sphere, like the other two, is self-governing in the realized threefold social order; it is responsible only for itself. This admittedly startling idea means that those who are authorized to legislate, interpret and execute laws, to define and preserve rights, are responsible *only* for that task. No individual or group of individuals has any power whatsoever to determine, control or manage *anything* to do with these other two spheres. Such an attempted assertion of power would be illegal and indictable.

Let us consider the situation in relation to a more differentiated threefold social organism than currently prevails: in most countries laws are in force which mandate a set school curriculum and this is linked to the governmental funding of the schools. In other words, the political sphere governs the whole of school educational life. It makes no sense, in any democratic nation today, to say that the political is only responsible for itself. Let us imagine that in a certain country a movement develops where many schools in that country assert the right to develop their own curriculum, to become completely free of governmental influence including the hold the government has over them through funding. A need develops in the cultural-spiritual life of this country for a law to be enacted which allows for such an educational freedom. *This need arises purely in the cultural-spiritual life, from those connected with the schools and has nothing to do with what those inhabiting parliament wish or do not wish.* Whether schools should have this right may need to be referred to the will of the community more generally, by means of a referendum. The independent parliamentarians' task is only to listen and perceive this need and then to debate whether and how these rights should be recognized and laws enacted.

To say it another way: the parliamentarians' only responsibility is to conduct parliamentary affairs in the spirit of the kind of enlightened democracy which has been pointed to on these pages. Their duty is to be able to govern their own sphere of activity effectively, ethically and perceptively, most specifically to cultivate and practise the art of listening. In the realized threefold social unity, this will be no loose matter; parliamentarians will have no *right* to develop and enact laws which have not originated specifically and clearly in the will of the people. There will be strict protocols, strong accountability in connection with this process. As discussed above, in most democracies today the political-legal sphere is tri-articulated according to the threefold archetype (the 'separation of powers'), and this means that a more or less healthy independence exists between the law-makers, the law-interpreters and the law-executers; this is the *trias politica*. In the *trias societa,* the radical independence of the three social spheres which is the realized threefold social unity, it will be obvious and incontestable that the political-rights sphere is responsible only for itself.

Governance of The Cultural-Spiritual Sphere

The power of the free human spirit determines what it wants, what it intends, out of its own sources and resources; it requires no governing by any kind of external organization or external individual. Steiner points out the absurdity of the idea that the free human individual needs governance, as if there could ever be a 'board of management for the spirit' (spirit meaning the 'I', the human individuality).[158]

Why then do we speak about governance at all in relation to the cultural-spiritual sphere? We must do so, even if the form of this governance is unusual in terms of conventional political theory—yet it is what people simply know and feel to be true. There are millions of individuals making up a society which means there are millions of individual governances—for each individual is sovereign over her or himself. Each sovereign individual is free to bring forth their unique capacities and determine their own life out of their own power of spirit—that is the meaning and significance of the cultural-spiritual sphere. In relation to the threefold social picture we are not dealing with a 'social contract' as proposed by Rousseau and others, whereby citizens cede natural rights and freedoms to the presiding state so that all people may be protected equally by the legal authority of that state. The justification in relation to the 'social contract' is that only the strongest individuals can actually realize and benefit from their freedom. By contrast, Steiner's picture of threefold governance is not about a community putting itself in the 'protecting' hands of the state but about forms of education and cultural life which enable all people to realize their freedoms, as unique individual wills.

We can take the example of school education: the cultural-spiritual aspect of a school has its focus in the classroom and the teacher body (the school also has a rights-legal dimension and an economic aspect). There of course will be a defined curriculum for every year of study; but the teacher does not govern a child in relation to their cultural-spiritual life—the child is self-governing. In this light we can consider the fundamental task of education as elucidated by Steiner:

> . . . the teacher must remove whatever might hinder the development of [the individuality of the child], and shield it with the utmost reverence . . . it is not necessary to intrude upon this individuality with any alien moulding process . . . for the individual knows through its own powers how to develop in a manner extending in its capacities far beyond what the teacher possesses. But this requires a veritable consideration for human freedom. Human freedom requires that man shall find within himself impulses that are to guide him and impel him in life.[159]

This is what Steiner wanted to be carried out through the schooling movement he initiated, in order for education to be a true expression of a realized cultural-spiritual sphere.

The human individuals who make up society today, each sovereign unto him or herself, do not exist socially like unrelated atoms. In the cultural-spiritual sphere many kinds of groupings of individuals form, some involving hundreds of people in relationship. There are research institutes, universities and schools, hospitals, orchestras, religious societies and so on. Each of these organs of the cultural-spiritual life needs to operate effectively and efficiently, even though they are made up of many independent but related 'wills'. In every case the guiding and inspiring ideal is freedom—but, depending on the grouping, cooperation (fraternity) is involved to some degree. Economic fraternity means people are working for each other whereas in an orchestra, for example, members are cooperatively playing with each other but not for each other. Certainly they are playing a predetermined score but they bring their free spirit to it in the interpretation. Their aim is not to produce a good or service but to bring into being a free spiritual creation. In a hospital there may be hundreds of individuals at work cooperatively, from cooks to doctors, and certainly a service is involved with each case. However, the inspiring ideal is always freedom—to 'set free' each individual into health and the possibility of personal realization.

In the independent cultural-spiritual sphere individuals are free but they are not equal. That is why the democratic principle doesn't apply in the cultural-spiritual life any more than the principle of rulership does. One musician may have immensely greater musical capacity than another; that is their gift, their individual endowment. Some people have a capacity for activities which others have no capacity for at all. To be the conductor of an orchestra requires a very special capacity which the members of the orchestra likely do not possess, but when the conductor is conducting the orchestra he or she is not governing it, acting as a kind of lord and ruler over the individual members. The conductor is using this unique capacity to allow the conditions to exist whereby the music can come forth in its most perfect form. Thus the conductor-as-artist works in the same way as the teacher-as-artist and does not seek to introduce any 'alien moulding process' but only a liberating process.

In such artistic realms we find the model of how the different organs of the cultural-spiritual sphere can 'govern' themselves—or perhaps we should say, 'conduct themselves'. In any grouping, any organization such as a museum, medical practice or scientific institute, church or school, there are going to be certain individuals who stand out as having the capacity to act as 'conductors' in the artistic sense. These people will be selected for tasks which may involve coordination of the institution, public relations, and representation at other institutions. If they misuse this role to lord it over others then their position is not going to last and there will need to be mechanisms to ensure this can happen. There is nothing strange about such an arrangement: it already takes place in many social situations. In a board of directors for example, the chairperson—selected because of a certain capacity—has responsibilities of coordination and representation, but in no sense is the governor of this board. Acting according to the ancient notion of 'first amongst equals' (*primus inter pares*) the chairperson is selected just so that his or her individual capacities can shine out, just as in different ways the other members of the board have the opportunity to realize their unique gifts.

Very often today in the organizations of the cultural-spiritual life—in schools, theatres and research centres for example—governance takes place through a hierarchical power structure adopted from the bureaucratic state and more specifically the military. There is a boss or chief executive officer and that boss makes decisions in relation to the entire operation of the organization including its cultural-spiritual direction and functioning. The truth is that, in the realm of freedom, every individual in such an organization is responsible for that organization in which they are unfolding their individual capacities. If they are simply under a boss who is making all the decisions then there will be limited opportunity to grow and realize freedom out of themselves. Many aspects of governance in cultural-spiritual organizations are going to need to be rethought—and in fact much of this kind of work has already been done. In the following chapter we look at the College of Teachers in the kind of schools instigated by Rudolf Steiner which are, or should be, differentiated in a threefold way. The issues and challenges of such non-hierarchical organizational governance are not necessarily fully resolved but a dedicated striving in this direction is what is of importance.

National and International Governance

A nation is a people, united through ethnicity or some shared cultural or spiritual value. Today we call a nation sovereign because it is recognized internationally as being self-governing. A nation is a 'one', an individual in a certain sense, and this kind of national individuality has come down to us from tradition. Ancient peoples experienced their individuality mainly through their identity with their tribe or clan. Today the nation, with its characteristic hierarchical form of governance, is the way this tradition lingers on, even though people experience themselves primarily as individual wills rather than a collective or 'folk soul'.

The picture of cultural evolution discussed in Chapter 3 was the slow, semi-instinctive development from a germinal unity to a more differentiated social condition in which the archetypal threefold has come progressively to revelation. If we are working toward forming the threefold social organism as a fully conscious creation, then, looking into the future, a specific picture of national and international governance emerges. No longer is the nation the fundamental social whole; people are also citizens of the world. The consciously created threefold social unity expresses itself in a relationship between national and international foci of governance.

We have just looked at how, in the threefold social organism, each of the three spheres is self-governing. Now we must consider how these autonomous spheres are 'held together' as an integrated, healthy whole. Most essentially, the three spheres inhere within the relatedness and lawfulness of the threefold archetype—a polarity and a mediating, binding principle. It would be somewhat atavistic to insist that the three governances must be held together 'at the top'. These fundamental spheres of social life are independent, entirely differentiated from one another, but at every level, at every interstice, they are in organic interaction. To take one of the spheres, the cultural-spiritual: this sphere is self-determining or self-governing, which means as a whole and in every part. In every one of the organizations, educational institutions, medical research institutes and so on, just as with those engaged in cultural-spiritual work in an individual way such as writing poetry, people are determining what is necessary and deciding how to bring it about. But this doesn't mean that what takes place in the cultural-spiritual sphere is somehow cut off from the other spheres. We have already looked at how, in a vast number of different ways, what arises as inspiration, invention, and initiative, fructifies the economic realm and how capital, distilled within the economic realm, supports all manner of cultural initiative. If we seek to develop an imagination of the threefold wholeness we arrive at a picture of a vast network of productive relationships.

Likewise, the autonomous, self-governing economic realm is in intimate relationship with the other two social spheres. What drives the economy forward is not key decisions made by governors 'at the top'; rather, the vast 'cooperative of expertise' is in constant internal dialogue, at every level and in every situation, from production to consumption. The entire working of the associative economy is the result of constant 'listening' and dialoguing, forming a network of communication and association. This dialogue shapes the working of the economic sphere in its wholeness, but this dialogue means nothing unless extended to the other two spheres. To take one example out of the very many possible: the price for any item is not something worked out by corporate bosses to maximize profit on the market. Price has a rights and cultural dimension. What today is called 'fair trading' primarily makes its appeal to certain ethically-minded purchasers. In the realized threefold social order, fair trading becomes a matter of *rights*, the legal right for every worker to have a fair share of the profit. It extends to the cultural realm in that every worker is not merely a 'production machine' but is bringing to the work their gifts and capacities, their right to work and their right to capital.

In the threefold social organism, the autonomous cultural-spiritual sphere expresses the unity of what today we call the nation. There are certainly elements of cultural-spiritual life which have an international character; nothing is rigidly demarked in the threefold social organism. For example, universities and medical institutions form relationships worldwide; likewise, orchestras may operate internationally. However, the greater part of the cultural and spiritual life of society relates to the activities and responsibilities of individual nations.

The economic life is also autonomous but its sphere of governance is international; it is in no sense bounded by the culturally-unifying characteristics of a nation. Modern economy is world-economy; production, distribution and consumption involve a vast number of international relationships and transactions. What we have been calling the associative economy are cooperative connections between people and groups, locally and across all countries.

The political-rights sphere operates on both a national and an international level; there are matters of international law and universal rights which play into the issues of law making, law interpreting and law enforcing on the national level. The political-rights sphere mediates between the national and international. However, the parliamentary process (the legislature) pertains only to the nation. The citizens of a nation democratically elect the members of parliament to represent their views. These views are usually connected with national issues but, if there are broader concerns relating to international affairs, these can be dealt with through the parliamentary process. The state, limited to the political-rights dimension of the threefold social whole, legally asserts and preserves the sovereignty of the nation.

All current efforts towards bringing into being a centralized global form of governance, a 'new world order', are working in a direction antithetical to the above picture of the threefold social organism in its national and international dimensions. In 1919, immediately after the cessation of the First World War, Steiner worked hard to present his picture of the threefold social order to counter what he called the 'mania for unification'.[160] By this he meant the race of governments, in response to the chaos of the war, to form a global cooperative body modelled on the centralized governments of particular countries. Such a body was founded in 1920 and was called the League of Nations, the chief architect of which was Woodrow Wilson. The 'mania' was to coordinate all aspects of human life—economic, legal, scientific, medical, educational, and so on—with the aim of achieving an enduring global peace. The onset of the Second World War represented the dismal failure of the League but this only intensified efforts in the same direction. In 1946 the League of Nations became the United Nations which spawned numerous specialist agencies, including the World Health Organization and the World Bank.

Steiner certainly recognized that humanity was moving into a new era of planetary consciousness and cooperation, but he indicated that the 'League' should be a caring relatedness of people everywhere, on every level, not an institutionalized unity. He wrote:

> . . . states and economic bodies become interrelated in formations that are extremely varied in shape and character. These link every part of mankind with every other part, in such a way that each is conscious of the life of the others pulsing through its own daily interests. A League of Nations comes into being out of basic impulses that correspond to actual realities. There will be no need to 'institute' one based on one-sided legal theories of right.[161]

Working in this statement is something of the wisdom expressed by Goethe in his *Green Snake and the Beautiful Lily* through the mouth-piece of the Old Man: 'One alone does not help, but rather he who unites with many at the right moment.'[162] When the need presses upon us we choose (as an individual, an organization, a whole nation), out of our own will and initiative, as a deed of conscience, to join with others in service to the world. That's how unity of purpose comes about; this is a spiritual unity, a true fraternity. Nothing is compelled, nothing mandated. The corollary is that we are also free *not* to unite with others if circumstances change or a different need arises.

A hundred years later, in the first years of the second decade of the twenty-first century, the 'mania for unification' has intensified to a very great degree. There are now seventeen specialized agencies which make up the United Nations, each of which has extended its reach into most countries of the world in relation to all aspects of social life. Now we have the World Health Organization's plan for One Health, gathering to itself responsibility for the health of humans, plants, animals and ecosystems on a global scale as well as for all medical modalities: conventional, traditional, complementary, and integrative. The United Nations and each of the agencies is an 'institutionalized unity', a hierarchical form of organization. In 1992 the United Nations created the Commission on Global Governance which was tasked with considering the weakness of national democratic political and economic processes in a rapidly globalizing world. Since then the tendency has been to seek to place the actual control of world affairs in the hands of these agencies, motivated by the view that the governmental processes of sovereign states are ineffective and outmoded.

In 2024 the sovereignty of nations is still a reality—just. Buoyed by the prominent role it had in the COVID 19 crisis, the United Nations has put to its member states the plan for Emergency Platforms which include climate events, pandemics, and unforeseen 'black swan' events, which means anything else deemed a 'complex global shock'. In the proposal, the Secretary-General of the United Nations will have 'a standing authority to automatically convene and operationalize an Emergency Platform'.[163] In conjunction with this the World Health Organization is seeking to modify its International Health Regulations in order to compel citizens in all member countries to submit to its pandemic counter-measures. In other words, governments of sovereign states will not have the final say on operations, of many kinds, which may be put into play in their country. Can there be any doubt that the United Nations and its agencies, motivated and feeling justified by the global 'pandemic emergency' and now the 'climate emergency', are seeking to put into effect what was only proposed by the Commission on Global Governance?

A century ago Steiner attempted to introduce his vision of a threefold social order as a counter-picture to the movement toward a global hierarchical form of governance or 'new world order'. Today the need to understand, promote, and educate the threefold social outlook has never been greater.

Part IV
Education Toward The Threefold Social Order

'The Waldorf school can be successful only if it is completely inspired by the spirit that aspires towards the threefold nature of the social organism.'

Rudolf Steiner[164]

'Young people need to experience with full hearts, with their entire souls, things that they are waiting to understand with maturity... What today's young people receive from our culture allows people to grow old but not to be young... Our civilisation has lost the spirit; its thinking encompasses only material things. Such thoughts can only be understood, not experienced. Once understood they are incapable of transformation and lie heavy in our souls like stones.'

Rudolf Steiner[165]

'I would say that some, or even the majority, of our university students go through their entire course of study without an inner experience of the academic disciplines they study . . . It sounds almost paradoxical to say that the hearts of university students should be addressed in everything that is brought to them. It sounds like a paradox, but it could actually be so!'

Rudolf Steiner[166]

'All knowledge, even purely scholarly knowledge, must merge into pure artistry.'

Rudolf Steiner[167]

Chapter 10
SCHOOL EDUCATION

School Education and The Threefold Social Order

The form of school education presently called Waldorf or Rudolf Steiner education came directly from the impulse of the threefold social order and was one of the very first objectifications and expressions of it. In reality, the endeavour of these schools can only be understood in connection with the threefold social impulse although this is not always evident in the schools' presentation of themselves. Nevertheless, if one seeks to penetrate to the meaning of any aspect of this form of schooling—the curriculum, the teaching methodologies, the form of governance, and the whole artistic ethos of the schools—one finds that all of these only make sense in terms of Steiner's specific conception of social organization and social renewal.

That being said, it is equally true that every form of schooling in the world today has before it similar social dilemmas and social challenges. Every child in the 'womb' of their education goes through the same stages of growth and is going to enter a very much more internationalized, digitized world than even fifty years ago. On the level of economy they are being prepared for the global reality of manufacture and trade; on the level of cultural-spiritual life most educational systems deal far more with the needs of the individual ('unfold your potential') than in Steiner's time. Likewise, in today's world issues of human rights have far greater emphasis than a century ago. Every school today lives and has its being within these three realms. Nevertheless it is still the case that Steiner schools can serve as a model for a consciously-articulated threefold organization *if the schools take up this challenge.*

An act of self-recognition which any school within any schooling system can undergo is to acknowledge and to assert that fundamentally, in its essence, it belongs to the cultural-spiritual sphere of society. Today even this basic point is clouded because the economic and political-legal aspects—which of course play an important role in the life of a school—are assuming an ever-more dominant character. In connection with school education we increasingly hear about 'standardization', 'regulation' and 'corporatization', 'performance indicators', 'quality assurance', 'services rendered for a fee' and other such concepts drawn from the political and economic spheres. This tendency stands as a danger to the free cultural and spiritual life of Waldorf/Steiner schools as much as to any other form of schooling. The danger is that the most significant aspect of a school, its essential gesture we could say, will be forgotten or underestimated. This is the moment of free, inspired interaction of teacher with student, based on yet transcending whatever may have been meticulously set down in the teacher's government-approved programmes. This moment is a purely cultural-spiritual event and is what actually defines a school as an organ of the cultural-spiritual sphere.

Freedom in teaching—in the sense that Rudolf Steiner meant it—is not merely doing whatever one feels like. Freedom means to teach with self-mastery, to be authentic in one's deeds, moment to moment, to be able to bring just the right stroke or gesture to the teaching and learning situation. Students recognize such authenticity and it is precisely that experience of individuality and authenticity which young people need—immensely more than mere instruction—in order for themselves to become authentic and free. One does not need to do away with programmes and daily teaching plans to achieve this; the programme is part of the materials with which the teacher can freely and creatively work. Whatever limits a class in terms of its material or conceptual requirements, the free deed of teaching is defined by none of these things. The free will of the teacher draws upon its own sources, not bureaucratic determinations.

The task of the authentic teacher-artist is to liberate the forces which belong to the individuality of each student, not merely to mould the students so that they become 'good productive citizens'. This liberation can take place—or is certainly promoted—when the students experience the free individuality of the teacher, something made much more difficult with online learning. In Steiner's time, through the influence of Pestalozzi in particular (and still today) the prevailing idea was that the essential aim of education is to be 'all round', to embrace both the sciences and the humanities, to address the physical, moral and intellectual aspects of human nature. This is important but if it is made the primary aim of education then a distortion occurs. Steiner insists that the aim of education to be 'all round' is actually still just seeking to mould a human being into a useful servant of the state.[168] Only an education towards radical freedom, he goes on to say, can ultimately bring new forces into the social fabric through the coming to fruition of individual capacities and individual initiative. And only through such freedom and authenticity in teaching will 'a society of individual wills' ever come into being.

To value this crucial cultural-spiritual moment of freedom in the everyday life of a school is to see that teaching is a creative art—or, at least, can and should be so. If it is truly valued as such, then, as with anything else we value in life, everything possible will be done to support and enable it. For the creative art of the teacher will either be practised at great personal cost by an individual teacher in the face of difficult or even antagonistic conditions, or it will be supported by many other levels of free organization within a school and society more broadly. The main support can come from the teaching faculty as a whole which, in Rudolf Steiner schools, is intended to make all decisions regarding the pedagogical work of the school and to assure the 'space' for the work of the teacher-as-artist. It is what, in the history of these schools, is called the College. The College will continue to exist when the creative art of teaching continues to be valued but will die and be subsumed by hierarchical business-type structures when it is not. When, in schools, the practice of teaching and everything to do with the spiritual-cultural life of the school comes to be controlled by those who are not themselves doing the teaching (the principal who is CEO in a corporate structure, plus the executive group), what then occurs in schools is the reflection of what happens in society more broadly when the free cultural-spiritual life of society is not self-determining and is subservient to the state. Then we have the absolutist control of schools, universities, research institutes through the mechanisms of a government bureaucracy which is primarily concerned with defining a 'correct' content and with quality control through econometrics.

So we see that the realization and emancipation of the cultural-spiritual sphere of society is not a matter of theoretical debate and conjecture but rather the kind of understanding which springs from the living, will-filled thinking which is actually able to bring about conditions in which such free creative acts are ever made possible. The formation and preservation of schools and free Colleges which offer unshakeable support to the art of teaching is a central task of all those involved, who, in one way or another, are on the road to becoming social artists. No formulas are available for assured success; when the group of people who constitute a College bring their points of view and inspirations into the open then anyone knows there is potential for conflict and for the dominance of certain personalities. And of course, it is much more 'efficient' if one individual is the final decision-making authority. But the result is that teachers do not grow inwardly and indeed, are forced to remain in a child-like condition where someone is always making the key decisions for them.

Steps have most certainly been made in these directions since the inception of the worldwide Waldorf teaching movement but sometimes the schools have lost their nerve and faltered when difficulties arose. These schools have become diluted and the impulse towards freedom and the art of teaching has died away. However, these efforts are never wasted and can help to engender new initiative through renewed understanding. The basic function of the College as a decision-making organ makes great demands on the social artistry of the participants and many educational activities need to be used to cultivate it. Above all, what is vital is that such organs of school life are not taken for granted and are tended with great care by all those concerned. A College meeting is a 'meeting' in a large cultural and spiritual sense; it is the organ of the free cultural-spiritual sphere of the threefold social organization of the school, where the free creative work of the teachers is supported. It is thus the heart of the school and a vital element of the 'hidden curriculum' of a school whereby the students, through the free, creative work of the teachers, are themselves learning what freedom means.

The Structuring Of School Life As A Social Art

Part of the work of a school College is the effort to understand the threefold structuring of the school. The threefold is the archetypal social form and is not culturally relative, any more than the physical-soul-spiritual constitution of the human being varies according to time and place. But in the actual lived reality of a school, in a particular place and time, there are going to be any number of features which are unique to that school and new situations and problems continually arise in the school's ever-changing life. A significant task of the College is to determine which element of school life belongs to the cultural-spiritual sphere, which to the economic-financial, which to the administrative-rights—or, more precisely, *to what extent* each element belongs to each sphere. This delicate sculpting of a school is an ongoing task on the part of teachers and other members of the school's working community.

As an overall picture, the College and the teaching work can be seen as the dynamic heart of the school, with associated organs of an economic and legal-administrative nature working to serve the College and connect it to the external world. A possible College imagination is to picture, in a shared way—perhaps through artistic exercises using 'colour conversations'—the fundamental *gesture* of this cultural-spiritual heart in relation to the other two spheres. For example, we could picture the College as a magenta quality—holding great depth of understanding and spiritual insight and proffering itself outwardly and without reserve, for the sake of the students and the community. The administrative-legal aspect—the school administration—could be pictured as having a green quality with its role of balance and providing for each individual or each element of school life equally. A yellow quality could represent the economic aspect (the Board plus representatives from the administration and the College), radiating out to the greater community the value and significance of the school. A blue gesture could, on the other hand, capture the depth and seriousness of the responsibility of the economic sphere. Such a picture would certainly have to be worked with, in which case it is likely to become more refined and subtle.

Next comes the more difficult task of considering particular elements of the school life and operation and assigning them to one of the three spheres (or perhaps to more than one in certain cases). This, without question, calls for a highly developed social artistry. What follows are just examples of what, in reality, would be a lengthy but highly enriching experience. To the economic sphere primarily belongs matters of accounts payable and receivable, fundraising, budget (funds available) and so on; these are unequivocally part of an 'economic conversation' and are inspired by the ideal of brotherhood because they reflect the entire working-together of the school community and the greater world. To the sphere of rights-legal primarily belong legal compliance, salary structure, occupational health and safety, personnel files, teacher search and teacher salary, discipline policies, budget (allocation of funds, social contract)—these all come within a 'rights conversation' and express the ideal of equality. To the cultural-spiritual sphere primarily belong curriculum, teacher employment, professional development days, child study, buildings and grounds, festivals, teacher evaluation and so on, with the ideal of freedom working within them because each relates to the spiritual and pedagogical life of the school. These are just indications; much more besides is of course involved in school operations.

Let us consider here in more detail the question of buildings and playground equipment. Without such engaged artistic research by the College or a group mandated by the College (which is either given final say or asked to report back to the College) it might be presumed that these are purely administrative-economic issues which involve balancing the budget in the best possible way. But if we enter into the gestural language of the physical context in which children are being educated, we find that these matters are thoroughly pedagogical in nature—the forms, the colours, the function of the buildings and equipment are all part of how the young person learns and how their own inner forces are liberated and not restricted or moulded in an alien way. They are part of a 'freedom conversation'. Any mathematics or science teacher knows that merely memorizing a formula for a certain process is as good as useless when it comes to actually using that mathematical or scientific knowledge in the world to solve a problem or develop something new. What is required is *understanding*. Likewise with the threefold ordering of a school—indications such as those above can only serve as guidelines for what in reality would need to be entered into with care and authenticity.

Schooling as The Womb of Social Existence

One of the fundamental indications Steiner gave regarding school education is the need to give children living ideas which can grow with the child. In his words:

> We must understand that the ideas, sensations, or will impulses we give children must not be formed in rigid concepts that children must then learn and heed; the ideas, impulses and sensations that we give them must be as alive as our own limbs. A child's hand is small, and it must be allowed to grow and not be constrained. The ideas and soul development of children are also small and delicate and we must not limit them with hard rules, as though such limits must be retained in the same form thirty years later, once children have grown up.[169]

This is what we were looking at in the previous chapter in relation to governance of the cultural-spiritual sphere where, in an education for freedom, the teacher does not introduce any 'alien moulding process' but only provides the conditions which allow the young person to find, within themselves, the forces for their own development. Such living, imaginative ideas which stimulate and awaken the young person's own forces are the basis for the curriculum at all stages of schooling. However, at the different stages there are very different methods in relation to the different phases of unfoldment.

The teacher-artist can become conscious of how the conditions and curriculum they provide for young people can help them to develop in a healthy way within the three spheres of the social organism. Children in the pre-school, kindergarten and classes up to about the seventh year are actively engaged in what Steiner calls 'true imitation', something which he says will have to become increasingly intensive and conscious in the future.[170] On the part of the teacher this means allowing only what is best for the child to imitate, what is good, what is true and beautiful. In practice this takes place through artistic experience, games and play. Children before the change of teeth are like one large sense organ he says; they live entirely outside themselves, participating in the things of their environment and responding instinctively to them. Through this immediate participation '. . . an impulse arises as an inner gesture to relive, with the intensity of their whole inner nature, what has been perceived'.[171] Through imitating what is wholesome the child learns that the world is good and this, Steiner indicates, plants the seed of *freedom*, the ideal behind the cultural-spiritual social sphere. Freedom, as an adult, means to live in a condition of balance and truthfulness which comes from self-responsibility; what is distorted, one-sided or compulsive is not free.

The impulse or inner gesture which the child responds to so openly, so instinctively—this is the 'small and delicate' idea which will grow as the child grows. We need to be able to imagine the metamorphosis of this embryonic idea. It is not really an idea at all in the sense of a concept; it is a will impulse, an experience. If we can imagine this will impulse growing, passing through the teenage years and into adult life when the conceptual mind awakens and the 'I' become fully incarnated after about the twenty-first year, then we can see what this will impulse transforms into. It becomes the sense that *I myself can act in the world, that I have the will power to do what must be done, out of myself in freedom—not through external compulsion.*

In the middle school, from the seventh to the fourteenth year, teaching should be practised through what Steiner calls 'true authority' which educates *equality*, the ideal of the political-rights sphere. By this he doesn't mean authoritarianism; he means the cultivation (far more necessary in the future than it has been in the past, he suggests) of 'a pure, beautiful feeling for authority', of reverence for the teacher who is able to say what should or should not be done. At this stage of schooling the feeling for authority doesn't come about in the intellectual sense of the teacher being an authority on any particular topic, in the sense of an expert. Rather it is the fruit of the teacher acting out of their free human individuality and who is experienced by the student as a 'natural authority'. It is an authority based on artistic feeling and artistic experience in relation to what is taught. Steiner advises that children before puberty shouldn't get used to making 'so-called own judgements' too soon. Such reverence for authority implants in children what can eventually become a sense of the inalienable rights of the human being, of what is equal for all and not open to argument.[172] It becomes the sense that *the people around me have dignity simply because of who they are and I have dignity and want to be recognized because of who I am. We are all equal with respect to our human beinghood.*

In the upper school, in relation to students of around the age of fifteen to twenty-one (which thus includes university years) the young adult is learning intellectual judgement. However, in contradistinction to what is normally regarded as intellectual education (and universities currently epitomize this) all ways of developing knowledge of the world should be infused with love; this is Steiner's striking pedagogical indication.[173] How can studies in chemistry, in physics, in mathematics, English and physical education, cultivate human love? This is the challenge which Steiner sets all teachers—topic to topic, class to class—in upper schools and colleges. He indicates that only through such teaching will *fraternity* develop and thereby prepare the student for healthy existence in the economic sphere. Can there be any doubt that the kind of intellectual education which constitutes the main thrust of senior school and university studies today does little or nothing to cultivate human love? Even the suggestion may seem absurd. Steiner isn't talking about the *concept* of love such as one might learn about in courses on Romantic literature. He means the development of a kind of living warmth-imbued thinking, developed in all areas of study, which can act as the seed of actual fraternal love in the social world.

What this points to is that a senior school or university education should never develop merely intellectually, through 'head thinking'. It implies that concepts presented and worked with by students need to have living force, concepts in which the cognitive feeling and cognitive will are in every respect active, where the whole person is involved in whatever they are learning to the point that ideas become actual inner *experiences*. When thinking learns to consciously participate in the form of another being in the manner anticipated by Goethe's way of science—whether it be the form of an animal, a chemical or mathematical process, a plant, a work of art—then the education is shaping and planting seeds which in a metamorphosed form *become the kind of fraternal love required for a flourishing and healthy economic sphere in which my work contribution is a deed of loving sacrifice.* The young adult 'learns to see what each single piece of work means for the combined fabric of the social order, to see it in such a light that one will learn to *love* it because of its value for the whole'. This, writes Steiner, develops the profounder principles of economic life which can replace the motives of personal gain whereby 'a love for the human social order springs up that is comparable to the love an artist has for the creation of his works'.[174]

The fostering of these three social ideals, in this developmental sequence, is what is predominantly the case in the education of the child. It's not as if the ideals are taught in blocks, side-by-side in the school curriculum. Steiner makes the point that these things are completely interwoven; in fact, he adds, the reverse order is true in a certain sense and to a certain degree. In the upper school the emphasis is on bringing an experience of cognitive love to the students, but 'if we do not develop love in the proper manner, freedom is missing'.[175]

The teachers who have an overall picture of the task of the school—not just their immediate classroom concerns—will thus understand that the threefold social order is being educated through the entire schooling process. In other words, a way of eventually participating in a threefold social life is being shaped by the *way* teachers conduct their classes, by the entire organization and creative formation of the school, not so much through the introduction of intellectual content, as if young people are going to learn the threefold outlook as a sociological theory.

Nevertheless, seeds are planted in many ways and in many places. Through the journey of the so-called Main Lessons in a Steiner/Waldorf school, in the lower and middle school much is explored about how the three social spheres slowly differentiated. In the great civilizations of the Near East (explored in Classes 3 to 5), in Ancient India and Ancient Mesopotamia, the economic aspect developed markedly, through trade, agriculture and division of labour. In the civilizations of Ancient Greece and Rome we see how the legal-rights aspect was differentiated and heightened as part of the broad picture of life in this time. And it is in the Christian civilization of Europe, with the waking up of the human individual (explored in Classes 6 and 7) that the cultural and spiritual life gradually became emancipated from the controlling influences of state and religion. For school students who are twelve or thirteen years old this is presented as pictures, stories, imaginative experiences. It is not dogma but simply represents the teacher's understanding of the evolution of human consciousness in Western civilization.

In geography studies in the middle school the relationship and development of these three social spheres is brought to certain clarity although, again, the threefold social organism is not taught as such.[176] Physical and human geography at this stage can present a picture of the way the human and natural worlds relate, showing how the economy is formed through transformation of nature's products, how the modern cultural and spiritual life is very individual and belongs to different peoples in different lands, and how the life of rights within the political sphere of a

State applies to all people equally. What is gained in geography studies can be brought to a higher level of understanding in the senior intensives, with freedom explored as an element of the Philosophy Main Lesson, fraternity or mutuality in an Economics Main Lesson, and rights and politics in a Main Lesson dedicated to that theme. In the senior years there is really no reason why the view that society has a threefold constitution should not be presented to the students and worked with entirely objectively, along with sociological theories such as capitalism and communism—not because one has to teach Steiner's 'theory' in a Rudolf Steiner school. After all, apart from Steiner himself, it is the perception of one of the most distinguished and influential social scientists and philosophers of recent times, Jürgen Habermas.[177]

These observations and suggestions apply to curriculum indications of Rudolf Steiner but in a general sense relate to all forms of schooling equally. The time has passed when school was seen as merely a way of ensuring that a young person performs adequately to a certain externally given standard so they may be equipped to carry out a certain role in society. Today, on very many fronts, the idea is taking hold that schooling is just as much about helping the individual young person to unfold their capacities so they will be able to realize themselves, out of their own potentials, as free adult individuals when they enter the cultural-spiritual sphere of society. Today, in our fraught economic world, every young person needs to learn how to participate in the economic life fraternally, out of love for their work and for how their work and the work of all others supports everyone mutually; and how, in a political world which is increasingly fractured, how every single person is equal in terms of human rights and laws.

Chapter 11

TERTIARY EDUCATION

The Threefold Social Order and The Idea of The University

The threefold social order must be taught in an appropriate, effective way in tertiary educational settings. If it is treated merely as a theory, as an 'alternative sociological system', then it may well be categorized as an intellectual curiosity and will be unlikely to advance. If it becomes the subject of a tertiary teaching where the thinking itself is so enlivened that it becomes a form of social artistry, then we can be certain that the threefold social picture will find a central place in the universities of the future.

Writers on the subject of the university and its possibilities speak of the 'idea of the university' which could also be called the 'university archetype'. They are seeking to understand what the university is fundamentally about in any different era, what its essential aims are in relation to the changing social circumstances. Out of the potential of the 'idea' come forth ever new forms. It might be asked whether the universities—the bastion of the intellectual mind—will be able to embrace the artistic ways of knowing which we are calling cognitive feeling and cognitive will, the forms of thinking necessary to properly understand the threefold social organism. The fact is that the university has undergone continual transformation since its inception in the late medieval period, and it will continue to change. There is an international conversation taking place today about the future of the university; this conversation is currently helping to shape many new developments. A critique of current tertiary educational practice has been building up over years and has produced a considerable literature.[178] If we take the broadest possible perspective on the development of the university there can be no reason to doubt that it has within it the capacity to become the situation for the cultivation of a truly living form of cognition.

During the century since Steiner presented the notion of the threefold social order this 'living idea' has scarcely penetrated the academic sphere. This is not surprising when we consider the nature of its origin. Steiner's vision of social renewal was brought forth in circles of influence entirely outside the academy. Steiner was a doctor of philosophy (the theme of his dissertation was the philosopher Fichte) and very scholarly in his method, especially in his early years when he conducted research in the Goethe-Schiller archives. However, he was not an academic and saw no reason to adjust his thinking to academic expectations. If one surveys his many statements about universities and academic life one cannot fail to detect a critical attitude; he once even spoke of 'the banal and philistine monstrosity that is called academia'[179], tempered, however, by his insistence that universities have a tremendous responsibility in relation to the human future.[180] Academics are unlikely to feel warmly disposed towards some of his views but they need to bear in mind that he was much more akin to the extremely independent personality of Nietzsche than to 'systematic' academic thinkers like Kant and Hegel. Nietzsche, for his part, had a rather jaundiced view of scholars, perhaps attributable to the years he spent working as a university lecturer. He saw scholars as those who harvested their subject matter from 'the yellow delight of the summer fields' and reduced it to the driest of intellectual dusts.[181] The criticisms of both Nietzsche and Steiner must be seen in a proper context in which they appear as entirely healthy. They are endeavouring to cut through the dross of superficialities in relation to the conventions and stereotypes surrounding universities in order to draw out from these central social institutions the highest human possibilities.

Outside the academic sphere those who have sought to understand and work with Steiner's ideas have made considerable progress in determining how this impulse is going to find its place in the modern world. Businesses and educational institutions have been founded and non-formal educational initiatives have kept the ideas alive. It still may not be that universities in their current form are the places in which the threefold social order can be taught, except in the most peripheral way. However, through these more background developments on a number of different levels, the way has been opened for the *kind* of tertiary institution to come into being in which the idea of the threefold social order will have a natural and necessary place.

Stages of University Transformation

The aims of the university have changed profoundly over the millennia since its beginning. Academics and futurists Otto Scharmer and Katrin Kaufer have pictured this transformation as taking place in three main phases—from the scholastic, to the classical, to what they call the postmodern university.[182]

The initial manifestation of the university in medieval times was the *universitas magistorum et scholarium*, the 'community of scholars' or body of teachers and learners. This was the university in its entirety; at that time it didn't involve researchers, administrative and management staff. In this scholastic phase the emphasis was on the dissemination of a given body of already-established knowledge, mainly by means of lectures and books. Here *universitas* means the 'unity of teaching'; everything in these earliest universities was concerned with the teacher-student nexus; *universitas* also suggests the 'wholeness of knowledge' meaning the totality of things known. The doctor or professor was the one who possessed this knowledge and the educational task was to transmit it to the students.

The classical phase begins with the University of Berlin founded by Wilhelm von Humboldt at the beginning of the ninteenth century; the university had now grown to incorporate a new dimension—that of research. The classical university recognized that it is research which underlies the generation of knowledge and so that dimension was incorporated into the work of the university—research which could take place 'in solitude and freedom' as Humboldt put it.[183] Humboldt meant research as a form of 'cultivation' (*Bildung*)—that is, self-knowledge as the basis of world knowing. He considered that all aspects of higher learning should be individually motivated and 'creatively sought in the depths of the human spirit'.[184] Thus the idea of the university had metamorphosed; *universitas* now means 'the unity of teaching and research'. As expressed in contemporary universities, this unity of teaching and research allows for seminar-style learning in which, through discussion and experimentation, students are developing skills in relation to the generation of knowledge, not just presenting themselves as empty vessels to be filled.[185]

The third phase of *universitas* is not just a vision of the distant future; according to Scharmer and Kaufer its emergence is everywhere becoming evident in our time. The postmodern university has grown from just teaching and research to engagement in praxis, to forming partnerships of researchers and practitioners in the world, so that the university becomes the birthplace of the entrepreneur. Now the *universitas* is 'the unity of praxis, research and teaching'.[186]

This third phase of the postmodern university is of focal interest to Scharmer and Kaufer. Here they see that 'the core processes of higher education—research and learning—will move beyond the walls of academe and into societal and personal realms'; this process is partly driven by the Internet, the information economy and by new tools which have been created for organizational learning. It is what they call (following the ideas of Joseph Beuys) 'the university as social sculpture'—the university with the capacity to bring about social transformation.[187] This change in the core process they see as coming about in two interdependent ways—the first through an outward orientation of praxis, in creative activity of effecting change in the world; the second through inward praxis, through methods of research which lead to self-understanding, specifically through the development of the 'will in thinking' as they express it (in other words, cognitive will), so that one's creative potential can be tapped. Scharmer and Kaufer are inspired by the idea that 'universities can grow from places for abstract reflection to dynamic sites that attract and propel new ideas into reality'; they see universities as becoming 'a home for entrepreneurial individuals and communities of creation that change the world'.[188]

At least in the overall thrust of Scharmer and Kaufer's thinking, this disquisition on the metamorphosis of the university is in accord with Steiner's views on the social needs of the modern age. Specifically, the effort of these writers in relation to the emergent postmodern university is a significant attempt to highlight and facilitate creative praxis in one of the principal organs of the cultural-spiritual sphere. There is no doubt that, in a general sense, they address Steiner's critique that the modern cultural-spiritual life is 'a sort of animated abstraction that runs alongside real economic and political events without having concrete effect upon them'.[189] It is important here to note Otto Scharmer's direct connection to the ideas of Rudolf Steiner and to the work of Joseph Beuys.[190] As indicated in Chapter 5, Beuys's approach to human creativity and social sculpture derives directly from Steiner's thinking on social art and the threefold social order. It was the inspiration of Steiner's social thinking which led Beuys in 1973 to found, in his studio, the *Free International University for Creativity and Interdisciplinary Research*.[191] Scharmer's 'post-modern university' actually has a great resemblance to Beuys's *Free University*; it could even be said to be Beuys's university resurrected and transformed.

Scharmer and Kaufer, working broadly out of Steiner's threefold picture, are seeking a way to address contemporary realities through a praxis which derives from the transformation of thinking. These writers get to the heart of the matter when they speak of the striving of the postmodern university for 'a science capable of grasping reality by contemplating the underlying forces of its genesis'.[192] Here we can recognize the significance of Goethe's way of science as an apprenticeship in living thinking, the will-imbued thinking which is capable of cognitively participating in the creative forces active in the world. The contemplation and experience of the underlying creative forces in the world is a profoundly artistic activity which, in the postmodern university, will require a special kind of orientation education, the fundamentals of which have been explored elsewhere.[193]

In other words, there is a vital place for *contemplative enquiry* in the postmodern university, the form of university which expresses the unity of praxis, research and teaching. It's not as if the whole orientation of research and praxis is real-world experience, putting into practice what one has learned theoretically. This traditional division between theory and practice really reflects the human being divided within itself and fundamentally at odds with itself—thinking from feeling and willing. To contemplate the form of a plant, animal, or social process Goetheanistically is to learn to make active the whole human being in knowing: cognitive feeling, cognitive will. This way of participating with one's thinking in the creative forces in the world can gradually transform the aims and methods of the faculties, the whole tenor of university life. Looking into the future we can envision the coming about of the 'communities of creation' which Scharmer and Kaufer speak of.

The Lecture and Seminar Re-Imagined

We have already noted aspects which make teaching the threefold social order at the tertiary level extremely unconventional—centrally, the way it draws upon an imaginative form of thinking in order to comprehend all social forms and processes. Moving from general considerations we now need to come to grips with how such a teaching can proceed within a re-imagined social science faculty. This involves re-evaluating the purpose and form of the lecture and the seminar, the two main teaching modalities of universities. Both of these have a long history in the evolution of the university.

There is a significant trend in contemporary universities which considers the traditional lecture outmoded; lecture halls in many universities worldwide are becoming a thing of the past. In the methodology of 'collaborative learning'—often presented as the next step for tertiary education—a lecture on a particular theme is not given on campus to an assembled body of students but is viewed beforehand, online, by students individually. The students then work in a group on campus (or possibly again online in a video-conference), with the assistance of the lecturer or a tutor, to engage in practical problems in relation to those facts and theories. Such group methods may involve collaborative research, case studies and role-playing. The rationale for such collaborative learning methods at universities is that students are insufficiently involved in the educational process, a hangover from the scholastic university which sees learners simply as vessels waiting to be filled with knowledge.

Without doubt the method of collaborative learning goes in the direction of the postmodern university as defined by Sharmer and Kaufer. The group activity aspect of this method is a form of praxis, an actual involvement in real-world situations through different 'hands-on' techniques. Collaborative learning goes a step in this direction but, even with its aim of solving problems and role-playing in real-world situations, it remains within the domain of intellectualism in the traditional academic sense; it is an attempt to deal with the rift between theory and practice without actually healing it. The students are presented with a theory or sociological concept, for example in relation to a specific social phenomenon; they then discuss it, work into it collectively, role-play it through group activity and other such techniques—yet the *form of thinking* remains the same in the passage from theory to practice. This is why it is valid to say that, no matter how progressive it is said to be in terms of real-world engagement, collaborative learning practice still belongs to the classical phase of the university.

Now the way toward re-imagining the lecture and seminar can become clearer. Rudolf Steiner gave indications to this end even before the start of the twentieth century.[194] Firstly, the aim of the lecture should not be to transmit to students a subset of current knowledge on a particular theme. This 'vessel waiting to be filled' approach is the traditional purpose of the lecture and, in a somewhat modified form, is still the intention of the initial online lecture presented as part of a collaborative learning strategy. The encounter with new theories and facts, Steiner comments, can be done by the student completely independently through library resources (and now by online methods). By contrast, the aim of the re-imagined lecture is to address not just the intellects of the students but as much their faculties of feeling and will. The lecturer can do this by taking 'great vantage points' as Steiner puts it, by speaking from personal experience, as someone who has not just read texts but who has inwardly experienced a broad area of life so that it lives within them as vibrant, living thoughts.

The lecturer needs to address what the hearts of the students need. This, we might say, is the demand which can both challenge and inspire every lecturer, at every lecture podium of the university of the future. What are university students seeking most profoundly, even if unconsciously, behind whatever motive led them to pursue their studies? We have already considered in the previous chapter that all teaching in the upper school and university, in all subjects, should be infused with love, for this is what educates true fraternal love in social life. The university lecturer opens to the students broad vistas on their subject which may take them into utterly unfamiliar territory; yet it is brought to them in such a way that speaks to their personhood, nourishes their soul and by no means merely casts them into a vast ocean of alien information and theory.

In relation to the teaching of social science, the content of the lecture would be any topic related to the multiple subject areas embraced by the social-science faculty; these include anthropology, archaeology, economics, human geography, political science, psychology, and history. In the present text we are specifically concerned with educating the threefold social picture and, as discussed in Chapter 4, the kind of artistic thinking required to understand the living, threefold social organization would be initially cultivated in an orientation programme of studies. This means that, at least at the beginning of a lecture series, only a broad picture of the social whole would need to be brought before the audience—the three principal spheres of social life and the relationships between them. Then, in the light of the whole, imaginations of any particular social-scientific topic could be brought alive for the students. In general we can say that all particulars gain their meaning and significance in terms of the whole.

The means of forming and communicating such social imaginations go far beyond what the 'talking head' experience of remote conferencing technology makes possible. Not just what is said but *how* it is said becomes something of great importance and so the living presence of the lecturer is necessary. This is not about rhetorical embellishment; a developed capacity of imaginative speech and 'speaking gestures' of the hands and arms help imaginations of the social organism become an inner experience for the listeners. If someone is able to deliver a lecture in this artistic way then it will inspire in the students the will to quest for social understanding out of themselves, to find their own great vantage points and living imaginations. The number of such lectures would not need to be large if they fulfil this aim; in a semester of study it may only be four or five.

The aim of the seminar, Steiner goes on to say, is for students to learn to become researchers. In relation to a re-imagined social-science seminar the specific task is to provide the means for students to engage with the social organism through an imaginative research process. The content of the lecture—a lecture which has brought before the student 'great vantage points' in relation to aspects of the social organism—can now be focalized and enriched in ways which involve a meeting of science and art. This training in social-scientific research can follow on from the kinds of exercises undertaken in the orientation programme, exercises which move from a Goetheanistic study of natural forms to a 'new Goetheanism'—that is, a training in imaginative social-scientific thinking, reaching toward cognitive feeling and cognitive will. Examples of such exercises have been presented in various previous chapters of this book but mainly in Chapter 4. The aim of the seminar is not to produce 'knowledgeable students' or even just 'practice-orientated students' in the sense of having some experience of situations they may encounter in the world. It is solely to allow students the possibility of applying a living form of thinking in any form of social-scientific research.

Let us consider the situation where a student has been tasked to research a certain social phenomenon or process—outside the lecture and the seminar. This is research in the conventional sense of information gathering and organizing, usually compiled from the research of others which is found in books or on the Internet but perhaps also from an original investigation, either quantitative or qualitative. This information is detailed enough to build up a general picture of the phenomenon in question. It may be factual, highly detailed, broad in scope, objectively true, and referencing all relevant literature; yet it is in a sense lifeless because it has been abstracted out of a living social reality. This sociological information is brought to the seminar where the task, under the guidance of the seminar leader, is to 'resurrect' what is lifeless or merely conceptual.

An economics student, for example, may have researched the role and process of banking in society today. No matter how detailed and technical this information is, every quantum of information may be envisioned from the great vantage point of the threefold social wholeness. Within the seminar this can be a collaborative activity. The student group would ideally, in the orientation programme, have worked together on Goetheanistic colour exercises which awaken the feeling and will cognition of the two polar spheres of activity and the mediating sphere, the copula. They may also have participated together in one of many possible exercises on metamorphosis in the social organism, such as is set forth in Chapter 4, which involves the transformation of money through the three spheres—purchase money, loan money and gift money. Now, together in a dedicated seminar within the social-science faculty, the students may be able to appraise the primary function of banking as a *rights* phenomenon, mediating between the economic and cultural spheres, as indicated in Chapter 6. Within these broad imaginations the details of the banking process, which the student has brought to the seminar, may be illuminated and given new meaning—for example, the role and legitimacy (or not) of charging interest, the relationship of banks to other social organizations such as economic associations, political organizations and universities.

In the seminar the threefold social outlook is not merely discussed and assessed in a theoretical way, although of course there must be room for such clarification and exploration in relation to other ways of viewing the nature of society.[195] To the extent that in the lecture the threefold social outlook has been brought alive for the students as a living, vibrant imagination, it will serve to galvanize and transform the students' research by bringing about a metamorphosis of thinking—from conceptual, analytical thought to cognitive feeling and cognitive will. When it comes to assessment, a hangover from the classical university is the academic essay, judged excellent if it is well researched, well argued, and well referenced. The problem for universities is that artificial intelligence, now readily available to students and teachers through the Internet, can create in a split second a 'perfect' academic essay on any topic—and it can 'perfectly' assess the essay to boot! If it wasn't apparent before, then the entrance of artificial intelligence into the basic activities of tertiary education makes it abundantly clear that the classical university has finally come to an end, although it may totter some steps further. Altogether new forms of seminar learning and assessment will need to be brought into being, forms which relate to the thinking of the whole human being.

Academic Freedom and University Governance

Any educational institution which understands itself as a true organ of the cultural-spiritual sphere of the threefold social unity will seek to be a clear and ever more perfect expression and embodiment of it. The university in its present form is far closer to this organization than is normally recognized, far closer than schools. This is in spite of the fact that, in terms of governance and their relationship to industry, universities have come to resemble economic corporations.

The modern university, deriving from the classical Humboldtian institution, has enshrined within it the key ideal of the cultural-spiritual sphere which is the well-recognized and universally accepted requirement of academic freedom. Wilhelm von Humboldt—through his work *The Limits of State Action*—was one of the first who gave expression to the need for a cultural sphere which is independent from the political-rights sphere. According to Humboldt, the limit of the political realm is that which impedes in any way the rights of individuals to unfold themselves, to freely realize their capacities. When he founded the University of Berlin in 1810 he instituted that freedom in the new university and academic freedom today is a key tenet of tertiary institutions worldwide.[196]

Academic freedom means the freedom of a professor or lecturer to undertake whatever research he or she chooses to, and work together with a student in similar freedom. It also means the freedom to determine the content of their lectures and to publish the results of their research without prior approval.[197] It also relates to the task of the university as a whole as a 'freedom being'. What follows is part of the Magna Charta Universitatum first signed in 1988 by 430 rectors of European universities and since by some 600 universities from all continents:

> [T]he academic mission to meet the requirements and needs of the modern world and contemporary societies can be best performed when universities are morally and intellectually independent of all political or religious authority and economic power.[198]

This is a clear and definitive statement of the aims of an autonomous cultural-spiritual sphere. A very important aspect of this statement is that this right to freedom is not understood in a self-serving way; it is *through* academic freedom that universities consider themselves best able to be of service to society.

It was noted above that the recognition of society as a tri-articulated whole has scarcely penetrated the academic sphere. However, this is a next step that could, or perhaps *should* be taken, by those following closely in the Humboldtian tradition. This is because, in a significant sense, the ideal and practice of academic freedom leads directly to the idea of society as a threefold unity. It is evidenced in the Magna Charta Universitatum which couldn't be a clearer statement of cultural-spiritual freedom. What can follow from this is the recognition that precisely the same requirement of complete independence from external political and religious governance applies to the economic sphere as well. The economy will only be able to meet the requirements and needs of the modern world and contemporary societies if it is, in practice and in terms of self-governance, independent of all political or religious authority and power. And when we have so defined the independence of the cultural-spiritual and the economic spheres, the integrity and independence of the political-rights sphere appear as a concomitant.

Let us imagine that universities do in fact take this step. Then it would surely follow that they would want to consolidate and reflect this understanding in their own structure of governance. For politics and economy are not only external realities; every cultural institution is a microcosm of the social world and, just as with schools, universities have all three elements within their internal functioning. Like schools, universities are principally organs of the cultural-spiritual sphere; as research and educational institutions they are not in the first place businesses or political entities although of course the economic and political-legal aspects are important elements. So the academic dimension (research and teaching) of every university should determine itself, should be independent of all political and economic authority and power *within the institution itself*. As already noted above, the concept and practice of academic freedom means that universities already embody, to a large extent, this autonomy and self-determination of the cultural-spiritual sphere. Universities will realize themselves as authentically threefold organisms when the same independence is achieved in their economic and rights-administration spheres, all three spheres working together to create a threefold wholeness. When universities step beyond the need to govern themselves through a centralized, hierarchical administration then they will become models for what may become possible in other social arenas and in the social organism altogether. This researching, teaching but also outreaching role is precisely the nature of the postmodern university.

The university is at a crossroads, which is really what is meant when we speak of 'crisis'.[199] It is a crisis of identity. Universities have made themselves financially powerful and this is why they have been able to undergo such expansion and diversification in the modern world. The commitment of universities to academic freedom has profound implications in relation to governance and, indeed, needs to be followed through conscientiously. At the crossroads Rudolf Steiner's indications concerning social renewal could be of great assistance and yield a pathway forward.

NOTES

1 See S. Fleischacker, *A Third Concept of Liberty: Judgement and Freedom in Kant and Adam Smith*, Princeton University Press, Princeton, 1999.

2 For example, the academic author Astrida Orle Tantillo makes a special point, in the Preface to her book *The Will to Create*, of alerting her readers to the 'problem' of Rudolf Steiner and his 'followers' who often write on Goethean science. By 'follower' she appears to mean anyone who even just quotes or mentions Steiner in their writings. Tantillo refers to Henri Bortoft who does just that in his important work on Goethean philosophy, *Goethe's Way of Science*. She says that these 'followers' tend to treat Goethe's science as 'a kind of mysticism or religion' and to look in Goethe's texts for 'messages of personal/spiritual guidance and fulfilment'. Tantillo wants to prove her point by going on to quote briefly from Bortoft and also from authors Mark Riegner and John Wilkes. Riegner and Wilkes, she reports, talk about coming to the experience of 'the idea within reality' through Goethe's precepts. Bortoft, she indicates, speaks of a new kind of education possible through Goethe's science which activates 'a different mode of consciousness which is holistic and intuitive', thus helping to bring about a 'radical change in our awareness of the relation between nature and ourselves'. Meanwhile, in the body of her own text (pp.37–8), Tantillo expresses no difficulty with Goethe's own views on a spiritual kind of consciousness. She writes: 'Throughout his *Theory of Colours*, Goethe discusses both the *physical eye* (the organ of sight) and the *spiritual eye* (the inner organ of intuition).' (A.O. Tantillo, *The Will to Create: Goethe's Philosophy of Nature*, The University of Pittsburgh Press, Pittsburgh, 2002. H. Bortoft, *The Wholeness of Nature: Goethe's Way toward a Science of Conscious Participation in Nature*; essays by M. Riegner & J. Wilkes in *Goethe's Way of Science: A Phenomenology of Nature*, State University of New York Press, NY, 1998.)

3 For Steiner's own account of this gathering see R. Steiner, *Freedom of Thought and Societal Forces*, SteinerBooks, Great Barrington, 2008, p.x.

4 In 1917, the year before the war ended, Otto Graf Lerchenfeld, a member of the Bavarian royal cabinet, began work with Steiner on articulating a proposal for implementing the threefold social organism. Steiner also prepared memoranda for Arthur Graf Polzer-Hoditz to present to the Austrian Minister of Foreign Affairs, who rejected them. Graf Polzer-Hoditz also discussed the threefold idea with the Austrian cabinet and a memorandum on threefold principles was sent to the Austrian Emperor. In that year also a presentation of threefold principles was made to Prince Max of Baden who was interested and met Steiner to discuss it in early 1918. Later that year Prince Max became

the German Chancellor and offered peace to American president Woodrow Wilson, based on Wilson's 14 Point Peace Program.

5 W.F. Lofhouse, *London Quarterly Review*, January, 1923. Raymond G. Fuller reviewed Steiner's *Towards Social Renewal* in a full-page article in the 14 January 1923 edition of the *New York Times Book Review* with the title 'New Scheme of Social Organization'.

6 R. Steiner, *The Renewal of the Social Organism*, Anthroposophic Press, Spring Valley, 1985, pp.130–1.

7 Victor Hugo, *Les Misérables*, Part V, Book I. (1862).

8 R. Steiner, *The Social Future*, Anthroposophic Press, Spring Valley, 1972, p.107.

9 R. Steiner, *The Spirit of Fichte Present in our Midst*, Rudolf Steiner Publishing Co., London, p.29.

10 See R. Steiner, *The Modern Art of Education*, Rudolf Steiner Press, London, 1972. Here he comments that, in the present age, the aim of education must tend toward superseding the 'doctor principle', and that the schooling movement he initiated seeks to turn this 'doctorial' education—which emphasizes the thinking function—into a education of the whole human being, balancing the thinking, feeling and will (p.44).

11 R. Steiner, *West and East: Contrasting Worlds*, Rudolf Steiner Publishing Co., London, p.149.

12 Ibid., p.215.

13 R. Steiner, *The Renewal of the Social Organism*, op. cit., p.32.

14 For Steiner's own views on Spengler's ideas see R. Steiner, *Otto Spengler: Prophet of World Chaos*.

15 R. Steiner, *The Renewal of the Social Organism*, op. cit., p.29.

16 See K. Kalimtzis, *Aristotle on Political Enmity and Disease*, SUNY, Albany, 2000.

17 W. Wilson, *The State: Elements of Historical and Practical Politics*, Nabu Press, 2011, p.26.

18 See Engels's book, *Die Entwicklung des Sozialismus von der Utopie zur Wissenschaft*, (The development of socialism from utopia to science), 1919.

19 M. Heidegger, 'The Word of Nietzsche' in *The Question Concerning Technology and Other Essays*, Garland Publishing, NY, 1977, p.61.

20 R. Steiner, *The Philosophy of Freedom*, (trans. M. Wilson), Anthroposophic Press, Hudson, 1964, p.138.

21 J. Habermas, *Legitimation Crisis*, (trans. T. McCarthy), Beacon Press, Boston, 1975, pp.5–6.

22 Quoted in R. Steiner, *Goethe's World View*, Mercury Press, Spring Valley, 1985, p.86.

23 R. Steiner, (eds. G. Lamb & S. Hearn), *Steinerian Economics: A Compendium*, Adonis Press, Hillsdale, 2014, p.8.

24 Ibid., p.5.

25 Without question, in the realized threefold social order, individual initiative and entrepreneurship are fostered in every possible way. The important point

is that these are *cultural-spiritual* activities; the entrepreneur is a *cultural*, not an economic worker. Only when such creative initiative fructifies as new forms of production, distribution, marketing and selling, provision of services, do we speak of economic activity where the fraternal spirit of cooperation and fairness reigns. That an individual has a creative input doesn't mean that vast profits have to flow directly to that individual. Creative initiative has rewards of a cultural-spiritual nature, as every mother knows who puts all her creativity into raising her children.

26 See R. Steiner, *The Philosophy of Freedom*, op. cit.

27 J. W. von Goethe, *Scientific Studies*, (trans. D. Miller), Suhrkamp Publishers, NY, 1988, p.156.

28 B. Matthews, *Schelling's Organic Form of Philosophy*, State University of New York Press, NY, 2011, p.166.

29 In Schelling's *Freedom Essay* (1809) he shows that the expression 'God is all things' does not mean that there is no difference between God and all things (which is pantheism). In this sentence 'is' is the copula, mediating both identity and difference. See M. Thomas, 'The Mediation of the Copula as a Fundamental Structure in Schelling's Philosophy', *Schelling-Studien*, 2 (2014), pp. 20–39.

30 See Chapter 4.

31 Quoted in G. W. F. Hegel, *Lectures on the Philosophy of Spirit* (1827–8), Oxford University Press, Oxford, 2007, p.26.

32 W. von Humboldt, 'On the Historian's Task' in *History and Theory*, Vol. 6 No. 1, (1967), p.64 (also at www2.southeastern.edu/Academics/Faculty/jbell/humboldt.pdf).

33 Ibid., p.65.

34 Ibid., p.64.

35 R. Steiner, *The New Spirituality and the Christ Experience in the Twentieth Century*, Rudolf Steiner Press, London, 1988, p.8.

36 O. Barfield, *Poetic Diction*, Wesleyan University Press, Middletown, 1984, pp.77–92.

37 See Mircea Eliade, *The Sacred and the Profane*, Harvest HBJ, NY, 1959.

38 Ancient Sanskrit texts such as the Mahabharata and the Puranas relate narratives that identify the lingam symbol found in Hindu temples as the phallus of the god Shiva. The lingam form and the yoni in which it rests together symbolize the union of the male and female principles and the totality of all existence.

39 See for example B. Pascoe, *Dark Emu: Aboriginal Australia and the Birth of Agriculture*, Magabala Books, Broome, 2018. Fire-stick farming was a method of controlled burning which, among other purposes, facilitated hunting and increased the amount and diversity of plant food available.

40 This monument was commissioned by the Roman Senate on 4 July, 13 BC to honour the return of Augustus to Rome after three years in Hispania and Gaul.

41 On the topic of mutual help and the guilds, see the lecture by Rudolf Steiner, 'Brotherhood and the Fight for Survival', Berlin, 23 November, 1905.

42 V. Hugo, *Les Misérables*, op. cit., Part V, Book 1.

43 R. Steiner, *Nietzsche as Fighter for Freedom,* SteinerBooks, NY, 1985, Chapter 1(1).

44 J.-P. Sartre, *Being and Nothingness*, (1943) Part. 4, Ch. 1.

45 R. Steiner, *The Challenge of the Times*, Anthroposophic Press, Spring Valley, 1941, p.120.

46 R. Steiner, *Social Basis For Primary and Secondary Education*, Lecture III. Lectures in Stuttgart, 1919, GA192.

47 Novalis, *Pollen and Fragments*, Fragment 32.

48 See G. R. MacLay, *The Social Organism: A Short History of the Idea that Human Society May be Regarded as a Gigantic Living Creature*, North River Press, Croton-on-Hudson, 1990.

49 See B. J. Cook, *Democracy and Administration: Woodrow Wilson's Ideas,* The John Hopkins University Press, Baltimore, 2007.

50 See his lecture on 12 November, 1917.

51 The phrase 'the true is the whole' is from the Preface to Hegel's *Phenomenology of Spirit*.

52 Marx used this expression in his *A Contribution to the Critique of Hegel's Philosophy of Right*.

53 K. Popper, *The Poverty of Historicism,* Routledge, London, 1986, p.3.

54 M. Stirner, *The Ego and Its Own*, Cambridge University Press, 1995, p.329.

55 Interview with Margaret Thatcher in *Woman's Own*, 23 September, 1987.

56 M. Weber, *Economy and Society*, University of California Press, Berkeley, 2013.

57 R. Steiner, *The Renewal of the Social Organism*, op. cit., p.126.

58 R. Steiner, *Freedom of Thought and Societal Forces*, op. cit., pp.98–105. As a scholar of twenty-one years of age, Rudolf Steiner was asked by Karl Julius Schröer—a major figure in Goethe scholarship at that time—to become the first editor of the scientific papers of Goethe, a large number of which had lain in the Goethe-Schiller archive in Weimar for around sixty years. This editorial work occupied Steiner for nine years, so it is unsurprising that the scientific methods of Goethe had a profound influence on Steiner's own work—in medicine, education, agriculture, architecture among other fields.

59 R. Steiner, Lecture, 22 November, 1920. In Goethe's own time one of his associates—the philosopher and man of letters Wilhelm von Humboldt—extended Goethe's methods to the social sciences. Humboldt applied Goetheanistic thinking to studies he undertook in anthropology, linguistics, and history.

60 R. Steiner, *Freedom of Thought and Societal Forces*, op. cit., pp.98–99.

61 See N. Hoffmann, *The University at the Threshold: Orientation through Goethean Science*, Rudolf Steiner Press, Forest Row, 2020.

62 From the Preface to Goethe's *Theory of Colour*.

63 See also N. Hoffmann, *The University at the Threshold*, op. cit.

64 See in particular W. Schad, *Threefoldness in Humans and Mammals: Toward a Biology of Form*, Adonis Press, Hillsdale, 2020.

65 C. Holdrege, *The Flexible Giant: Seeing the Elephant Whole*, The Nature Institute, Ghent, 2003, p.4.

66 Ibid., p.4.

67 Ibid., p.5. The quote from Goethe comes from J.W. von Goethe, *Scientific Studies*, (ed. D. Miller), Suhrkamp Publishers, 1995, p.57.

68 Most prominent in this area is Wolfgang Schad and his book *Understanding Mammals*, op. cit. Animals studies, carried out in the exact imaginative ways Schad indicates, are foundational to a re-imagined life science.

69 During the years 1794 and 1795 Wilhelm von Humboldt and his brother, the geographer Alexander, were in Jena working daily with Goethe on the dissection and observation of anatomical specimens. Through this work Wilhelm von Humboldt came to understand how a transformed thinking—a thinking which unites the artistic and scientific—is required in order to comprehend living form. He went on to apply such thinking to studies he undertook in areas of social science. Wilhelm von Humboldt was the founder of what is regarded as the first modern university—the Humboldt University of Berlin. See Chad Wellmon, *Becoming Human*, The Pennsylvania State University Press, University Park, 2010.

70 See Chapter 3.

71 P. Tillich, *The Courage to Be*, Yale University Press, New Haven, 2014, pp.97–8.

72 Ibid., p.96.

73 For Sartre, the universe has no inherent meaning and since the human being has no determinate essence, the human individual is thrown back upon him or herself and has to create his/her own meaning through his/her own decisions and actions. For Goethe and Romantic thinkers, the alienated self-consciousness is an important stage in the evolution of consciousness and the process of individuation.

74 Ibid., p.97.

75 Ibid., p.97.

76 See A. Wiedmann, *Romantic Art Theories*, Gresham Books, Henley-on-Thames, 1986, p.99.

77 D. Roberts, *The Total Work of Art in European Modernism*, Cornell University Press, NY, 2011, p.243.

78 A. Bely, *Revolution and Culture*, p.287.

79 F. Nietzsche, *The Birth of Tragedy*, §1.

80 A. Bely, op. cit.

81 R. Steiner, *The Arts and Their Mission*, Anthroposophic Press, Spring Valley, 1964, Lecture 7.

82 A. Bely, op. cit.

83 'I Am Searching For Field Character', 1973; translated in: Caroline Tisdall, *Art Into Society, Society Into Art: Seven German Artists : Albrecht D., Joseph Beuys.*, Institute of Contemporary Arts, London, 30 October–14 November 1974, London, 1974.

84 A. Bely, op. cit.

85 Ulrich Roesch, *We are the Revolution! Rudolf Steiner, Joseph Beuys and the Threefold Social Impulse*, Temple Lodge, 2013.

86 See the discussion of this point at the beginning of Chapter 3.

87 R. Steiner, *Education as a Force for Social Change*, Anthroposophic Press, Hudson, 1997, p.9.

88 See: https://www.news-medical.net/health/The-Size-of-SARS-CoV-2-Compared-to-Other-Things.aspx; https://www.fda.gov/medical-devices/personal-protective-equipment-infection-control/n95-respirators-surgical-masks-face-masks-and-barrier-face-coverings.

89 See website of World Health Organisation, accessed May 2022: https://www.who.int/news-room/feature-stories/detail/the-race-for-a-covid-19-vaccine-explained.

90 R. Steiner, *Anthroposophy and the Visual Arts*, Lecture in The Hague, 9 April, 1922.

91 See the discussion about animal physiology in Chapter 4.

92 See for example: https://www.abc.net.au/news/2021-01-27/china-coronavirus-new- invasive-quarantine-rules-lunar-new-year/13094370.

93 See for example, the capsule technology developed by scientists at the Massachusetts Institute of Technology: www.technologynetworks.com/biopharma/news/capsule-for-oral-mrna-delivery-developed-and-tested-358093. See also S. N. Langel et al., Sci. Transl. Med. 10.1126/scitranslmed.abn6868 (2022) 'Adenovirus type 5 SARS-CoV-2 vaccines delivered orally or intranasally reduced disease severity and transmission in a hamster model'.

94 See https://en.wikipedia.org/wiki/Senatus_consultum_ultimum.

95 See https://en.wikipedia.org/wiki/State_of_emergency.

96 See https://www.legislation.vic.gov.au/in-force/acts/charter-human-rights-and-responsibilities-act-2006/015.

97 It might be protested: isn't mandatory vaccination a public health measure in the same way as the sanitization of streets and the fluoridization of water are public health measures? It is not. Actually fluoridization of the public water supply as a 'community medication' comes close in that it involves a medical procedure (a medicine) which is forced into people's bodies. That is why it has been stopped or was never started in most European countries. Only 2% of people in Europe drink artificially fluoridated water. See: https://en.wikipedia.org/wiki/Water_fluoridation_by_country. Also fluoridization does not attract penalties for non-compliance and is easy to avoid by using a water filter.

98 R. Steiner, *World Economy*, Anthroposophic Press, NY, pp.201–5.

99 From a live interview, filmed on 11 November, 2016, www.youtube.com/watch?v=e3svbmlMALM&feature=youtu.be

100 Sir Ken Robinson, https://www.ted.com/talks

101 R. Steiner, *Education as a Force for Social Change*, Anthroposophic Press, Hudson, 1997, p.19.

102 R. Steiner, *The Social Future*. op. cit., p.111.

103 C. Houghton-Budd, *Prelude in Economics*, New Economy Publications, 1999, p.27.

104 'People will increasingly see that money is a commodity, in other words an economic value . . . that it is an economic value and we have to reach a stage where it must become a necessary potential, must act as a *rights document* for all the creative processes of human work . . . ' J. Beuys et al, *What is Money?: A Discussion*, Clairview Books, Forest Row, 2010, p.17.

105 R. Steiner, *The Renewal of the Social Organism*, op. cit., p.101.

106 To administer this transference doesn't necessary mean deciding who the successor will be. The particular entrepreneur or those who developed a business, through their experience and technical knowledge, are best suited to judge who is most equipped to continue or revive a business (which might involve productive land and factory equipment). A group of qualified individuals or non-profit organizations in the cultural-spiritual sphere, acting as stewards of the capital, can ensure that the transference never becomes a matter of nepotism. The role of the political-rights sphere is only to provide the legal framework by which such transferences can take place.

107 Active, deliberate thought processes like philosophical analysis or problem-solving are a form of work.

108 Certain cooperatives go a long way in this direction of the associative economy and a prominent example is the Mondragon Corporation in the Basque region of Spain, founded by a young Jesuit priest José María Arizmendiarrieta after the Second World War. This today is a flourishing group of 261 enterprises, including a bank and a university, which currently employ about 80,000 people. All workers participate in management processes on a democratic basis. It is the tenth largest business group in Spain. Mondragon Corporation is administered in a way that reflects consideration for its many stakeholders including its educational institutions. It cannot be sold off by investors, since as a cooperative it is not merely the creation of investors. Mondragon Corporation is a business enterprise but one element in particular of Jesuit practice found its way into its business ethic and this sets it apart from the normal methods of worker participation in cooperative management. It is what they call 'the sovereignty of work'. In their principles they state that 'the systematic recruitment of salaried workers has been abandoned' and that capital is considered 'an instrument subordinate to labour'.

The way the cooperatives are run promotes work being honoured and valued as a way of individual and social transformation. This accords with the idea of an associative economy articulated by Steiner in which labour comes more within the sphere of rights and is not something which can be manipulated to allow the few to reap maximum profits.

109 An example of an initiative which works more broadly and specifically in relation to the idea of a threefold social organism is Sekem, north of Cairo in Egypt, which has been developing for forty years. It was founded by Dr Ibrahim Abouleish who had learnt about the work of Rudolf Steiner when studying in Austria to be a pharmacologist. Sekem now includes biodynamic farms, a number of trading companies, a medical centre, a Steiner school and community school for disadvantaged children, a research institute and Heliopolis University for Sustainable Development. Sekem is founded on what they call an 'economics of love'. This is only referring to caring relationships between human individuals—the producers, traders and consumers—in a conscious practice of associative economics and humanistic management. Within the whole assemblage of institutions embraced by Sekem the threefold social order has been carefully articulated—so that workers in the trading companies, for example, all take part in personal development within the cultural-spiritual organization, especially through the arts, to realize their individual potential. And a rights organization has been created to ensure that workers experience work and capital as a right and that added value from business operations is fairly distributed along the supply chain, to the local community, to education and research into sustainable practice.

110 The connection between slavery and capitalism permeate Marx's writings.

111 See M. Large, *Common Wealth*, Hawthorn Press, 2010.

112 V. Hugo, *Les Misérables*, Part V, Book I.

113 R. Steiner, *World Economy*, op. cit. In recent decades the Fair Trade movement has come into being; this takes a large step in the direction of what Steiner referred to as 'true price'. In the Fair Trade process farmers and other producers achieve sustainable and equitable trade relationships. The Fair Trade movement combines the payment of higher prices to exporters with improved social and environmental standards.

114 GLS Bank (full name GLS Gemeinschaftsbank eG, Community Bank for Lending and Giving) is a German ethical bank that was founded in 1974 by Wilhelm Ernst Barkhoff and Gisela Reuther, out of the economic ideas of Steiner. It was the first bank in Germany that operated with an ethical philosophy. Triodos Bank was founded in 1980 as a sustainable bank based on ethical principles, also out of the work of Steiner. It now has branches in a number of European countries.

115 V. Hugo, *Les Misérables*, Part V, Book I.

116 See for example K. Marx *On the Jewish Question* (1843) and K. Marx and F. Engels, *The German Ideology* (1846).

117 R. Steiner, *West and East*, op. cit., p.225.

118 Change or Suppression (Conversion) Practices Prohibition Bill 2020. The Bill bans *any* conduct (including a conversation) by *any* person directed towards *any* second person on the basis of the second person's sexual orientation (or gender identity) where the conduct is intended to 'suppress or change' the second person's sexual orientation (or gender identity). The Bill makes illegal all practices and conduct (including a conversation or family discussion, counselling, pastoral care, prayer) engaged in for the purpose of 'suppressing or changing' a person's sexual orientation or gender identity, even if the conduct was requested and consented to by the person and even if that person experienced the conduct as beneficial rather than harmful.

119 In England this began with the Education Act 1880.

120 Plato, *The Republic*, (444e).

121 R. Steiner, *The Social Future*, SteinerBooks, Great Barrington, 2013, p.62.

122 R. Steiner, *Education for Adolescents*, Anthroposophic Press, Hudson, 1996, Lecture 2.

123 Plato, *The Republic*, (444e).

124 See Suolahti, J. *The Roman Censors: A Study on Social Structures*, Suomalainen Tiedeakatemia, Helsinki, 1963.

125 Such a standing outside the law, however, is normally considered to be not possible, for the law conceives of a 'natural person' as a legal entity, inseparable from the actually existing human individual. We cannot transform the law by means of the law, for that is really only perpetuating it in its current form. It is a well-known principle, which applies in many other fields of endeavour as well, that you can't solve a problem with the same thinking which caused it in the first place. The law, just as the economy, calls for an entirely new form of thinking in our time and for the future. The sovereign citizen movement asserts that the living human being has natural rights entirely outside any legal framework.

126 R. Steiner, *Education as a Force for Social Change*, op. cit., pp.18–19.

127 R. Steiner, *The Renewal of the Social Organism*, op. cit., p.36.

128 In the final chapter of his *Tractatus Theologico-Politicus*.

129 F. Nietzsche, *Twilight of the Idols*, §38.

130 F. Nietzsche, *Beyond Good and Evil*, §21.

131 See for example A. Ridley, 'Nietzsche on Art and Freedom', in *European Journal of Philosophy*, Vol 15 (2), 2007, pp.204–224.

132 Karl Marx and Friedrich Engels, *Communist Manifesto*, Chapter 2: 'You must, therefore, confess that by "individual" you mean no other person than the bourgeois, than the middle-class owner of property. This person must, indeed, be swept out of the way, and made impossible.'

133 R. Steiner, *The Renewal of the Social Organism*, op. cit., p.68.

134 See the discussion of Steiner's years at this college in the Introduction. See also R. Steiner, *The Course of My Life*, Anthroposophic Press, Hudson, 1986, pp.284–288.

135 R. Steiner, *The Renewal of the Social Organism*, op. cit., p.68.

136 The pathway of social art developed here proceeds in stages which can be broadly defined. In all types of creative actions there is a preparatory stage, sometimes called the 'research stage', where an area of life or an important theme relevant to a particular life situation is researched and internalized. The 'incubation stage', taking no defined length of time, is where the creator's mind contemplates and works through this problem or situation, to the point when there can be a motivating, inspiring impulse of insight or intuition, called the 'illumination stage' and may lead to a 'manifestation stage' where the insight or intuition takes physical expression. In what is called the 'verification stage' there is an assessment of whether what emerged in illumination and manifestation fulfils the criteria defined in the preparation stage and satisfies broader social requirements. See G. Wallas, *The Art of Thought*, Solis Press, Tunbridge Wells, 2014.

137 V. Hugo, *Les Misérables*, op. cit. Part V, Book 1.

138 R. Steiner, *The Renewal of the Social Organism*, op. cit., p.36.

139 See the chapter entitled 'Capitalism and Social Ideas' in R. Steiner, *Towards Social Renewal*, Rudolf Steiner Press, Forest Row, 1999, pp.63–102.

140 A social credit system such as is in place in China.

141 See the vision of the World Economic Forum and their plan for a Great Reset.

142 Quoted in P. Harrison, *The Disenchantment of Reason*, SUNY, Albany, 1994, p.57.

143 R. Steiner, 'The Threefold Social Order and Educational Freedom' in *The Renewal of the Social Organism*, op. cit., p.76.

144 See for example: www.weforum.org/agenda/2019/04/the-benefit-workers-want-most-is-less-work/

145 R. Steiner, *The Renewal of the Social Organism*, op. cit., p.82.

146 R. Steiner, *Education as a Force for Social Change*, op. cit., p.52.

147 H. Marcuse, *One-Dimensional Man*, Routledge, London, 2013, p.10.

148 W. Wilson, *The State, Elements of Historical and Practical Politics*. The point about the will of the state is discussed by Rudolf Steiner in *Ideas for a New Europe*, Rudolf Steiner Press, Sussex, 1992, Lecture VII.

149 Not so far back in European history religious life was entirely bound to the state and there are vestiges of this today. For example, the governor-general or head of state of Australia must be an Anglican because he or she is the King of the UK's representative and the King is the Supreme Governor of the Church of England. Under the Australian constitution the King, through the agency of his governor-general, has the power to disallow a bill of the Australian parliament.

150 'There is only one thing I fear in life . . . one day, the black will swallow the red'. From *Red*, a play about Rothko by American playwright John Logan.
151 R. Steiner, from Memorandum (1917).
152 R. Steiner, *Ideas for a New Europe*, op. cit., Lecture VII.
153 Plato, *The Republic*, (444e).
154 Ibid.
155 J. Habermas, *Legitimation Crisis*, op. cit., Chapter 2.
156 On this point see J. Rohen, *Functional Threefoldness in the Human Organism and Human Society*, Adonis Press, Hillsdale, 2011.
157 R. Steiner, *Education as a Force for Social Change*, op. cit., p.27.
158 R. Steiner, *The Renewal of the Social Organism*, op. cit., p.36.
159 R. Steiner, *West and East*, op. cit., p.149.
160 See R. Steiner, *Toward Social Renewal*, GA 23, Chapter 4 'International Aspects'.
161 Ibid.
162 Goethe, *The Green Snake and the Beautiful Lily*, Chapter 4.
163 See https://jordan.un.org/sites/default/files/2023-03/2302794E_Policy-Brief-2.pdf
164 R. Steiner, *The Spirit of the Waldorf School*, Anthroposophic Press, Hudson, 1995, p.7.
165 R. Steiner, *Youth and the Etheric Heart*, SteinerBooks, Great Barrington, 2007, p.91.
166 R. Steiner, *Awake! for the Sake of the Future*, Great Barrington, 2015, p.18.
167 R. Steiner, *Youth and the Etheric Heart*, op. cit., p.76.
168 R. Steiner, *The Renewal of the Social Organism*, op. cit., p.70.
169 R. Steiner, *The Spiritual Ground of Education*, Anthroposophic Press, Great Barrington, 2004, p.11.
170 R. Steiner. *Education as a Force for Social Change*, op. cit., Lecture 1.
171 Ibid., pp.10–15.
172 Ibid.
173 Ibid.
174 Rudolf Steiner, *The Renewal of the Social Organism*, op. cit., p.82.
175 Ibid., p.14.
176 E. Stockmeyer & R. Steiner, *Rudolf Steiner's curriculum for Waldorf schools: An attempt to summarise his indications: a collection of quotations for the benefit of the different Waldorf schools*, Steiner Schools Fellowship, London, 1969, p.81.
177 See Chapter 2.
178 See for example: A.T. Kronman, *Education's End: Why Our Colleges and Universities Have Given Up on the Meaning of Life*, Yale University Press, New Haven, 2007; B. Readings, *The University in Ruins*, Harvard University Press, Cambridge, 1996; P. Smith, *Killing the Spirit: Higher Education in America*, Penguin Books, Harmondsworth, 1990; A. Bloom, *The Closing of the American Mind: How Higher Education Has Failed Democracy and Impoverished the Souls of Today's*

Students, Simon & Schuster, NY, 2012; F. Donoghue, *The Last Professors: The Corporate University and the Fate of the Humanities*, Fordham University Press, NY, 2008; W. Chapman (ed), *The Western University on Trial*, University of California Press, Berkeley, 1983.

179 R. Steiner, *Problems of Society*, Rudolf Steiner Press, Forest Row, 2015, p.72.

180 R. Steiner, *Youth and the Etheric Heart*, op. cit., pp.11–13.

181 F. Nietzsche, *Thus Spake Zarathustra*, Section 38.

182 O. Scharmer and K. Kaufer, 'Universities as the Birthplace for the Entrepreneuring Human Being', in *The SoL Journal on Knowledge, Learning and Change*, MIT Press, 2000. www.ottoscharmer.com/sites/default/files/2000_Uni21us.pdf

183 Ibid.

184 W. von Humboldt, *Humanist Without Portfolio*, Wayne State University Press, Detroit, 1963, p.134.

185 For a key example, see the University of Adelaide's (Australia) new *Beacon of Enlightenment* strategic plan, which introduces key elements of the Humboldtian methodology—specifically, research possibilities for undergraduate students, and small group learning experiences rather than lectures. See www.adelaide.edu.au/VCO/beacon/beacon-ofenlightenment.pdf.

186 O. Scharmer and K. Kaufer, op. cit.

187 Ibid.

188 Ibid.

189 R. Steiner, *The Renewal of the Social Organism*, op. cit., p.29.

190 C. O. Scharmer, *Theory U: Leading from the Future as it Emerges*, Berrett-Koehler Publishing, San Fransisco, 2009, pp.30–31.

191 https://sites.google.com/site/socialsculptureusa/freeinternationaluniversitymanifesto

192 O. Scharmer and K. Kaufer, op. cit.

193 N. Hoffmann, *The University at the Threshold*, op. cit.

194 See http://wn.rsarchive.org/Articles/GA031/English/UniEdu_index.html

195 Any thinking which develops within a strictly intellectual-logical orientation works itself out within the tension of assertion and refutation; one side presents an argument and the other seeks to argue against it in order to move toward truth; this is the dialectical method adumbrated by Aristotle which evolved into the culture of disputation and painstaking logical analysis in the medieval universities and the methodology of debate in the modern seminar system. The possibilities and limits of the true are considered to arise only within this tension between conjecture and refutation. In relation to the dialectical method is a notable fact that it is possible to present a powerful argument for any particular case without having any commitment whatsoever to that case. In disputation it is all a matter of logic; what an individual feels or wills to do personally is not the main concern.

196 B.R. Clark, *Places of Enquiry: Research and Advanced Education in Modern Universities*, University of California Press, Berkeley, 1995, p.21.

197 See https://www.britannica.com/topic/academic-freedom

198 Recommendation 1762 (2006), Point 7. The Parliamentary Assembly of the Council of Europe that recalls the Magna Charta Universitatum opened for signature by 430 rectors of European universities in 1988 on the occasion of the 900th anniversary of the University of Bologna (Italy). So this is not research freedom as an individual right but as a public responsibility, to benefit society.

199 From Greek *krisis* meaning 'decision'.

Picture Credits

Fig. 9: Shiva as Natajara, Lord of the Dance © LACMA (Wikimedia, Commons); Fig. 10: Chefren and Horus © Soutekh67 (Wikimedia, Commons); Fig. 11: Ancient Egyptian government pyramid © Reptail82 (Wikimedia, Commons); Fig. 13: Marble statue of a kouros © www.metmuseum (Wikimedia, Commons); Fig. 14: Kroisos kouros © User:Mountain (Wikimedia, Commons); Fig. 15: Ara Pacis relief © Miguel Hermoso Cuesta (Wikimedia, Commons); Fig. 17: Vincent van Gogh, *Sower at Sunset* © vggallery (Wikimedia, Commons); Fig. 18: Honoré Daumier, *The Third-Class Carriage* © Walters (Wikimedia, Commons); Fig. 19: Caspar David Friedrich, *Wanderer above the Sea of Fog* © StellarHalo (Wikimedia, Commons); Fig. 27: Drawing – A. Gack, M. Budschigk, J. Pekarsky; Fig. 28: Drawing - U. Winkler; Fig. 41: Goddess Maat © TYalaA (Wikimedia, Commons).